WOMEN IN A
VIOLENT WORLD

WOMEN IN A VIOLENT WORLD

Feminist Analyses and Resistance Across 'Europe'

Edited by
Chris Corrin

EDINBURGH UNIVERSITY PRESS

Edinburgh University Press
22 George Square, Edinburgh

Typeset in Linotype Sabon
by Hewer Text Composition Services, Edinburgh and
printed and bound in Great Britain by
the Cromwell Press, Melksham, Wiltshire

A CIP record for this book is available
from the British Library

ISBN 0 7486 0804 4

Contents

Introduction

Chris Corrin

This book is about politics and power — the political use of power within patriarchy and the politics of feminist resistance and development of alternative ways of being. The contributions to this volume are not setting out to give 'answers' to set 'questions' nor to provide solutions to problems. One aim of this book is to formulate questions that are relevant to women's political work in resisting male sexual violence and to show the connections and linkages across the range of such violence. Such aspects include violence which takes place in the home or workplace and on the street corner; violence involving racism, homophobia,[1] xenophobia and other prejudices; violence on international and global levels including trafficking in women and women's experience of war violence.

Another major aim of this book is to stress the need for recognition and remembrance. To recognize that is has been feminist activism and resistance to men's violence against women that has made visible the causes and consequences of this violence and to remember this work and some of these campaigns. Against many barriers (legal, political, social, cultural) feminists have sought to speak out against men's violent use of power over women, and in favour of making available public resources to support women who survive violent situations, to bring about changes in legislation (such as rape in marriage), and to develop educational, training programmes and public awareness campaigns. The public acknowledgement of men's violence against women has been an important step in exposing this social problem. As several contributors illustrate, in countries where this public recognition does not yet, or not fully, exist, challenging men's informal and formal power over women is much more difficult.

We also need to remember, how long and hard feminist activists have worked and campaigned — from 'Reclaim the Night' marches to years of unpaid labour in Rape Crisis Centres and Women's Refuges to making 'pilot studies' from which others could build — for the gains now apparent. This work has continued in very different social and political circumstances. That such gains are currently under attack through various 'backlashes' — from Tory policies in the UK, resurgent Christian and other religious fundamentalisms across much of Europe, in war situations and ethnic cleansing and in social, political and economic transitions — also deserves our consideration.

Another aim of this collection is to examine the links between male sexual violence in local and domestic contexts, and across the international systems of violence. These links were considered at the Fourth World Conference on Women in Beijing within the framework of the human rights standards. As Charlotte Bunch notes in her work on 'Transforming Human Rights from a Feminist Perspective':

> In order to respond to the brutal and systematic violation of women globally, governments and the human rights community must move beyond male-defined norms, a move that requires examining gender biases and acknowledging the rights of women as human rights. (Bunch 1995, p.15)

In this work the links are made within the context of feminist analyses while resistance and consideration is given to the complexities raised for individual women and groups of women when assessing 'global' claims across cultures and over time.

In her opening keynote address to the NGO Forum on Women in Huairou, Aung San Suu Kyi explained that:

> The last six years afforded me much time and food for thought. I came to the conclusion that the human race is not divided into two opposing camps of good and evil. It is made up of those who are capable of learning and those who are incapable of doing so. (Aung San Suu Kyi 1995)

The main aim of the contributions in this book is to offer analysis, information and some questions, as to why women suffer male sexual violence and how feminists are both taking issue (with patriarchal assumptions and 'explanations') and taking control (of political movements and agendas for progressive change). It is, then, intended for those who are capable of learning.

This book raises questions about how women experience male violence exercised against them in various contexts (social, economic, cultural and political) across 'Europe'. It considers some of the analyses and forms of feminist resistance that have developed from such experience. Whilst authors within various chapters refer to specific instances of resistance to male violence by women in order to survive and/or escape situations of violence, the term 'feminist resistance' is here used to refer to feminist research, support services, theorising and activism to resist male violence. Power, patriarchy and privilege are important concepts in this work. The use of power by men within patriarchal societies to privilege themselves over women is at the core of male sexual violence. The recognition within feminist analyses that 'each of us views societal concepts and institutions from a different lens depending on our consciousness and our place in society' (Bunch 1995, p.11) is an important starting point.

The context of 'Europe' is explored in its complexities, of what is 'European'. The focus on 'Europe' has been chosen since the impetus for this collection came from a 'pan-European' workshop. This offers an opportunity to highlight both the diversity and ambiguity concerning what being 'European' means within the context of male violence against women, and what is considered 'European' in terms of inclusion and openness and questions about the refusal of acceptance of people who are not seen to share 'European' culture. Much of this exclusivity, which defines 'Europe' in terms of a limited cultural history rejecting anything different as 'non-European', so inferior and anti-modern, underlies the refugee situation across 'Europe'. This politics is apparent in several 'numbers games' including that of who are 'acceptable' refugees. Aspects of this example are highlighted in the Swiss study of feminist campaigns and in the consideration of the work of Southall Black Sisters in the UK.

Whilst the focus is on 'Europe' it is clear that the overarching systems of male violence against women operate on a *global scale* and have implications for women everywhere.

> Significant numbers of the world's population are routinely subject to torture, starvation, terrorism, humiliation, mutilation, and even

murder simply because they are female. Crimes such as these against any groups other than women would be recognised as a civil and political emergency as well as a gross violation of the victim's humanity . . . (Bunch 1992, p.5)

The contributions have both a wide comparative frame and a narrower focus. The wide comparative frame considers the many different ways in which women experience violence across different countries of Europe and in terms of the various sections chosen — others could have included more specific focus on women's reproductive health and sexuality (*see* Davies 1994), the relationship between militarism and sex industries (*see* Enloe 1993 and Cleaver and Myers 1993). Women are oppressed on the basis of gender, 'race', class, sexual orientation, disability, religion. The exclusion of any groups becomes a basis on which violence can be tolerated and even supported. Recognising 'race, class and gender as interlocking systems of oppression' (Hill-Collins 1990, p.223) is a shift that Black feminist thought has made in terms of rethinking social relations of domination and resistance.

It is important to make the distinction clear between power relations and patriarchy. Space is not given here to full theorizations around power and its use in relation to violence. The primary concentration is on male violence within patriarchal societies. Bell hooks pointed out in 1984:

It is essential for continued feminist struggle to end violence against women that this struggle be viewed as a component of an overall movement to end violence. (hooks 1984, p.118)

The contributors to Section Two illustrate that there can be no ordering of oppressions. It is the case that violence occurs in many human relationships — for example, adults (women and men) are violent towards children, and violence occurs within lesbian relationships. As is also apparent within Section Two, racist groups across Europe are actively and violently controlling certain political agendas which dictate core aspects of people's lives. In her essay 'There can be no hierarchy of oppressions' Audre Lorde writes:

I have learned that sexism (a belief in the inherent superiority of one sex over all others and thereby its right to dominance) and heterosexism (a belief in the inherent superiority of one pattern of loving over all others and thereby its right to dominance) both arise from the same source as racism — a belief in the inherent superiority of one race over all others and thereby its rights to dominance. (Cleaver and Myers 1993, p.17)

In their work various contributors echo these thoughts by emphasizing the need to continue to work on various levels and in various struggles simultaneously in order to achieve freedom for all.

Women in a Violent World is then a beginning, in terms of considering male violence against women across 'Europe'. It is not a comprehensive research project in which all contributors follow a similar rubric. This is precisely its strength. The feminist voices here collected come from various locations — they are activists, academics, practitioners, theorists and campaigners. Some contributors are involved in all five areas. The strength of our joint effort lies in speaking out our different experiences, theorising from our and other feminist experience, in an effort to move forward some thoughts on how male violence against women is being resisted and can be further resisted.

HUMAN RIGHTS ARE WOMEN'S RIGHT

Internationally some feminists and feminist groups and campaigns have put an enormous amount of work into the various human rights non-governmental forums and official tribunals over the last twenty years. Yet the 'human rights' perspective in many European countries is only recently becoming accepted as an important current feminist approach to highlighting governmental responses and responsibilities towards ending male violence against women. One recent turning point was the Vienna UN Conference on Human Rights in June 1993 when the Vienna Declaration and Programme of Action was adopted. This action programme declares that violence against women in public and in private, as well as all forms of sexual harassment and exploitation, are violations of human rights.

The run-up to the Beijing conference in 1995 meant that many women's groups around the world had meetings to discuss human rights issues and to attempt to make demands upon their governments. Yet for many feminist groups there is a reluctance to expend energy on large public (public relations) gatherings such as the Beijing governmental conference or the Huairou non-governmental conference, recognizing the problems of implementation and the prior agreements made at the governmental levels. As both Stella Jegher and Hannana Siddiqui point out in their considerations of these conferences, particularly at Huairou, feminists were active in defining human rights abuses arising from structural inequalities, from patriarchy and racial dominance within our societies. The important influence of feminist debate in extending human rights considerations is vital in furthering international discussion and action towards ending women's oppression. As Charlotte Bunch notes:

The specific experiences of women must be added to traditional approaches to human rights in order to make women more visible and to transform the concept and practice of human rights in our culture so that it takes better account of women's lives. (Bunch and Carrillo 1992, p.6)

Such considerations and some of the strategies in which feminists in 'Europe' are involved are returned to in the conclusion.

COMMON THREADS AND DIFFERENCES

It is important to be clear about the common ties amongst women before our many differences can take on meaning. One common aspect in women's lives can be the likelihood of them being subjected to male violence as a form of social control. The forms taken by male violence are shaped by the specifics of women's positions in terms of power relations and cultural contexts. If crimes of violence were against other groups than women, they would be responded to differently. Such violence is not only personal or cultural — it is political:

Female subordination runs so deep that it is still viewed as inevitable or natural, rather than seen as a politically constructed reality maintained by patriarchal interests, ideology, and institutions . . . If violence and domination are understood as a politically constructed reality, it is possible to imagine deconstructing that system and building more just interactions between the sexes. (Bunch and Carrillo 1992, p.8)

As several of the contributors demonstrate one common tie for women is that their bodies can become used as battlegrounds in struggles for control and domination. Issues of control over women are highlighted in struggles over laws and social changes that give women some measures of control over their own bodies — be this in terms of abortion, or resisting enforced sterilisation, enjoyment of sexuality (heterosexuality or lesbian sexuality) or laws that criminalise rape in marriage. By denying women rights to enjoy their sexuality or to choose when or whether to have children, political power is being exercised to oppress women. The varying responses to male violence at a community and societal level, and within the international arena, are also shaped by specific contexts and women's locations within them.

Feminists in Europe have been forced to consider the differential impacts of competing patriarchal power structures on women's lives in terms of 'race', culture, class, ethnicity, sexuality and physicality (age and disability). When considering women's situations there is a need for care in thinking about which women are speaking and/or being spoken of, and to engage with issues of inclusion and exclusion in dominant representations. In the context of racism Jill Radford points out that:

> White feminists have had to acknowledge that black women's experiences are rooted in histories different from white women's. White colonial and imperial rule considered the rape of black women to be the slave owner's privilege.
>
> The influence of this history persists today: it is expressed in the stereotypes of black women portrayed in the media and in pornographic celebrations of violence against black women, and it is expressed in the response of the police and other professionals in the legal system to black women experiencing male violence — a response dictated by racism. (Radford and Russell 1992, p.8)

The need to recognise the complexities of such power relations present in different women's lived realities is essential to all feminist strategies of resistance aimed at changing women's lives for the better. As Hannana Siddiqui shows in Chapter 4, there are many dilemmas and contradictions faced by Black women in simultaneously taking on a multiplicity of struggles against racism and patriarchal oppression.

PATRIARCHY

Contributors highlight such dilemmas and contradictions and note the pervasiveness of patriarchal power structures having different impacts over time, across cultures and in different situations. In the UK debates have arisen over the usefulness of the concept of patriarchy (*see Sociology* 23(2) May 1989). Yet many feminists have found the term particularly useful in analysing the systematic organisation of women's oppression. There remain various uses of this term with differing emphases (Rich 1977; Delphy 1984; Walby 1990). Christine Delphy's account of patriarchy focuses on household production. As men benefit from women's provision of domestic services, childcaring and production of goods, so for Delphy, the main form of women's oppression is men's exploitation of women's reproductive and productive capacities in the household. In Sylvia Walby's six structures of patriarchal society the focus is on: employment; household production; the state; sexuality; violence; and culture. Jackie Stacey notes that questions of identity and lived experience are not apparent in Walby's model, thus leaving it open to:

the criticisms of much structural analysis: it fails to explain how people negotiate such a system, how they resist or conform, and how and why it affects different women differently, according to class, 'race', ethnic and sexual identity. (Stacey 1993, p.57)

In this context the work of Adrienne Rich has been useful in acknowledging the ways in which the nature and extent of patriarchal control differs within and across societies. Rich states that patriarchy is:

a familial-social, ideological, political system in which men by force, direct pressure, or through ritual, tradition, law, and language, customs, etiquette, education, and the division of labor, determine what part women shall or shall not play, and in which the female is everywhere subsumed under the male (Rich 1977, p.57)

Rich does not imply that no women have power, nor that all women in a given culture may not have certain powers. What Rich is emphasizing is that patriarchy is a difficult reality to perceive because it permeates everything including how we speak and think of our his/herstories. The key to Rich's consideration of patriarchal systems of control is that it is not inevitable and can no longer be denied or defended. Yet, in acknowledging this:

we tear open the relationship at the core of all power-relationships, a tangle of lust, violence, possession, fear, conscious longing, unconscious hostility, sentiment, rationalization: the sexual understructure of social and political forms . . . (ibid., p.56)

Within debates concerning women's oppression and resistance, arguments about the 'universal' nature of such oppression have produced useful shifts in thinking. Certainly some of the early feminist thinking about women's positions within their societies tended to universalise an idea of women — as white and heterosexual. Yet much of the creative drive in women's movements over the last twenty years has been in expanding concepts to address women's needs and interests across cultures and over time. The work of Black feminist thinkers has caused fundamental shifts in terms of how we think of oppression. In placing Black women's experiences at the centre of our analysis Patricia Hill-Collins argues that:

By embracing a paradigm of race, class and gender as interlocking systems of oppression, Black feminist thought reconceptualises the social relations of dominance and resistance . . . offering subordinate groups new knowledge about their experiences can be empowering. But revealing new ways of knowing that allow subordinate groups to define their own reality, has far greater implications. (Hill-Collins 1990, p.222)

Other shifts have occurred, in thinking about heterosexuality, as a certain component in patriarchal systems. In this connection Adrienne Rich questioned the assumption that 'most women are innately heterosexual':

To take the step of questioning heterosexuality as a 'preference' or 'choice' for women — and to do the intellectual and emotional work that follows — will call for a special quality of courage in heterosexually identified feminists. (Rich 1980)

In their work Celia Kitzinger and Sue Wilkinson (1993) argue that lesbianism is a political challenge to the institution of heterosexuality. As such lesbianism challenges patriarchal oppression.

MYTHS AND REALITIES

By examining the range of forms taken by male sexual violence it is possible to acknowledge and respect women's many strategies of resistance. Powerful myths concerning aspects of male violence against women have grown up, and are being (re)formulated, in many societies. Such myths are often very difficult to challenge. How debates and discussions around male violence against women have been structured in the past have radically affected women's ability to think through strategies of resistance. Such barriers to resistance include not only arguments concerned with 'universality' addressed above, but also with the 'private' nature of family life, in that support from the police for women experiencing male violence, or the provision and resourcing of refuge space for women, has been denied in some countries, as the chapters on Hungary, Russia and Spain highlight. For Black women and women living in minority ethnic communities the potential for racism in official responses has to be taken into account. In countries at war particular ethnic groups can become vulnerable to attack. The raping of enemy/'other' women is a classic instrument of war and highlights the use of power by men to objectify and to divide women — as 'good' or 'bad', as 'ours' and 'theirs'.

Public discussion of violence has been a key feminist campaign so that much of the hidden, privatized nature of male sexual violence can be overcome. In this context the old adage 'knowledge is power' is appropriate, certainly in terms of challenging myths. When women experiencing male violence have no opportunities or spaces in which to analyse and better understand the structures which engender and/or encourage the situations in which such violence occurs, developing strategies of resistance is made more difficult. In this context many of the myths surrounding male sexual violence in cases of domestic violence, rape, and femicide have been powerfully challenged by feminist writers. (Brownmiller 1975, el Saadawi 1980, hooks 1984, Kishwar and Vanita (eds) 1984, Kelly 1988, Bunch and Carrilo 1992, Radford and Russell 1992, Maynard 1993). Discussion of such myths are linked to patriarchal thought and ideologies — such as the 'woman blaming' that is often apparent. Men's 'uncontrollable' sexual drives are an other example, as are considerations of 'privacy' in terms of social control within households which can often be used as 'excuses/explanations' of male sexual violence. The opening statement in Susan Brownmiller's book *Against Our Will: Men, Women and Rape* clearly counters some such myths:

> Rape is nothing more or less than a conscious process of intimidation by which *all* men keep *all* women in a state of fear. (Brownmiller 1991, p.15)

In the London inquiry into rape and sexual assault (Hall 1985) an excellent example is offered of certain engendered myths around rape:

> It is often said that women are prone to 'lying' in relation to rape and sexual assault, or at the very least we make 'too much of a fuss' over 'trivialities' (such as being raped), or that we exaggerate the details of our experience. As a result our experiences and fears walk around with us — in many cases never being revealed, discussed, reported or acted upon. Accusations about women's wild imaginations and/or 'complicity' in sexual offences ensure that there are many people we cannot tell the truth to, and our assaults remain invisible or trivial — particularly in the eyes of those who are supposed to protect us from rape. (Hall 1985, p.158)

This quotation gives rich examples of the many ways in which women can be blamed for the male violence against them thus swerving the focus of analysis away from the violent men and, at the same time, from the patriarchal political context in which the violence occurs.

Hall also points out that for Black women the harassment and violence suffered can be 'racist violence' and gender issues cannot easily be separated. In terms of our understanding of the ways in which men are able to exercise power over women key terms are 'men's violence against women' and 'male sexual violence'. In her explanation of the continuum of male sexual violence, Liz Kelly notes that it: 'ranges from extensions of the myriad forms of sexism women encounter everyday through to the all too frequent murder of women and girls by men' (Kelly 1988, p.97). Terms such as 'male sexual violence' and 'men's violence against women' cannot be reduced to 'violence against women', because, as Ailbhe Smyth points out in Chapter 3, to do so leaves out men as the perpetrators and contributes to the construction of women as 'victims'. The terms 'male sexual violence' and 'male violence against women' includes a range of violent harm deliberately inflicted upon women — physical, psychological and sexual.

Feminist considerations of the ways in which patriarchal ideologies work to establish other discourses, highlight both how such changes in perspective privilege male power and oppress women. In Section 1 consideration is given to naming and defining men's violence against women and in outlining the feminist gains in placing such violence onto political agendas. Contributors to Section 2 consider men's violence against women within the international context of the power of prejudice, such as racism and ethnic nationalism, violence by which women who are poor, are refugees, are from 'minority' communities or 'enemy Others', and/or are 'non-citizens', are oppressed. In considering the contradictions of human development and violence, Roxanna Carrillo explains how women's dependence upon men is socially constructed:

> Women are socialised to associate their self-worth with the satis-faction of the needs and desires of others and thus are encouraged to blame themselves as inadequate or bad if men beat them. This socialisation process is reinforced by cultures in which a woman is constantly diminished, her sexuality commodified, her work and characteristics devalued, her identity shaped by an environment that reduces her to her biological functions. (Bunch and Carrillo 1992, pp.18–19)

Often women's economic dependency, citizenship status and/or socio-psychological dependence make it very difficult for women to leave situations of domestic violence. Often there is literally nowhere for women to go.

EUROPE

It is important to pose some questions regarding 'Europe'. Where is 'Europe' historically, culturally, politically? A very loose geo-cultural outline could stretch from Western Ireland to Eastern Siberia and from Iceland to the Balkan Peninsula. Yet, given the patterns of European colonisation worldwide, which have thwarted other developmental tendencies such a definition means little. From another perspective, millions of people from Africa, the Indian sub-continent and other 'non-European' countries live within the loose boundaries of 'Europe'. The economic controls and powers still emanating from Western European member states of the European Union, certainly continue to distort notions of 'Europe'.

With the start of European colonial expansion from 1492, nationalist and racist tendencies extended further afield. The development of such 'European' values as respect for human rights, equality and tolerance began to have relevance after the mid-1700s. The two-faced aspects of 'European' values became more visible in political arenas in the nineteenth and twentieth centuries — apparent tolerance (equality and rights) and intolerance (racism and oppression of minority communities). Whilst nationalism and racism are deeply rooted in the 'European' political and cultural heritage, any 'pluralism and tolerance' is very deeply gendered. The selective use of historical notions of 'tradition' particularly with regard to women is an essential element in the process of nationalism. This is clear from the contributions in Section 2 concerning the use of myths and symbolism surrounding 'mothers of the nation' and images of women and men in Croatia and Serbia during wartime.

Examples of male abuse of power can determine life and death decisions about whether or not women must have children as in the 'five children' rule in Ceauşescu's Romania and in the legisla-tion which criminalises abortion in Poland and Ireland or enforces sterilisation upon some Albanian women in Kosova. Examples of the exercise of male violence abound in the 'sex' trade and in trafficking in women, in which women are quite literally, and violently, bought and sold. In many instances 'definitional' problems appear to hinder international implementation of policies to combat trafficking. An example is noted in the recent International Organization for Migration (IOM) Report *Trafficking and Prostitution: The Growing Exploitation of Migrant Women from Central and Eastern Europe* (May 1995). The lack of clarity in the use of the terminology of trafficking is explained in part because trafficking covers a wide variety of situations, not all of which involve illegal migration or exploitation.

> In discussions with officials and NGO representatives in the four countries visited, it was found that the term 'trafficking in women' was interpreted in different ways. Some officials do not seem to make a clear distinction between the form of exploitation suffered by trafficked women and other forms of trafficking. On the other hand, at least one NGO would prefer to see the term 'trafficking' reserved exclusively to describe forced prostitution amongst migrant women. (IOM Study 1995, p.6)

It is apparent that in many countries the terms of reference differ regarding the exploitation of women who become caught up in trafficking.

It is apparent that across 'Europe' great social and political changes have generated massive upheavals with wide-ranging consequences including increasing crimes of violence against women. Within the context of the militarism of social values, analyses are made regarding ways in which certain aspects of women's lives such as child bearing and the cultural education of children become 'dangerous' for women. In the rapidly changing political landscapes of the 1990s contributors to this volume challenge many accepted myths and wisdoms regarding women's politics and women's activities towards change.

Violence, or the threat of it, is something that women live with every day of their lives all over the world. Male violence against women is the most forceful evidence, much of it only now becoming 'visible', of the oppression of women. Women's public discussion of male sexual violence has illustrated that women share common problems concerning patriarchal conceptions about women as inferior (to men), as subject to the rule of men and about the unequal distribution, and use, of power within societies.

FEMINIST ANALYSES

Feminism is above all about *praxis*. Feminist critiques of mainstream views about men's violence against women link with women's activities towards progressive change, i.e. change that matters in the lives of women and children. In recognising the importance of theorising in challenging ideas and creating further debate, feminists couple this with organizing to actively seek change. Keeping these streams running is what feminist politics is about. As noted, the central argument of feminist explanations of male violence against women is that all such violence is a product of unequal power relations in society. It is about the exercise of power leading to a social control by men over women. Our experiences of power can be positive and negative, individual and systematic. The focus of 'power' in this book is on men's use of power over women and on the power of feminist analyses and resistance. Despite widespread evidence of much male sexual violence certainly in terms of physical assaults upon women, the extent of this violence has remained hidden for a long time. One major use of power within patriarchal systems is apparent in the 'normalising' or legitimising of men's violence against women. In turn feminist resistance has succeeded in challenging such 'normalisation' or legitimation.

THE STRUCTURE OF THIS BOOK

Women in a Violent World is divided into three sections: analyses and challenges to male sexual violence in local/household contexts; feminist campaigning within racialised political contexts and within war situations; and feminist interventions in state structures. Of course, there is a good deal of overlap between all sections, given the nature of the analyses and the feminist support and campaigning work to which they are linked. The sections are different only in terms of the concentration of focus on the various aspects under consideration.

In the first section chapters considering male sexual violence in Russia, Hungary and Ireland offer analyses of the patriarchal oppression apparent in these societies. In her introduction to Chapter 1 — 'Sexism and Sexual Abuse in Russia' — Natalia Khodyreva notes that 'contemporary violence against women in Russia has its roots in historical specificity as well as patriarchal attitudes towards women, anarchy and impunity in the legal sphere and women's poverty'. These experiences connect with 'sexist approaches' and Khodyreva's analysis highlights other aspects — such as women's low self-esteem — which aggravate the situation in the post-perestroika period. Her perspective, from working with the Crisis Centre for Women in St. Petersburg covers issues arising from the ways in which crimes of violence are reported to authorities and legal proceedings are enacted and how domestic violence is still regarded as a 'private' problem with a consequent reluctance to intervene on the part of legal protection bodies.

From her consideration of the first Hungarian hotline for women and children experiencing domestic violence, Kriszta Szalay, in Chapter 2, makes links within a 'systems oriented approach' which views 'domestic violence against women in Hungary as inseparable from its social context'. Education is viewed as a key by Szalay in attempting to prevent domestic violence — both at the levels of students and staff in educational institutions and in public awareness campaigns. It is clear that lack of resources is a major problem in Budapest. Within a population of two million there are less than 100 places in shelters for women and their children. The history of NaNE (Women working against violence against women) is very much a history of the power of women's self-organization.

In her work reviewing what is known of male violence against women in the Republic of Ireland, Ailbhe Smyth focuses in Chapter 3 on how feminist activism has 'challenged and changed the ways in which Irish society both sees and does not see men's violence against women, and what this means for women'. Smyth is able to demonstrate that men's violence against women has been exposed as a massive social problem, translated from a private realm into the public arena in Ireland. Whilst there has been some amendment of laws, and education and training programmes have been initiated, it is apparent that the power of Church and State is seen to 'function in powerful tandem to 'legitimate' men's dominant position'.

The second section focuses on feminist campaigns in their broad political contexts. In the chapters considering the Swiss feminist campaigns and the support and campaigning work of Southall Black Sisters in England, the powerful impact of such campaigns within their political arenas is apparent. Issues of racism and the dominance of certain beliefs and behaviour are highlighted in the context of the use and abuse of power and privilege within both of these societies. In various ways such considerations are also central for many women from so-called 'minority ethnic communities' within larger and often racist 'dominant' communities in Central and Eastern Europe. Aspects of racism within state structures and police forces act as powerful deterrents. For those women living in Central and Eastern Europe considerations regarding the 'over-reaching arms' of state structures have also been such that many of them (from both minority and majority communities) have not been prepared to invite external forces into their homes at times of violent confrontations (Corrin 1994). Sexist attitudes within police forces and judiciaries not only prevent women reporting crimes of violence to authorities but form barriers in terms of the redress/justice for women who do choose to report.

In Chapter 4 Hannana Siddiqui draws out the particular hardships faced by women from minority communities in England. Whilst domestic violence 'cuts across class, race, religion, nationality — it exists all over the world', it is of crucial importance to recognize differences and inequality in terms of racism. Within this is the necessity for recognition of the needs of minority ethnic and Black women. In her discussion of their campaigns, Siddiqui notes that such issues as 'redefining family honour' provoked many different reactions. In dealing with racism the workers in Southall Black Sisters have to consider the policing of Black communities in the context of the policing of domestic violence. Immigration problems are also having to be faced as are the dangers for some women in resisting violence. Women are often criminalised, and as recent legal cases show, reform of the homicide laws in Britain, and no doubt elsewhere in Europe, is required to prevent further discrimination against women in this area. In order to demand rights for all, campaigning groups such as Women Against Fundamentalism work alongside Southall Black Sisters in attempting to pursue many struggles simultaneously in ways that are neither racist nor fundamentalist.

In her work on Swiss feminist campaigns Stella Jegher considers in Chapter 5, the struggles for 'the rights of all' in the ironic context of 'the oldest democracy in the world'. The irony is apparent in the double or triple struggle in which Swiss feminists engage:

> To change the situation of women inside the ruling structures, to criticise the latter in solidarity with those who are kept outside, and to change them on the basis of our own experiences, biographies and utopias, diverse as they may be.

Concentration is on statist aspects of men's violence against women in order to move forward analyses of the structural aspects of patriarchal rule. The many changes in immigration and asylum law in Switzerland have focused feminist attention on the inequality and hardships faced by migrant women. The politics of the foreigner police and the development of the so-called 'coercive measures' indicate a massive growth in powers which are open to abuse. All such measures affect women, especially women without independent residency who are living with violent male partners.

The experience of Swiss feminists and members of Southall Black Sisters at the Fourth World Conference on Women in Huairou/Beijing make evident the links apparent in both the second and third sections — in finding common strength between women and involvement in various struggles simultaneously. As the 'letter to our sisters in Sarajevo' (Chapter 6) shows, feminists in Bosnia, Croatia and Serbia have been working to deepen their common strengths. On feminist campaigning in war situations, the original talks given at our workshop in 1993 have been reproduced to emphasise how women's analyses and realisations of violence have changed over time and how feminist campaigns have continued and developed through the twists and turns of war. Lepa Mladjenović in Belgrade emphasizes the strength of feminists and their inventiveness in initiatives ranging from continuing the SOS hotline to developing second-hand shops. In detailing some of the meetings between groups on women such as the International Women in Black meeting in Vojvodina or that with women in Sarajevo, Lepa Mladjenović allows us to see both the pain and the joy in feminist networking towards changing women's lives for the better. Meanwhile in Chapter 7, Rada Boric emphasizes the complexities apparent for women living as refugees and the power women gain from working together. The Centre for Women War Victims is one of the first organisations linked to the feminist and anti-war networks in Croatia, and their work shows the desire of women from the former Yugoslavia to stay in contact and to work on women's solidarity. As Rada Boric notes: 'we share the experience that war is an extreme pattern of patriarchal social structure, and that civil violence against women and war violence have things in common'.

In the third section links are apparent too at state-structural levels, to which various feminist campaigns against male violence have been targeted in Spain and in Scotland. Here some considerations are made of elements of 'feminization of state policies', or more accurately, of the work of feminists active within state structures. This is highlighted in the Spanish and Scottish Chapters 8 and 9 in terms of women working within bureaucracies and state organizations in order to further the aims of feminist groups wishing to create change for all women. In terms of change, this is an area of significance, given that the bridging of the gap between grass-roots work and that of institutions and governmental offices is a matter of considerable debate in feminist circles. Questions raised by both Celia Valiente and Katie Cosgrove include 'how such bridges can usefully be built?' and 'what levels of compromise can be accepted and/or negotiated?' Hannana Siddiqui gives an example of one consideration of negotiation with state structures regarding the acceptance of state funding by voluntary groups, and the uses to which such funding can be put, or the 'strings' which can be attached to it.

In the concluding chapter a wide survey of women's activities towards change is undertaken to emphasize women's coalition-building not just in feminist networking against men's violence against women but in terms of the connections women are actively making across all the disconnections and barriers placed against women's ways. From the global context of male sexual violence involved in trafficking in women;

to women's human rights; to international coalitions across 'Europe'; to national connections in Poland and local affiliations in Glasgow, feminist resistance comes full circle, giving evidence of the strength and diversity of feminist campaigning work in challenging and resisting men's violence against women on many fronts simultaneously.

Note

My thanks to Liz Kelly for her comments and to Jill Radford for her very thoughtful and thought-provoking notes on an early draft of this introduction.

1 Celia Kitzinger (1987) points out that homophobia is actually something of a contradiction, in terms of lesbians, in that the term implies an irrational fear of homosexuals. As lesbians have a politicized identity of resistance, it is rational for men in power positions to fear them.

Section One

Introduction: Making Men's Violence Visible

Chris Corrin

In this section the three authors consider men's violence against women within their own countries and the consequences and impact of this for women. Consideration is given to the ways in which feminist campaigning work has changed some social and state views of how male violence is perceived and, in turn, what this has meant for different groups of women. The services which have been made available for women are outlined, as are the ways in which feminist theorists, practitioners, campaigners and activists are interacting with other groups to challenge existing practices and to create new practices and services which are woman-centred. What comes clearly through these chapters is the overarching message concerning male sexual violence — that it is political in nature and it is about domination. As Charlotte Bunch has noted:

> Victims are chosen because of their gender. The message is domination: stay in your place or be afraid. Contrary to the argument that such violence is only personal or cultural, it is profoundly political. (Bunch and Carrillo 1992, p.8)

Many attempts have been made throughout the last twenty years across 'Europe' and globally, to name and define male sexual violence. For the purposes of this introduction I touch only upon terms used by the authors and do not attempt to give a global, historical overview of these complex debates.

NAMING AND DEFINING MALE VIOLENCE

Male violence against women is an everyday reality for women everywhere in the world. This is the case in terms of the threat, if not the reality of violence. As the Popular Education Research Group note:

> When we speak of male violence against women, a myriad of images come to mind; a battered wife, a rape victim, pornography, or the fear on a woman's face as she walks down a dark street at night. Our images of violence against women are shaped by the context in which we live, by our social class, personal experience, education, culture and — of course — the media. These images are different in different societies and cultures . . . (Davies 1994, p.223)

Women's groups throughout the world have been successful in different way's in challenging patriarchal claims and images of men's violence against women as being somehow 'natural' and neither criminal nor systematic. In theorizing about the ways in which to consider male sexual violence certain terms have become important. One such is that of 'continuum' which, Liz Kelly notes, connects women's different experiences of sexual violence, as it:

> enables us to document and name the range of abuse, intimidation, coercion, intrusion, threat and force whilst acknowledging that there are no clearly defined and discrete analytic categories into which men's behaviour can be placed. (Kelly 1988, pp.75–6)

This is important in connecting women's different experiences of male violence, such that the expressions of 'men's gender power through the routine use of aggression against women is connected to 'non-routine' assaults, such as rape, which are extensions of more commonplace intrusions' (Kelly 1988, p.27). It does not imply any 'weight' as to the situation in which the violence occurs or the 'seriousness' of such violence. This continuum of male sexual violence is important, as Jill Radford notes:

> it provides a broader perspective that more sensitively reflects the experiences of male violence as named and defined by women and children. Rather than forcing experience of sexual abuse into discrete legal categories the concept of a continuum allows us to identify and address a range of forced or coercive heterosexual

experiences. The notion of a continuum further facilitates the analysis of male sexual violence as a form of control central to the maintenance of patriarchy. (Radford and Russell 1992, p.4)

In the context of political attempts to define male sexual violence in terms of male control, discussion in the European Parliament has raised several key issues. A resolution was passed there in 1986 concerning 'violence against women and girls'. This was taken to refer to:

> situations where women are forced into a relationship, contact or act whereby it is obvious that they have no independent rights to determine how they are to relate to others, in this case men. In such situations women are restricted in terms of their freedom and independence . . .
> Although violence is frequently expressed in a sexual manner, it is not always a case of sexual actions. The characteristic feature is that, in the case of violence against women and girls, the relationship between those committing the offence and their victims is sexualized. This means that women are judged against their will by their sexual characteristics and that their own experience of sexuality is subordinated to that of the man. (Acker undated, p.6)

This definition of 'violence against women and girls' is similar to that of 'sexual violence' used by feminist theorists (Bunch and Carillo 1992, Kelly 1988, Radford and Russell 1992). The Socialist Group of the European Parliament express the necessity to link male sexual violence with the domination of men by women economically:

> The more disadvantaged a woman's economic situation is, the harder it is for that woman to escape from sexual violence. This means, according to the resolution, that the search for a policy to combat this violence is part of an emancipation policy aimed at ending the unequal division of power between men and women. (Ibid.)

It is clear from the contributions in each of the three sections that it is precisely these types of policies that are the most difficult to develop and to promote as there is often a strong resistance, from those in power, to their incorporation into legal and social policy frameworks.

> The importance of control over women can be seen in the intensity of resistance to laws and social changes that put

control of women's bodies in women's hands: reproductive
rights, freedom of sexuality whether heterosexual or lesbian,
laws that criminalise rape in marriage, etc. (Bunch and Carrillo
1992, p.8)

It is to the development and implementation of such policy measures
that we return in conclusion.

DOMESTIC VIOLENCE, FAMILY VIOLENCE, VIOLENCE IN THE HOUSEHOLD

The approaches considered in this section are primarily concerned
with what has been termed 'domestic violence' or 'family violence'.
Domestic violence has become an overall term used to define violence
which takes place in or around the home. Some writers use this term
to define violence by adult, current or former intimates. It can also be
used to consider violence in the household perpetrated by a woman's
partner, parent, child or other relative. Some uses of the term 'domestic
violence' include forms of child abuse and elder abuse. However, as
Kathy Silard points out the term 'domestic' can be used to trivialise
such violence:

> The legal system is indifferent and casual in its treatment of domestic
> violence. The family is seen to be a shrine to be protected — violence
> is called 'a domestic' which totally trivializes the real pain, fear
> and horror that occurs and also hides the fact that it is women
> and children who are the victims of this prolific violence. (Silard
> in Davies 1994, p.241)

Other terms have been used in literature and policy-making documentation — such as family violence, wife battering, wife abuse and
woman abuse.

'Domestic violence' has been commonly used in certain Western
industrialised countries, including the UK, in policy-making circles.
Women experiencing violence in the home do not always think, or
speak, of their experience as 'domestic violence'. Male violence from
fathers, uncles, or brothers against women is not always specifically
addressed within this term. Nevertheless, it is most often in 'privatized'
situations, those that are viewed socially as 'safe', that women experience
domestic violence.

Family violence is a broad term. It can include experiences of incest
and child abuse but this is not always clearly specified. Nor is defining
what a 'family' is, by any means a straightforward matter. Diana

Gittins argues the controversial nature of claiming such an entity as 'the family':

> Childbearing, childrearing, and the construction of gender, allo-cation of resources, mating and marriage, sexuality and ageing, all loosely fit into our idea of family, and yet we have seen how all of them are variable over time, between cultures and between social sectors. The claim that 'the family' is universal has been especially problematic because of the failure by most to differentiate between how small groups of people live and work together, and what the ideology of appropriate behaviour for men, women and children within families has been. (Gittins 1985, p.70)

Terms such as 'wife battering/wife abuse' commonly used in the 1970s, again can assume men exercising violence against adult female partners within heterosexual marriages, common-law or otherwise. Feminist definitions reject the assumptions in such terms due to their restriction to legitimized unions. The term 'battered women' was also used to describe the violent consequences that women experience in various situations of domestic violence. Again, some feminist definitions have rejected the word 'battered' as many women do not identify with it, especially if the abuse is primarily emotional and/or psychological.

In the UK there have been many studies concerned with outlining the important considerations and debates about defining violence against women (Dobash and Dobash 1980 and 1993; Stanko 1985; Hanmer and Maynard 1987; Kelly 1988; Smart 1989; Maynard 1993). It is feminist thinkers who have highlighted the contradictions in much of the non-feminist literature in terms of patriarchal assumptions concerning women's oppression. Non-feminist approaches do not view male sexual violence in the same ways as feminist theorists and do not make connections with wider issues of male violence against women. Feminist considerations view most of the non-feminist theories as serving to disguise or deny men's positions of dominance within patriarchal systems. From non-feminist perspectives certain everyday assumptions can arise which are detrimental to offering women useful analyses of male violence. Such assumptions can include aspects of 'rights' within families (men's 'rights' over women and children), understanding of violent behaviour in men as something 'abnormal' (rather than common) and suppositions about how to 'deal with' violence and what are 'appropriate' responses (within 'private' families).

Aspects of the 'privacy' of family life can assume importance in non-feminist considerations both in that family members could be assumed to have rights to behave as they please in their own home and that families can solve their own problems without outside interference. That 'families' differ tremendously in their forms and that many people do not live in any socially-recognised form of [heterosexual-nuclear] 'family' is seldom considered within such studies. Nor are the different contexts in which minority ethnic communities' living conditions are structured in relation to the state. Racism within police forces, social services and the judiciary seriously affects the outcome of intervention within people's homes and lives. Assumptions from limited, non-feminist perspectives still often shape men's and women's thoughts on how to assess and deal with violent situations.

In her work 'Violence Towards Women', Mary Maynard outlines three significant kinds of definition — legal; professional/expert and those of women themselves. As with all attempts at definition the political nature of male sexual violence means that the narrower, non-feminist proposals in legal or expert areas can and are being challenged by feminist perspectives which are very much built upon the experiences and definitions of women themselves. Maynard notes the need for widening the parameters of research, as in her study she found that:

> the experiences of Black women and those from different cultural groupings are hidden in the literature. In addition, the violence experienced by lesbians, both as women and as a result of anti-lesbianism, is largely ignored. Most material is overwhelmingly about white, apparently heterosexual women and, where there has been research which includes women from other backgrounds, this tends to ignore issues of racism and heterosexism in analysing its findings. (Maynard 1993, p.119)

The interrelationships between the range of different types of violence against women is something that most of the contributors to this volume have been at pains to highlight. In this way the contributions gathered here attempt to widen the parameters of study and extend the comparative frame within the 'European' dimension. Many of the issues raised in Section One are taken up by the contributors in Section Two in connection with the linkages between systems of gender, 'race', economic oppression and the violent consequences for women's lives.

1

Sexism and Sexual Abuse in Russia

Natalia Khodyreva

Contemporary violence against women in Russia has its roots in historical specificity as well as in patriarchal attitudes towards women, anarchy
and impunity in the legal sphere and women's poverty. Sexist approaches
on the part of most specialists (lawyers, physicians, policemen, psychologists, psychiatrists) to women, and women's low self-assurance and
self-respect, aggravate this situation in the post-perestroika period.

BACKGROUND

Until recently the phenomena of rape and sexual violence were practically
ignored in Russia. Despite the fact that the country's Constitution
declared equality of men and women, men still dominated. The first and
foremost indicator of such domination, and consequently, of women's
discrimination, is the extent of violence of men towards women. It was
as late as 4 February 1989 that detailed statistics regarding rape and
other violent-related crime was published at last. Even from the official
figures one can see that the number of registered rapes grew unfailingly,
even though this kind of crime is characterized by greatest latency.

Figures of registered rapes in Russia and in the integrated Soviet Union

	1987	1988	1989	1990
Russia	10,902	11,560	14,597	15,010
USSR	16,756	17,658	21,875	22,467

(Zhenschiny v SSSR (Women in the USSR) 1992, p.771)

REPORTING OF VIOLENCE

These figures differ drastically from the real number of rapes. This is attested by information supplied by the recently established independent women's organizations and centres providing help for victims of sexual violence.

Natalia Gaidarenko from Moscow was the first to organize in 1989 a hot line for rape victims. Natalia wrote an article for *Komsomolskaya Pravda* and since then has received over 750 letters from sexually abused women. According to the figures given to her by the prosecutor's office there were 3,148 sexual crimes committed against girls-teenagers in 1991 in Russia. She answered about 50 calls in the first half of 1993.

Only three women of those she worked with reported to the police. All the others preferred not to report the rape for two main reasons: attitudes of the police and people of legal professions to these things and the women's conviction that the crime was to some extent their own fault. Gaidarenko reports that often young girls who were raped are held responsible for what happened and are accused of inventing a story of rape instead of admitting that the sexual act was their own free will or that they turned on the boy(s) intentionally.

After the First Women's Forum in Dubna (First Independent Feminist Conference, 1991) some volunteers (M. Aristova, G. Bratukhina, I. Lunin, O. Kocharian, N. Khodyreva and T. Fedorova) joined their efforts to organize a hot line and special service for victims of sexual violence. It was based in the state medical department 'Children's Psychiatry' located in St. Petersburg.

After the service was announced over the local radio and a corresponding article appeared in the press we received plenty of calls. Most of them were from teenagers — victims of sexual violence (55.5 per cent). Women between eighteen and twenty-one made up one third of all cases. Those between twenty-one and fifty made up about 14 per cent. According to the results of our research 93 per cent of sexual assault victims were women. During the one-year period of our work only four women of out of 333 (that is about 1 per cent!) reported to the police.

The statistics uncovering the problems of rape in Russia are frightening: only 10 per cent of rape involved robbery; 75–80 per cent of attackers acted in groups of about three or more men; 64–84 per cent of defendants were under the influence of alcohol (Martin 1976). According to the estimations most Soviet women experienced at least one rape or attempted rape in their life. Rape made up 75–95 per cent of all cases of sex crime (Mamonova 1984).

According to the conclusion of our modern researchers (I. Korneva 1993, I. Lunin 1993, N. Khodyreva, 1993) up to 60 per cent of women and girls encounter sexual violence in their lives. Thus official statistics reports only one of ten or of a hundred cases. As an example, 288 rape cases were registered by the police or first-aid station in 1992 in St. Petersburg. If we multiply these figures by something between ten and a hundred we shall get — to this or that extent — the real situation regarding rape and sexual assault in St. Petersburg. By estimates the real figure of sexual abuse in 1992 was 2,880–28,800 cases. It is peculiar that only 40 per cent of cases mentioned (of 288 reported) were taken into account. And though the number of cases registered increased by 18 per cent in 1993, the number of court proceedings was even less than before. (In St. Petersburg and its environs there are about six million residents.)

In 1993 the information of the criminal situation in our city was made known to the public. But the absolute figure of rapes was not given. Regardless of the rise in percentage of cases as compared with average figures over Russia — from 3 per cent in 1987 to 63 per cent in 1992 — a conclusion was made about relatively stable levels of sexual violence (though there was a remark that the problem needs further investigation and interpretation). It was also noted that the criminal activity of teenagers involving rape and robbery is four to six times higher than the similar adult's activity (*Smena* 21 September 1993).

During nine months of 1994, the law enforcement bodies of St. Petersburg and Leningrad administrative rural region registered 212 complaints from rape victims. This makes only 0.25 per cent of the total figure of criminal cases. Only one victim was raped and threatened with a pistol. Forty-nine rapes took place in public places and sixty rapes were disclosed (*Komsomolskaya Pravda* 21 October 1994).

LAW AND LEGAL PROCEEDINGS

The criminal law of Russia is not so bad as such. In the clause on rape not only physical violence and threats on the part of the attacker are taken into account, but also the victim's helpless situation. The maximum punishment envisaged for the rapist is 15 years of imprisonment or even the death penalty. But in reality if the victim has no visible physical injury, it is hard to bring an action against a rapist.

The most difficult technical task concerns the collection of evidence (sperm, for example). This test has to be made within forty-eight to seventy-two hours after the crime was committed. Thus, the victim of violence who is in a grave psychological condition must go to the police, wait for an investigator, give accurate evidence, and afterwards, get a permit for a forensic examination by waiting in a queue. This procedure should be changed, and medical tests should be made in some friendly environment. The woman could undergo medical testing there as the first step, and then decide whether she should go to the police or not.

It should be noted that the plenary Session of the Russian Federation Supreme Court, having adopted a decree on 'practice concerning rape cases', inclines courts of law, when setting a penalty, to take relations between the victim and defendant prior to the rape into account. That gives a chance to the abuser's defence to extenuate his guilt if he and his victim were in marital or partner relations or even were just acquaintances.

There is a clause on sexual harassment in the criminal law. It reads that forcing a woman to enter into sexual relations if she is dependent on the assaulter either materially or as his subordinate entails punishment (up to three years of imprisonment).

But in practice this clause does not work. Not more than eight to ten related cases are brought before the court during one year. That is because, first, it is extremely troublesome to produce evidence and, second, in the sphere of private business (when salaries are rather high) a woman has to suffer serious oppression from her employer. In case of her refusal to obey she immediately is sacked.

Often one can see advertisements in the newspapers that there are job openings for secretaries (strictly young, attractive and without complexes) who are supposed to provide sexual services for the boss or his clients. Women's organizations succeeded in making the officials responsible admit that publication of such advertisements is discrimination against women and asked them to stop publishing them.

What is typical for the actual work of law enforcement bodies with victims of violence? Being asked: 'Why didn't you report to the police and have criminal proceedings started?' the victims mentioned first of all the uselessness of such appeals, their own unwillingness to be improperly treated by police workers, and their fear of the violator who often terrorized the victim and her close relatives.

Among the case stories of those applying to our centre there are cases of girls being raped by police and state security bodies' workers. We managed to institute proceedings on one of these cases, but at the moment the action is suspended. Victims of violence also told us that they were persuaded by the police not to institute proceedings; also they were misinformed concerning the possibility of undergoing medical testing for examination by legal experts and they were given invalid examination permits.

'A situation when a woman accuses a man of rape for the sake of saving her face in the situation when their liaison became known is typical. What for? To make the chap marry her. 15 per cent of all rape reports are false' — that is written by workers of an institute reporting to the Ministry of Internal Affairs of Russia (*Krestyankar* 6, 1994). All this is characteristic of the attitude of people working for investigation bodies towards the victims of violence, as well as of their inability and unwillingness to provide help and protection to rape victims required from them according to appropriate instructions and the law.

It is no wonder, because in the course of lawyers' instructions they are taught first of a victimological approach. ('Victimity' is a personal predisposition to become a crime victim.) 'Again we confirm our assurance of the fact that the victim's role is great in the genesis and mechanism of violent sexual crimes'. Antonyan and Tkatchenko make this claim in their book *Sexual Crimes* (Antonyan and Tkatchenko 1993). They continue: 'Women who are accustomed to behave themselves unduly, for example, drink hard permanently, easily enter into relations with dubious people, etc. become, *as the natural result* (my emphasis), victims of sexual transgression' (ibid., p.175).

Theoretically, contemporary Soviet law can even be considered progressive as far as rape is concerned. However, irrespective of progressive laws the facts indicate that the judicial criminal system is against rape victims. For example, a Soviet reference book for judges warns a lawyer that he must be aware that sometimes a woman who agreed to sexual intercourse with a man can later claim that it was a rape, 'because she may feel ashamed, or influenced by her friends or relatives, or pursuing some certain private objectives. Teenagers, in particular, easily fall under pressure of their associates' (Juviler 1977).

A Soviet handbook on forensic medicine gives detailed advice to doctors engaged in the examination of rape victims' warning them that rape is sometimes 'feigned'. Finally the doctors are recommended to examine the evidence closely and to analyze the victim's prior sexual experience. This tendency 'to accuse the victim' is extremely firm in contemporary juridical institutions since medieval times (S. Kuznetsova and N. Khodyreva, 'Study of lawyers' and doctors' attitude to sexual and domestic victims of violence in St. Petersburg', 1994).

DOMESTIC VIOLENCE

14,000 women were killed and 57,000 battered by their partners in 1993. At present the police cannot apply any specific laws protecting women in families. In cases of family violence men are just tried for hooliganism.

What can be resorted to in cases of violence to women in the family, in the first place, something like 'infringement of the public order' or 'manifestation of obvious disrespect of the society'. Domestic violence has never been considered in Russia as a social domain, especially since, according to the Russian tradition it was the husband's duty to educate the wife by lashing; and the whip hung over the matrimonial bed (in ancient Russia). So, domestic violence is still a 'private' problem in contemporary people's minds rather than 'breach of the peace'. The situation is also characterized both by failure to understand and to disregard it on the part of legal protection bodies. None of these bodies know how to intervene in a family conflict. For that reason women are often told, as explanation, that it is she who provokes aggressive actions on the part of her husband or partner by her behaviour.

So far neighbours, relatives and acquaintances are still guided by the principle 'Lovers' tiffs are harmless'. However, in 1987 a Soviet Minister of Interior A. Vlasov claimed that 70 per cent of all murders were domestic murders. Other sources give a lower estimate of murder committed at home — only 44 per cent. Research into homicide shows that 'women are the victims in over one third of the most serious form of homicide' (Shelly 1987).

CULTURAL SITUATION AND SEXISM IN RUSSIA

A superficial view of the situation might make one think that cultural traditions were ruined after the revolution (1917). But in reality they are still the same. Though women were urged to work in industry equally with men, they were traditionally engaged in housework, child-rearing, looking after elderly and sick people. Moreover, all the responsibility for relations in the family, solving conflicts with children and relatives and maintaining the family was laid upon women. For that reason in case of divorce or the 'husband' drinking heavily it is the woman who has always been blamed, evidenced in present-day sayings like 'a husband never leaves a good wife' or 'a good wife's husband would never drink hard'.

Prior to *perestroika* there existed an official image imposed by the press, television, cinema and school system according to which men and women in Soviet society lived and worked together in ideal harmony being united by their common commitment to the building of communism. And it is true, women were employed in industry on an equal footing with men, but the top positions, which implies better-paid positions, were filled by men. One should remember that a position at the top ensured privileges to men (something that other people could not have or receive). In particular those priveleges included infringing upon other people's rights and committing violence over women. These people were never made judicially answerable for their crimes (Vasilyeva 1993).

It was only after the start-up of *perestroika* in 1985, that materials appeared in the press about women's treatment in Stalinist camps. A woman recollects the practice of mass rape when guards let the other non-prisoners rape imprisoned women for bottles of vodka (Glinka 1989). These facts backed by the knowledge of crying transgressions of human rights in the USSR on a mass scale, confirm the existence of gender violence despite the fact that official statistics have never provided such information.

The illusion of equality of men and women in the USSR was created due to promotion of some selected women to 'masculine' (in the traditional sense of this word) professions. Thus, we could be proud of the fact that we had a woman-cosmonaut, a woman-marine captain, as well as a test-pilot, academician and a member of the Communist Party Politburo. At the same time a whole lot of women were engaged in unhealthy laborious trades with bad labour conditions for scanty earnings. The Soviet cinematograph formed an image of a merry and energetic woman, a bit rude, and able to stand up for herself. The man was either a romantic or artless simpleton. A wise wife always knew how to treat him including when he was drunk. All this looked quite inoffensive. Gradually, an image was formed of a strong dominating woman and her man being under her thumb giving up all his salary to his wife.

In the environment of permanent disproportion between the male and female population, and demographers' articles about the lack of men compared to women in number, women are encouraged to believe in the necessity to take special care of men, and a certain anxiety to marry was engendered. Demands concerning marriage partners were rather low, and cases of family violence were not made public because women were reluctant to 'wash their dirty linen in public' for lots of reasons.

All these peculiarities as well as the consequences of traditional gender relations resulted in a specific men's and women's attitude to equality in the post-*perestroika* period.

Many young women ask in bewilderment what should they have equality with men for. They claim they are not at all interested in the problem of violence against women. In fact most women associate equality with hard working industry and with an image of a non-sexual 'emancipated' woman. Even in modern marriage advertisements the first thing women do is assure male readers that they do not belong to the category of 'emancipated' woman. Many people don't understand the word 'discrimination'. Women's activity against violation of human rights is not popular.

The traditional distribution of roles in the society still exists in reality notwithstanding some progress in declarations concerning other men and women (not oneself). 'Yes, I am a progressive-minded person; let women take part in politics, but in my family she wants to look after the house and the children and is not going to work' (typical statements of popular actors and film directors). It is probably hard to find any other country where popular showmen and actors so much adored by women would state so frankly their sexist attitude to women.

RESEARCH UNDERTAKEN

My students and myself worked on the problems described in the researches 'The Rape Myths and the Myth of Protector' (V. Getman and N. Khodyreva 1993). The initial findings showed that over 50 per cent of respondents — victims of sexual assaults — had a deeply ingrained conviction that men (husbands and partners) were their physical defenders, and the psychological trauma they experienced being raped or subjected to domestic violence was intensified by the destruction of that perception of gender roles.

Some psychologists and psychiatrists who worked on the hot line laid specific emphasis on traditional concepts concerning rape. They used to tell those calling that the crime took place by accident, that the victims happened to be in the wrong place at the wrong time, that it wasn't the end of the world and they should just try to forget about it. The most tenacious myth is that rape is provoked by a woman's behaviour and outlook and that she is to blame for what happened just for that reason. The next group of myths is representation of men as creatures not to able to control their sexual drive and for that reason committing rape impulsively or after long abstinence. Then there goes a myth that the rape is mostly an act between an assaulter and victim who were not acquainted before. Marital rape is still a topic absolutely not developed.

The opinion that 'in no circumstances can one force somebody to have sexual intercourse' ranks eighth among the other opinions (Levitskaya, Orlik and Potapova 1993). Violence is accounted for in these researches by the different nature of male and female sexuality.

The public attitude towards rape victims must be changed as well. The existing stereotype — that it is women who are to blame — must be turned the other way round.

The research made at first-aid clinics (Kuznetsova 1993) proved that

80 per cent of female victims were injured by a man they knew, 10 per cent by men they didn't know and 10 per cent by other women. Among those coming to the clinics mentioned, only 3 per cent were raped, and so one can suppose that women are not in a hurry to go there with their problem because doctors also are seriously prejudiced against raped and assaulted women.

RAPE AS IT IS COVERED BY MASS MEDIA

Before *perestroika* the issue of rape and sexual violence received almost no attention on the part of the press. Now there is a tendency to exploit the 'hot subject' to titillate the readers. There are lots of articles about maniacs with plenty of details of the awful events. Even in more serious articles the idea seems to be that men have a sexual urge they are not able to control and that it is up to women to try to avoid dubious situations. We have been very concerned to challenge this manner of media coverage.

One of the latest television programmes was concerned with problems of abortion and violence in the society. It was shown unambiguously (on the background of a series of bloody events in Russia) that violence has its sources and is engendered by the very fact that women commit a 'murder' of human being (abortion). Thus it is true that women are primarily sinful, and all evil originates from them.

The orthodox church has already issued its brochures about the sin of abortion. The society 'Pro life' is now established in St. Petersburg. According to Levin, the Russian church attributes rape to the type of crime which 'dishonours' the victim (Levin 1989).

Recently, we were approached by a representative of the church who offered his help to our Crisis Centre — work with victims of violence. The help he proposed was to teach women prayers in order to build protection against the devil. As far as it is the devil who has an effect upon men through women, it is women who are to blame for the incest between a father and a daughter and other sexual abuse.

Our last interview (*Smena* 2 December 1994) was devoted to the creation of a system of women advocacy and recruitment of volunteers to our Crisis Centre. Presently we cooperate with a number of women journalists to cover these subjects.

PROSTITUTION

In Russia prostitution is prohibited by the law. But in fact, according to police information, there are about five thousand professional prostitutes operating in St. Petersburg; for them prostitution has been the main source of income over the past few years. Apart from these there are women who occasionally resort to prostitution as a means of making quick money.

Taking into account that 73 per cent of the city's unemployed are women, the total number of those involved in prostitution is far greater than the number of professionals. In former times (1980–5) most prostitutes worked as hairdressers, medical nurses, school cleaners or hotel maids. Now over half of them have no permanent place of work. Currently the difference between the professional prostitute's earnings and those of an 'ordinary' woman is huge. On the other hand, that is an indication of discrimination in the sphere of women's employment.

According to results of the research carried out among female students, some of the them consider prostitution a 'legitimate form of obtaining money'. Others claim that 'Prostitution stops the growth of unemployment, especially in the environment of sharp rises in prices for food and clothing' (Kozlova and Slucski 1994). There is almost no street prostitution in St. Petersburg. Occasionally one can see the so-called railway station prostitutes. They are usually inveterate alcoholics, in hopeless condition, and they do not account for more than 2–3 per cent of the total number of prostitutes.

The data collected during criminal investigations show that the majority of prostitutes are under thirty. A third have completed or nearly-completed higher education. One quarter of them started the 'work' before the age of eighteen. One in eight has a child. About 10 per cent of those arrested for prostitution in the city are students of higher educational establishments and technical colleges.

There exists a specific practice of involving underage children in prostitution and using them in sexual commerce; 45 per cent of hotel prostitutes had their first sexual experience before they were sixteen. There are groups of little girls whose job is providing sexual services to long-distance lorry drivers. The reason for teenagers being engaged in prostitution is their desire to earn money as well as grave problems in the family (Afanasiev and Skorobogatov 1994).

According to the data provided by *Tchas Pik* Newspaper (September 1994), currently 130 agencies operate in the city providing sexual services through different clubs, saunas and salons functioning within dating services advertised widely in the newspapers. The pay varies from twenty to one hundred US dollars, depending on the class of services provided. But the prostitute gets only one third of this amount, while the remaining amount is taken by the boss.

During the first half of 1994 forty criminal proceedings were instituted for keeping 'pandering agencies' and spreading sexually transmitted diseases (*Delovoy* 1994). Lawyers and police representatives have already started discussing the problem of legalization of prostitution: 'We see the outcome in setting up a network of brothels in the city. Only in that case we could raise taxes on that kind of activity and take spreading of sexually transmitted diseases under control' (*Delovoy* 1994). For reference — in 1990 there were 1232 brothels in St. Petersburg (*Argument and Facts* 1994).

No doubt, the state is interested in collecting taxes on prostitution for replenishing the budget. It is annoying that it is members of Mafia concerns and rackets who gain all of these earnings. As we can see, the arguments for legalization of prostitution are: 1. the struggle against sexually transmitted diseases, 2. protection of prostitutes against violence. But as we could see above, no woman (even a teenager) is guaranteed support in the case of violence, and in the case of reporting to the police she faces sexism and neglect.

Some workers in law enforcement bodies claim that 'a considerable percentage of sexual offences is provoked by victims themselves. A view of a provocatively short skirt is sufficient'. If so, then it is 'natural' to suppose that prostitution as such might be considered as a provocation for rape on the part of prostitutes themselves.

Moreover, being engaged in prostitution as an occupation may affect the course of criminal proceedings leading to extenuation of the rapist's guilt. 'Notwithstanding the gravity of the offence [murder of one woman and rape of the other woman] it was hard to fix exact punishment, because in the course of proceedings it was found out that both of the girls were prostitutes' (*Smena* 10 September 1994).

As far as sexually transmitted diseases are concerned, 80 per cent of women get them from their regular heterosexual partners because they 'trust' them and don't use condoms. But 96 per cent of prostitutes, in comparison, use condoms in their work. Many prostitutes take enough care of their health and call private doctors to be examined at home.

PROSTITUTION AND TRAFFICKING OF WOMEN

The Russian Federation took on itself the obligations of the UN Convention on fighting human trade and exploitive prostitution by third persons. This Convention was ratified in the 1954.

At present under the Criminal Code there is no article covering prostitution. However articles 210 and 226 of the Criminal Code cover: drawing a minor into prostitution, being held in a brothel of debauchery and pimping. Women working as prostitutes can be prosecuted and fined under articles 164–2 of the Administrative Code. In St. Petersburg for 1993 only ten people were charged under the above statutes. In 1994 it had risen to 40 people.

Russia's National Report to the UN World Conference in Beijing states that there is no special department in Russia dealing with prostitution. The drawing of minors into prostitution is brought to light only in cases of some other criminal code violation. 'This acts as a barrier to government control of this process and does not allow for a realistic appraisal of scale of this phenomenon' (ibid.).

In 1995 the newspaper *Tchas Pik* carried an article entitled 'A new involuntary market has opened in St. Petersburg' about prostitution rings. In the course of many years some men have been involved in kidnapping women. Women were taken away to Viborg (a city near St. Petersburg, bordering Finland) and were forced to work as prostitutes for several months. Out of ten incidents officially uncovered four girls were kidnapped on the streets of St. Petersburg. Two of them were juveniles.

In this incident the brothel consisted of an average two-room apartment where the girls serviced Finnish workers for 150 FM a session. In the absence of clients they serviced their kidnappers. It is interesting to note that when one of the girls managed to get to a telephone she called not the police but her mother who then called for help. The police pulled her away from the brothel. Being beaten down to animal condition the girl refused to press charges. This was enough for the Viborg procuracy to, in turn, refuse to file a criminal charge.

The following year (1993) five girls went to the Viborg procuracy. Three had been prostitutes and two were kidnapped while returning home from work along Nevsky Prospect (St. Petersburg's central street). When they ran away from their kidnappers and filed a complaint it did not prove convincing enough for the Viborg procuracy. In other incidents several times police officers during routine investigations of motor vehicles were confronted by female passengers claiming to have been kidnapped, then taken to a brothel where they were raped and beaten. The police refused to file a complaint. Receiving a $400 bribe from the kidnappers the police threw the women out into the cold (the girls did not even have any warm clothing on). They once again fell into the hands of their kidnappers and were once again raped and beaten. This is how they spent the next three months. In the end the mother of one of the victims filed a complaint with the procuracy and at long last after three years of existence the brothel was closed down. The regional procuracy overturned the decision of the Viborg city procuracy and filed charges in the above described cases.

The article ends with several suggestions for women kidnapped: 'Do not be shy about screaming and never get into a car with strangers. Do not be afraid to go to the police. Believe in the police's absolute power to neutralize any threat'. This incident characterizes the reaction of the legal authorities to such incidents, the completely non-existent protection of women, and their disbelief that they can be protected.

Women from the former Soviet Union are sold abroad as well. Mafia gangs, with well-established and efficient practices of making money from prostitution, act as suppliers usually.

Brothel keepers in Western Europe pay up to two thousand dollars for each woman to the Russian mafia. Often the girls used in cross-border trade of women are quite inexperienced and come from relatively low social backgrounds. Some of them were taken abroad being promised a temporary job (not in the sphere of sex services), then they were deprived of their passports, and forced to deal in something they hadn't expected. Others hoped to earn some money abroad because of the severe unemployment at home, and afterwards, return to Russia, to start their own business (*Komsomolskaya Pravda* 21 October 1994).

As these women work illegitimately, they are not subject to protection by local law in case of infringement upon their rights. Nevertheless, in experts' opinions, the scale of Russians getting into 'flesh commodity' markets is quite sizeable. Already now the appearance of prostitutes of Slavonic origin promotes the development of sex-business in Western Europe and Scandinavia, as Russian girls are unpretentious and are ready to work for lower prices than local prostitutes (ibid.).

PORNOGRAPHY

It is hard to find a city in Russia now where pornographic editions are not sold at every corner without hindrance. They are sold by teenagers and aged ladies willing to earn some money for everyday needs. Many television channels show pornographic films that were banned for show in other countries. After a long-time ban on 'sex', people greedily devour the forbidden fruit. In this environment of a low sexual culture, as well as traditions of sexism and violence towards women and children, pornography continues to spread the woman's image as a sex-object.

VIOLENCE DURING HOSTILITIES

Refugees from Chechnya told us about the grave situation of women in military conflict zones. Moslem traditions and judicial lawlessness resulted in situations when women after being raped were driven out of their own families. It is dangerous for women to appear in the street after 5 p.m.: they are shot at, they are dragged into cars and taken to military camps, where they are raped or made servants (according to the testimony of refugees from Grozny, September 1994).

OUR ACTIVITIES

Since we started our work in 1992 we have developed a number of programmes aimed at the following categories of people:

1   Teenage girls who participate in the school programme 'sexual safety' introduced in St. Petersburg and other Russian cities. We believe that such a special course for girls should be introduced in every school in order to prepare girls for dangerous situations. The boys also need a special course on non-violent communication with girls.

2   Students, psychologists, social workers and volunteers who take part in workshops on feminist counselling. In our opinion a special psychological service should be established to help women-victims of sexual violence.

Experience shows that psychologists are not always able to provide competent help without special training.

3   Single mothers, divorced women, lesbians who are members of training courses in assertiveness and self-defence. We are continuously developing ties with professionals in the community who might be able to help our clients.

We conducted as well a workshop for men — 'Men can help stop the rape' — with participation of teachers and managers working in the field of education.

The Centre's workers have taken part in political actions for women's rights, they are well-known in the circles concerned about violence against women. In October 1994, nine crisis centres from different Russian cities decided to set up an Association of Crisis Centres for Women. The Centre 'Sisters' (N. Gaidarenko), the Crisis Centre from Moscow (M. Pisclakova) and the Crisis Psychological Centre for Women in St. Petersburg (N. Khodyreva) are planning to arrange a joint action 'Safety for Women'.

The problem of violence against women is probably one of the few able to unite women's social organizations in order to take part in making new laws and supervising their observance by working in the Social Chamber of St. Petersburg. This work began in November 1994.

2

Domestic Violence Against Women in Hungary

Kriszta Szalay

In the first part of this paper I intend to outline some of my observations and ideas concerning domestic violence against women in Hungary. Since no serious research has so far been done into this topic in Hungary I will rely on my personal experience and knowledge whilst being fully aware of the limitations of such an approach. The age-old methodological problem applies to me just as much as it would to anyone trying to write about something of which she is very much part. Indeed, who knows more about the porcupine: the porcupine herself or the zoologist who observes her? At this point I think it necessary to clarify my position as the author of this chapter. I am a woman of forty who has spent all her life in Hungary and has survived violent relationships both as a child and as an adult. Whether I like it or not I am, in many ways, the product of the so-called socialism that was the ruling ideology in this country till the late 1980s. In other words, this is the porcupine in me. I am also a university lecturer and a volunteer of NaNE (Women working with Women against Violence), the first-ever hotline for battered women and children in Hungary. In these latter capacities I would call myself the zoologist.

In the second part of my paper I take on the role of the record-keeper and familiarise the reader with the objectives, activities and achievements

of those twenty-odd brave women who have been operating the above
mentioned hotline for over eighteen months now amidst all the inevitable
ups and downs of such a venture. I know that most of them are simply
too modest or practical to speak about NaNE at length. One of my
objectives with this work is to honour and to thank them.

IDIOSYNCRASIES OF DOMESTIC VIOLENCE AGAINST WOMEN IN HUNGARY

The problem of domestic violence against women anywhere in the world
is inseparable from the social climate in which it occurs. Assessing this
social climate in Hungary now is particularly difficult since for five years
the country has been in the process of transition from so-called socialism
to a market economy with all the accompanying social, economic and
psychological consequences. It seems that a great price has to be paid for
political freedom and national sovereignty especially by those who are
traditionally the farthest away from the springs of power: i.e. women,
children and the elderly. Together with the poor, they constitute the
most vulnerable strata of Hungarian society today.

In trying to assess the causes, patterns and modifications of domestic
violence against women in Hungary one has to face other difficulties as
well. The lack of statistics, surveys and scholarly interest in the topic
combines into a vicious circle with the lack of realisation of how great
the problem really is. But even if interest were higher — one suspects —
latency would prevent women from coming forward with their miseries.
The often hostile social attitude — blaming the victim — the humiliating
police procedures, the lack of sympathy and expertise in many who meet
the victims result in women becoming shy and ridden with guilt. They
get isolated and so uncertain about themselves that they do not ask
help even from their family members or friends. Assessment is further
made difficult by the inadequacies of the Hungarian penal and civil
law system. The Hungarian penal code does not recognise marital
rape. So as far as official statistics are concerned, it does not happen
in this country. Little wonder then that only one case of rape in ten
gets reported to the police. It is telling that the only statistics so far
(*see* Appendix 1) that focus on women crime victims in Hungary were
not produced by the official Central Statistical Office but ordered by
one of the parliamentary parties, the Free Democrats, from a market
research agency. Another source that could supply data about domestic
violence against women could be the divorce courts. Here again our
vision is occluded by the fact that the complicated and long-lasting
divorce procedure together with the housing problems (the batterer

often remains in the same flat after the divorce) keeps many women back from turning to court. Normally, the police with their records and experience could be of great help. However, the overburdened and in this respect untrained Hungarian police tend to banalise family problems, and even often will not take records. It is not completely a legend that they will not interfere until 'blood flows'. Traditionally, the church is looked upon as a reliable source of information concerning all sorts of social problems. But although the importance and influence of the church has been steadily growing in this country over the past five years, many victims of violence are still not in the habit of turning to clerics with their problems, or indeed, to anybody. Another factor that makes assessment difficult lies in violence being a culturally defined phenomenon. What counts as gross violence in one culture might go unmentioned in another. Indeed, it is hard to define where exactly violence begins: verbal aggression, light physical violence such as pushing, pinching or serious physical violence? In defining violence, it seems, there are a great number of varieties even within Hungarian culture itself. In this respect there are great differences between, say a Roma family and a Magyar one, between an urban family and one in the provinces, between a professional family and a working-class household. Generally, it can be stated that violence for most Hungarians begins at the physical level.

The difficulties of assessment however, should not keep one back from pondering upon the causes of the high incidence of domestic violence against women in this country.

The first such cause might lie in the fact that up until the 1880s Hungarian culture was a basically agrarian one. Endurance and patience have a great ethical value in such cultures, especially as far as women are concerned. Traits of this endurance can be seen in films that have been made about peasant cultures in Sweden, Russia or Hungary, for example. Folk-tales and folk-songs also corroborate the evidence that women were expected to be immensely patient, waiting many a year for 'Johnny' who has gone away to be a soldier. Peasant culture also means a highly hierarchical family structure, where the father, or, should he be missing, the eldest son is head of the family. Domestic violence was often seen as part of the woman's lot, as something inevitable and socially accepted. This seems to be true even if one knows what a crucial and influential role women did play in the economic management of the family.

Another cause of the high level of violence in a society has often been linked with that society's exposure to grand-scale aggression — war. It has been observed that all sorts of violence show an incidence in those European countries that have experienced war not very long ago within a few generation'. In that respect Hungary is most unfortunate: two world wars and a revolution (the 1956 Civil War and War of Independence) have left a lasting mark on the country. It seems such experiences teach people (how) to be aggressive and also banalise 'minor' forms of aggression, such as domestic violence.

Next, it should be kept in mind that forty years of a totalitarian regime in Hungary resulted in a general erosion of human rights. Human dignity had never been a serious issue except in slogans. The fact that in such circumstances people could not direct their aggression upwards, whatever it stemmed from, contributed to the general practice of what is known as the downward delegation of aggression. The lack of opportunities for social negotiation plus the undeveloped conflict-resolving skills all resulted in a generally high level of tolerance towards all sorts of violence. One should not forget that domestic violence against women in Hungary is part and parcel of a more general practice of violence that is still all too frequently visited on children in the family, pupils at school, young men in the army, mental patients in the hospitals, suspects at the police stations, or, considering not only the human world, animals as well. I would say that the despairingly high rate of suicide in this country can also be interpreted in this context as an extreme form of violence directed against oneself.

Partly as a result of socialist protocol and partly dictated by economic necessities old family patterns loosened and finally broke up in the course of women becoming independent breadwinners. In 1994 80 per cent of women were at work. This otherwise positive change has had its dark sides: women became overburdened and often frustrated in their many roles while men also reacted ambiguously. On the one hand, they enjoyed the benefits of the increasing family income, on the other, they had to deal with their growing anxiety over gender roles. Many of them were unable to cope with the new situation and canalised their anxiety into aggression. It is also of great significance here that on the average, women in Hungary are better trained than men (*see* Appendix 2). More girls finish the eight grades of elementary schools than boys, more women students choose secondary grammar schools rather than secondary vocational ones, and almost as many of them get a university degree as men. A 'white-collar' wife and a 'blue-collar' husband — although the latter may earn three times as much as his wife — is a set-up which is often a 'problem' in itself in Hungary.

After forty years of a somewhat artificial full employment, the deep running economic changes that began around 1990 brought with them the hitherto unknown experience of unemployment. Up till December 1994 a significantly higher percentage of men had been out of work than women. The reasons here are manifold. Since for decades women have been doing the same job for less money than men, it was 'logical' on the part of the employer to send men away first. Also, the first target of the economic transformation had been the highly unprofitable heavy industries and mining, these traditional catchment areas of unskilled and skilled male labour power. So even if we know that many women simply did not register as unemployed because they, unlike men, were able to compensate themselves by returning to the traditional family roles, it can safely be said that until quite recently unemployment had hit Hungarian men harder than women. Now that unemployment has reached the traditionally female professions, education and health care, the situation is changing. Nonetheless, no researcher of domestic violence fails to point out the correlation between the loss in social status and the growth of violence at home.

As one looks around in Hungary today one sees a deep eco-social crisis, a crisis in the system of values, in self esteem — for which, yet again, the most vulnerable will have to pay the price. After a couple of years of stagnation, or even decreasing, alcoholism, abortion, suicide and divorce rates are rising again. The same lack of conflict-resolving skills that drives Hungarian men mad and violent, drives them to the grave as well: the mortality of Hungarian men in the age bracket forty-five to fifty-five is the highest in the world. Also, their life expectancy is seven years less than that of Hungarian women. Among a thousand other things this means more widows and more single-parent families.

I would like to dwell on this last point a little to make it as clear as possible that domestic violence against women in Hungary is inseparable from its social context. That is one reason why many generalisations about this problem will not work. That is why the *net* import of foreign ideas, procedures and ideologies should be avoided. That is why no-one should identify domestic violence as a problem for women and children only. Only a system-oriented approach seems productive which understands that the batterer is also a victim. Therefore, do not scapegoat men. Do not antagonise men and women. In the years of 'socialism' civil society was more or less united in their hatred/suspicion/reservations felt towards the regime: men in Hungary did not hate women and women did not hate men. Let not that be wasted: the war between the sexes only benefits the oppressor, whatever you conceive that to be.

What can be done then to put an end to domestic violence? To get our bearings, professional, unbiased research should be done into the problem. Everybody who is committed to fighting violence at home should know what exactly he or she is fighting against so that they could adapt their moves and policies accordingly.

In trying to prevent domestic violence happening education campaigns should be initiated targeting schoolchildren, men and women alike, plus teachers and educational authorities. Conflict resolution, negotiation of problems, consensus-making skills should be taught at schools. In parallel, the already existing school and family counselling units should be reinforced by adequate staffing and funding. Awareness raising campaigns should be organised to call public attention to the problem and also to make it easier for survivors of violence to tell their stories. This is often the first step towards the solution of the problem. Self-help groups should be set up for battered women and violent men. Efforts should be made to make people who meet survivors of violence more tolerant and sympathetic. Doctors, police officials, judges, priests, social workers and lay helpers should be trained in how to face the problem and how to handle it effectively and tactfully. More hotlines should be set up, also for the batterers themselves. Widespread experience has corroborated what one had suspected already, namely that many violent men are very unhappy about their own aggression and would like to find ways in which to get rid of it. At the same time, more shelters for battered women and their children are needed. Although a nationwide network of these is slowly developing they often fail in the present economic crisis. It is telling that in Budapest (two million inhabitants, high incidence of domestic violence) there are less than one hundred places in shelters for women and their children. Further civil organisations should be founded and funded that could combat violence in the homes. Also, some kind of national machinery should be implemented to help in diagnosing and fighting the problem.

This national machinery together with the civil organisations could exercise pressure on the government for more involvement and for adequate legislation. Reforms in law and legal procedures should be initiated. At present, it seems, both legal philosophy and practice are lagging behind the events. And last, but not least, communication between groups and individuals committed to work against domestic violence should be improved. It seems, we have not quite managed to avoid the pitfalls of mistrust, jealousy, rivalry and ideological fights. This is very sad and also a waste of time and energy.

In conclusion, domestic violence against women in Hungary has its local shadings and variations. Any successful attempt at trying to stop it will have to bear that in mind. The problems are many, the resources scarce. Only by a cautious, clever and benign attitude do we have a chance to implement changes. Difficult as it may seem, even on perhaps the most horrendous territory of gender inequality — domestic violence — all our moves have to be based on the ethics of care and understanding.

FIGHTING GENDER INEQUALITY

The history of NaNE began sometime in 1993 in Bratislava where a couple of women from Hungary took part in a women studies seminar and met representatives of the Belgrade hotline set up for battered women and women war victims. Inspired by the congeniality and camaraderie of the event, they immediately decided to set up a similar hotline in Budapest as well, where, they believed, the situation (though by far not as bad as in Belgrade) was grave enough to call for action. On arrival home they started the tiresome work of gathering licences, writing applications and petitions, searching for suitable premises. In less than a year's time their efforts materialised in a precious document whereby the Municipal Court of Budapest registered NaNE as an independent, non-party, non-partisan civil organisation. Finally, suitable premises had also been found in a central, yet 'un-posh' location in Budapest. In January 1994 the fourteen founding members moved into Vámház körút and soon transformed the somewhat drab and run-down place into a most cosy one by sticking up posters, nailing bulletins on the wall and furnishing the flat with second-hand, rickety pieces of furniture. And there was NaNE . . .

The acronym NaNE stands for *Nők Nőkért az Erőszak Ellen* — Women Working with Women Against Violence. It also has a pleasant slang overtone to it, meaning something like 'Come Off It!' in English. The name so inventively chosen has attracted much interest since then and has given information about the style and attitude of this organisation to whoever was interested. NaNE has four explicit aims:

— to operate a hotline for victims/survivors of violence,
— to reduce the present high level of violence against women and children,
— to press for change vis-a-vis relevant laws and policies concerning violence against women and children and the way those are applied,
— and to improve the provision of support services for survivors of physical or sexual violence.

Media interest in NaNE was considerable from the very beginning with articles and interviews appearing in a wide variety of newspapers, as well as radio and television programmes, already in the first month of NaNE's existence. This coverage meant that NaNE started to get calls for help earlier than it was planned.

In order to respond to this need, volunteers were recruited and trained. Leaflets, newspaper advertisements and several public infor- mation meetings brought twenty-two volunteers to take part in two consecutive weekend training sessions in January. These were given by means of trainers from the former Yugoslavia, one from Zagreb and one from Belgrade, who had several years' experience of running helplines and shelters for battered women and children. These training sessions were extremely inspiring and successful; and they were also filmed for documentary and future training purposes.

As soon as the line was opened NaNE started getting calls, most of them from Budapest, but about 20 per cent from other cities or villages. By now the helpline has become well established. NaNE volunteers have advertised it in Budapest with leaflets, stickers and posters, and the phone number is regularly listed in national papers and magazines that publish hotline numbers. NaNE has received some 500 calls to date. Records are kept of every call for help along with details of what help NaNE was able to give the callers and the follow-up information if such is received. We do our utmost to protect callers' privacy and have resisted the siren songs of the media to supply their articles and TV appearances with, as it were, some 'interesting' details.

In the course of the past eighteen months, work on the hotline has crystallised around two major functions. One of them is what might be called dispatching information. It is astonishing and also very sad how little Hungarian women know about their rights and their chances. Their ignorance in legal matters is all too often turned against them by blackmailing or threatening partners or family members. Many women do not know that often there *is* help and that the awful situation they are presently in is unjust, illegal and should no way be tolerated any longer. So NaNE volunteers have frequently found women in need, shelters, free legal or psychological counselling; they have put them in contact with self-defence groups or have initiated police intervention.

Here a digression needs to be made into the social composition of our callers. Although domestic violence penetrates Hungarian society at all levels and in all spheres and knows no territorial boundaries either, most of our callers seem to belong to the under-privileged. One supposes that better-educated women of better means tend to find the way out of difficult situations more easily or they have the circle of acquaintances and friends through whom they finally get to the right lawyer, psychologist or police person. Also, if the situation gets intolerable at home they simply can afford to move out, at least temporarily.

The other function NaNE seems to have been performing is listening, simply listening to women who, often after much hesitation, finally come forward with their stories. Often the only thing they want is a sympathetic, non-judgmental listener who is prepared to devote fifty minutes of her time to listening to accounts of ten or fifteen years of solid suffering. It has turned out in a number of cases that the NaNE volunteer was the first person ever to whom that women dared to reveal her story. If I consider what we normally do in fifty minutes — have a leisurely breakfast or bath, travel from home to work, scan through the papers — I am stunned and shaken by how little those women would have been asking had there been anybody to care about them.

Such experiences and revelations indeed are bound to put great stress on volunteers. Mindful of the importance of personal and professional support for the volunteers, several further training sessions have been held enabling them to acquire co-counselling and other techniques for dealing with emotional overload, as well as giving them opportunities to discuss and practise difficult situations they are confronted with when answering calls. Also, we hold regular meetings to discuss cases and methods under the supervision of a psychologist who works for NaNE on a voluntary basis. In order to put NaNE on the map and also to call public attention to the greatness of the problem of domestic violence, NaNE organised, in May 1994, a conference on 'Violence and Democracy'. Hungarian, Croatian, Serbian, German and American activists came together to discuss the state of affairs, to do networking, to exchange ideas and methods, to share experiences, good and bad alike. As regards establishing contacts and learning about various patterns of domestic violence, the conference was a great success. Also, it was followed by sound media coverage which NaNE could not have attracted otherwise. But there was also a lesson to learn: the perceived imbalance between Western and Eastern contributors prevented the conference from becoming as useful and effective as it perhaps could have been, had it been more about the specific problems of women in this region of the world. For however charming, witty and non-violent it might be to try and fight domestic violence, as some women do, by gathering around the house of the batterer, chanting mocking songs and thus making him flee and hide in the forest in his shame, this is something that surely will not work in an Eastern European village where there is a batterer in almost every house. What if they join forces? One had better not think of that.

Our attempts at networking did not stop after the conference was over. NaNE activists have participated in international conferences in Belgrade, Novi Sad, Vienna, Ljubljana and Birmingham, not to mention the various conferences and training sessions that have been organised in Hungary. Longer lasting and more direct contacts are being built with shelters and hostels offering temporary accommodation to women and children in Budapest, with Family Assistance Centres and other providers of social services operating both in and outside the city. This both enables us to keep abreast of the developments in the field, so that the information we pass on to callers is up-to-date, and also means we can turn to experienced professionals for advice.

Relationships are forming on another level too. We have so far been contacted by two groups of women in the provinces who wish to set up helplines or provide assistance to battered women and children in their regions. Helping them benefits us as well, since this way we can get acquainted with specific problems, variations of infra-structure, finance, local habits of thought inside Hungary and yet still outside our experience.

LEARNING TOGETHER

Working on a hotline, among other things, is a great learning experience. Volunteers in NaNE have had a chance to look into the often grave state of affairs within the Hungarian legal, health care and education system. During training courses, and also whilst listening to unknown callers on the phone, we had a chance to see ourselves function in yet unprecedented ways. We had the opportunity to get to know each other. Blissfully, NaNE volunteers have come from all walks of life and have colourfully different views on life, love and on less important things like politics and institutions. The common denominator is the realisation of how downtrodden Hungarian women often become, and the desire to change this situation. For well over a year now, some twenty women have been sticking together through thick and thin, despite arguments, moments of frustration or despair. Although rising social tension is affecting NaNE as well, and although no civil organisation can be completely different from the society that surrounds it, NaNE's aim has been to develop into a place where it is simply good to be.

We all know, how rare and precious this is and how vigilant we have to be to resist distracting and disintegrating tendencies. The closer we get to ourselves in this process of co-operation the closer we get to each other and to those callers who might just now be searching in their pockets for a coin to dial 216-1670.

APPENDIX I

Women Crime Victims in Hungary

	1988	1989	1990	1991	1992	1993
1.1 Crimes against (the person)						
Women crime victims over 14 years of age	2789	2905	3157	3370	3654	3688
Victims of domestic crimes	971	916	985	922	1075	1101
Percentage of Total	35%	32%	31%	27%	29%	30%
1.2 Homicide						
Women crime victims over 14 years of age	145	109	107	141	143	153
Victims of domestic crimes	101	76	59	81	80	91
Percentage of Total	70%	70%	55%	57%	56%	63%
2.1 Assault						
Women crime victims over 14 years of age	1733	1811	2003	1945	2143	2239
Victims of domestic crimes	795	763	833	731	881	903
Percentage of Total	45%	42%	41%	37%	41%	40%
2.2 Sexual Crimes						
Women crime victims over 14 years of age	369	390	390	388	376	346
Victims of domestic crimes	11	10	5	8	4	11
Percentage of Total	3%	3%	1%	2%	1%	3%
2.3 Hooliganism						
Women crime victims over 14 years of age	824	894	986	1207	1330	1482
Victims of domestic crimes	107	125	123	160	166	213
Percentage of Total	13%	14%	12%	13%	12%	14%
3.1 TOTAL						
Women crime victims over 14 years of age	3982	4189	4533	4965	5360	5516
Victims of domestic crimes	1089	1051	1113	1090	1245	1325
Percentage of Total	27%	28%	25%	22%	23%	24%
3.2 Crime clock (hour/crime) of domestic violence against women	8.0	8.3	7.9	8.0	7.0	6.6

Notes to Appendix 1:
1 The statistics include only the so-called 'major crimes' and only those where the offender became known to the police.
2 'Domestic crime' means that the victim is the wife (partner) or the ex-wife (ex-partner) of the offender.
Source: MEDIAN Market Research Agency, December 1993

APPENDIX 2

Seven-Year-Old and Older Population as Divided by Highest School-Degree in Hungary in 1990

	Male	Female	Total
Elementary school, less than 8 grades	28.3	34.7	31.6
Elementary school, 8 grades	30.3	33.4	32.0
Secondary vocational school	17.8	7.0	12.1
Secondary grammar school	15.5	18.9	17.3
High school and university	8.1	6.1	7.0
TOTAL	100	100	100

Source: Hungarian 1990 Census

Note

This paper grew out of the talk I was asked to give at the 'ESCR Seminar on Women and Gender Relations in Russia, the Former Soviet Union and Eastern Europe'. The seminar was organised by Linda Edmondson and Hilary Pilkington at the Centre for Russian and East European Studies in the University of Birmingham in March 1995.

I wish to make a public thank you to all of the organisations and individuals that have funded and supported NaNE. In recording NaNE's early history, which I was not part of, I relied on various English-language material written by others at NaNE. Thank you Zsuzsa, thank you Antonia.

3

Seeing Red: Men's Violence Against Women in Ireland

Ailbhe Smyth

Yes, my father was a butcher,
and kicked me down the stairs
before going to the slaughter-house
because he had no choice
and I must know that I could not choose.
But he had all the strength,
and I kept my tiny rage
intact behind silent tears
until soon I overcame that too,
and there were no tears, just silence,
and blood dripping passed my eyes,
I saw him through it
and I saw red.
              (Rita Kelly, from 'The Patriarch')

I saw red long before I saw the full picture, long years ago when I was
a young woman, fresh to feminism and quick to anger, both equally
new, for rage had been forbidden us. I thought I knew so much. Now I
see that what I saw then was only a first pale wash of colour, although
enough, more than enough to see red. I still can't see the full picture

— who can? — but I know better now why it has been hidden and, perhaps, how to look through it. The rage is still intact.

But why, if I have been enraged for 20 years and more, have I never written before about men's violence against women in Ireland? Of course, violence is not my 'field' — I am not a sociologist or a psychologist or a counsellor — but so what? Lack of a 'field' hasn't been much of a deterrent for other things I've done. I don't altogether know why not, except that maybe the rage — the quality of that red rage — has something to do with it. There is fear in it, and shame and pain. And a failure of courage, I have no doubt. I am not apologising, rather trying to work out why rage is not always enough, and why it is (still) so difficult to write through.[1]

3.1   SEEING AND NAMING MEN'S VIOLENCE AGAINST WOMEN

I want to do two things in this paper: first of all, I want to try and review what we know about violence against women in the Republic of Ireland,[2] to see how much we can now see of the 'full picture', and to consider how we are prevented from seeing more; and not secondly, but throughout, I want to focus on how feminist activism has challenged and changed (Hanmer and Saunders 1984) the ways in which Irish society both sees and does not see men's violence against women, and what that means for women.[3] For there is no doubt that feminists working to identify and stop men's violence against women have made a literally incalculable contribution to the on-going achievement of freedom and autonomy for women in Ireland.

> It gets to a point where you think that death would be easier than living like this, I had a bottle of pills. I was ready to take them when I telephoned a refuge. (Marian, cit. in Shanahan 1992)

There is no way of knowing how many women's lives have been saved, physically or psychologically, because they have had a refuge to go to. Through their emergency assistance, legal and medical support and counselling, Rape Crisis Centres have helped thousands of women in Ireland to deal with the traumatic aftermath of their ordeal.[4] We cannot even begin to calculate the vital difference made to children's lives, through the provision of support for children by Women's Aid and sister organisations: 'One simple and key principle which we can begin from is that woman protection is frequently the most effective form of child protection' (Regan 1994). How many children will be helped both to avoid and to reveal abuse and violence against them through the introduction in schools of a new 'Stay Safe' programme, which would never have come into being without the analysis of patterns and strategies of male dominance identified and developed by feminists?[5]

> I hid what was happening to me from everyone. I made excuses for my bruises and marks. I thought I should put up with it, [I] accepted my lot as being part of marriage. (Lily, cit. in Casey 1987)

The collective socio-cultural prohibitions against the naming of men's violence, experienced by individual women at an intensely personal and painful level, are a key factor in the enforcement of patriarchal rule. Hiding violence from others, from society as a whole, is also crucially about hiding it from ourselves. What is abundantly clear, for Ireland as for elsewhere, is that the silence enshrouding men's violence against women was broken by feminist anti-violence activists, groups and campaigns. Home-based violence, child sexual abuse, rape, prostitution, pornography, sexual harassment have been identified and named as systematic and institutionalised strategies for the sexualised oppression of women. (*See for example*, Steiner Scott 1985; Casey 1987; Corcoran 1989; O'Connor 1992; Shanahan 1992; Leonard 1993; O'Connor 1994.)

> Rape is a terrible crime, yet in Ireland it is surrounded by a terrible silence. (Mary Crilly, Cork RCC, cit. in Shanahan 1992)

Feminist anti-violence activists have enabled women to speak by providing them with shelter and support, with a sense of legitimacy, and with a vocabulary and a framework through which to recount their experiences. The 'secret and unshareable' (Dobash and Dobash, 1993) has now a common and public language which has become increasingly explicit and insistent over the past twenty years.

> Public statements of disapproval [of men's brutality] are now made by activists throughout the world, and their echoes can be heard in the media, in houses of government and in everyday conversation. (Dobash and Dobash 1993)

This has actually enabled us to *see* men's violence against women and to call it by its proper names. Men's brutalisation of women in body and mind is no longer minimised (by women at least) as just 'a few slaps' or 'knocking her about a bit'.[6] That is why throughout this paper, as in 'real life', I use the phrase 'men's violence against women' because the shorter and more usual 'violence against women' speaks/writes out men's agency. Implying by ellipsis that such violence has no perpetrators, the phrase 'violence against women' erases men's responsibility for violent criminal acts and contributes powerfully to the paradoxical construction of women as simultaneously 'victims' (but of whom?) *and* as responsible for their own fate. *She brought it on herself; she was asking for it; she should never have . . .*

> Elsie Martin's husband beat her unconscious because she called him twice for his dinner while he was talking to his brother . . . Afterwards, his mother said that if Elsie had fed herself better, instead of wasting good money on them fags she'd have been able to take the few wallops and got over them the way any normal woman would. 'He didn't mean nothin', the elder Mrs Martin said. 'He got a bit ahead of himself'. (Maeve Kelly, from 'Orange Horses')

The existence of refuges and Rape Crisis Centres, the impact of 'Reclaim the Night' marches in the late 1970s and 1980s, of education programmes, of media campaigns — the multi-faceted forms of feminist activism highlight and define the issue of men's violence, its complex dimensions and its absolute unacceptability:

> The new attitude to violence against women is that we have *zero* domestic violence in Ireland. That has to be our goal. (Joan Burton, TD, Minister of State, National Federation of Women's Refuges press conference, 15/5/95)[7]

Ministerial statements such as this clearly indicate that ending men's violence against women is, in the view of at least some members of government, a national project, and those who work towards achieving this objective are to be encouraged, supported and treated with respect.[8] In Ireland, Women's Aid and Rape Crisis Centres are increasingly solicited by the media and by government for their views on matters related specifically to violence, but also more broadly on women's human rights issues.[9] At moments of controversy and crisis — and in contemporary Ireland crisis is more of a constant than a moment (Smyth 1995a) — these organisations are appealed to for information, for advice, for ways of thinking our way collectively to a more just and egalitarian society. It doesn't mean they are always listened to, nor that their advice is followed, but in a relatively short space of time they have become an effective voice in Irish socio-political discourse. Recently for example, Women's Aid, the National Women's Council of Ireland and other women's organisations had formal meetings with the Minister for Justice to discuss a range of issues including the implementation of the law relating to prostitution, proposals for a new women's prison, family courts, rape and sexual assault sentencing policy, Gardai (police) policy on violence against women, and other matters (*The Irish Times* 17 January 1995)

Men's violence against women has therefore been exposed as a massive social problem, despite the ferocious taboos against doing so. Services have been set up by feminist groups and, because of these groups' unremitting pressure, by State agencies. Oppressive and inadequate laws have been amended, new laws have been made. Education and training programmes have been initiated. Women violated and abused by men are discovering a measure of hope and some means of survival.

It is impossible to evaluate the precise impact of these initiatives or of this changed and constantly changing discourse, but that doesn't matter: what matters is that violence as an issue and a reality is being translated from the realm of the private and personal into the public arena where it is defined as a serious social problem.[10]

In the case of Ireland, a markedly traditional and Church-dominated society, it is particularly important to recognise the strength and persistence of feminist activism around violence. The continuing denial of rights to divorce and abortion, despite a quarter century of feminist struggle, is a sobering measure of men's power to define and control women's sexuality, reproduction and labour. In Ireland, the patriarchal subordination of women is blatantly achieved by coercion and force: women are forced by the Constitution to carry unwanted foetuses to term (Hoff 1994), just as they are forced by the Constitution to remain in unwanted marriages. These Constitutional prohibitions against women's freedom and autonomy are crucial foundations of the edifice of male ownership and regulation of women (Smyth 1992a).

Irish women are confined to marriage and motherhood through a complex weave of gender ideologies, institutional arrangements and social attitudes and practices, with Church and State functioning in powerful tandem to 'legitimate' men's dominant position.[11] In such a tenaciously patriarchal Roman Catholic culture, getting men's violence against women onto the political agenda, keeping it there and thus daily challenging men's private and public power over women, has been a difficult and brave thing to do. It is important for that achievement not to be obscured, nor attributed to others. If men's violence against women is now recognised as a social problem requiring a variety of

State responses, that is due to feminist politics and activism, and not to any other agency.

I see that, you see that, we all see that. Or do we? There was the man at the National Refuges Federation press conference who kept saying 'My God, I don't believe it'. He was shocked by the Federation's statistics, which the woman beside him said was only to be expected since men's violence against women was regarded as a 'women's issue' and given the 'invisible treatment' (*The Irish Times*, 16/1/94). I am far more worried by a conversation I had shortly afterwards with a woman who told me how 'stunned' *she* had been to discover the extent of men's violence against women in Ireland. This woman is much the same generation as myself, has been active in a major women's organisation for many years and has a real concern for women in this country. How can she not have known until now? If we only see what we want to see, why could she not see this before now? There are certain things we are not allowed to see at all.

And then he came home tight.

Such a simple definition!
How did I miss it?
Now I see
that all I needed
was a hand
to mould my mouth,
to scald my cheek,
was this concussion
by whose lights I find
my self-possession,
where I grow complete.
(*Eavan Boland*, from 'In His Own Image')

3.2   THE EXTENT OF MEN'S VIOLENCE
AGAINST WOMEN IN IRELAND

Silence is never broken all at once and of a piece. It breaks now and then, here and there, voice by voice, gradually making sound and sense where before there was none.

In Ireland, the silence surrounding the issue of violence against women is clearly demonstrated by the serious lack of statistical data. (O'Connor 1992)

As researchers and activists everywhere have pointed out, it is exceptionally difficult to arrive at an accurate assessment of the extent and precise nature of men's violence against women. Women do not reveal or admit to men's brutality because they are afraid, because they think it is 'natural', or unimportant, because they think no one will believe them or care, because they do not or cannot identify with the role of victim, because they are ashamed, because they think they are to blame, because it is too painful to even admit it to themselves (*see* McWilliams and McKiernan 1993; Kelly and Radford 1991; Hanmer and Saunders 1984). The problem of seeing the extent of men's violence against women is compounded in Ireland where there is no funding for research, where services have not had resources to develop computerised data-bases;[12] where record-keeping by the Gardai (police) is inappropriate and/or sporadic, and altogether non-existent in Accident and Emergency hospital units; where GPs could not or would not diagnose women's injuries as the result of men's violence.

You cannot understand what is kept hidden from view.

Research and Documentation

It has taken twenty years for feminist groups and organisations to even begin to document men's violence against women in Ireland, and there is still no comprehensive, nation-wide numerical-statistical data available. Virtually every report or paper from service groups and organisations notes that funding for research is an urgent requirement. It is clear that a major national study of men's violence against women is long overdue, and vitally necessary for policy development and service provision. Such research as has been carried out, has had to be (under)funded in a piecemeal, hand-to-mouth way and rarely extends beyond short-term, once-off projects on necessarily limited aspects of the issue. Women's Aid, for example, carried out an *unfunded* pilot project on the identification and treatment of women admitted to an Accident and Emergency unit, which is now being extended to other hospitals in the Eastern Health Board area (Cronin and O'Connor 1994). They have recently obtained limited funding (50 per cent through private sponsorship and 50 per cent from the Department of Social Welfare), to research the prevalence of violence against women through a postal *questionnaire* and a community-based survey in the North Dublin area.[13] And the Dublin Rape Crisis Centre initiated a research programme in 1990 which has so far focused on an evaluation of counselling and therapy programmes and the development (with the support of the Eastern Health Board) of a data collection system which will eventually enable them to compile information on the sexual assault of adults and on child sexual abuse. They have also recently completed a survey of sexual harassment in the workplace.

The first-ever survey of women working in prostitution in Ireland was carried out in 1994, funded by the European Union on a very small budget (O'Connor 1994).[14] I know of no data of any kind on the nature and availability of pornography in Ireland (but *see* the discussion in Corcoran 1989). A Garda 'Woman and Child' Unit was set up in 1993 where reported incidents in the Dublin Metropolitan area are being recorded (Morgan and Fitzgerald 1992).

Statistical and other information about the prevalence of violence, about professionals' responses and provision of services must therefore be culled from a variety of sources, including relatively small-scale or local surveys (e.g., Casey, 1987; Ruddle and O'Connor 1992); the annual reports of Women's Aid, refuges and Rape Crisis Centres; Gardai reports (see Morgan and Fitzgerald 1992); Law Reform Commission reports (1988; 1990); or extrapolated from studies on other issues (e.g., Kellegher *et al.* 1992).[15]

From this uneven mosaic, we can determine the following:

Service Provision

1 There are ten refuges in the country, catering for a maximum of 213 people.[16] There are no community outreach services.
2 Rape Crisis Centres exist in six Irish cities or towns.
3 Advice and Information telephone 'Helplines' are provided by Women's Aid and by Rape Crisis Centres in Cork and Dublin.
4 The Women's Health Project runs a drop-in/health centre for women working in prostitution in the Dublin south city area. Major hospitals have STD (Sexually Transmitted Diseases) clinics, but no special services are provided for women working in prostitution with the exception of Baggot St Hospital where the Women's Health Project is based.
5 The Employment Equality Agency in Dublin deals with cases of sexual harassment in the workplace, as do the trades unions.

Rape and Sexual Assault: Statistics

The number of rapes reported to the Dublin Rape Crisis Centre (DRCC) has increased from 76 in 1979 (when the DRCC opened) to 408 in 1984, to 1479 in 1990 (DRCC Annual Reports, cit. in Shanahan, 1992). In 1993, DRCC received a total of 5129 calls on its twenty-four-hour telephone crisis line, 84 per cent of which were from women: 64 per cent of these calls concerned child sexual abuse, while 36 per cent related to adult rape/sexual assault; 86 per cent of those counselled by DRCC in 1993 were women; 58 per cent of the total were counselled for child sexual abuse, 42 per cent for adult rape/sexual assault, and 17 per cent for both forms of abuse.

Rape Crisis Centres throughout the country maintain that rape and sexual assaults are seriously under-reported. They note that rape or assaults which occurred in the past are also now being reported, with a rapidly increasing number of contacts concerning child sexual abuse. The most common scene of the rape, abuse or assault was the victim's home. Limerick RCC has noted 'an increase in the number of women disclosing marital rape' (Shanahan 1992).

The DRCC estimates that fewer than 30 per cent of adult rapes/sexual assaults are reported to the Gardai (DRCC Annual Report 1993). In 1991, fewer than one per cent of cases recorded by Clonmel RCC had been reported. Limerick RCC estimated that an average of 10 per cent of cases were reported to the Gardai, while in Cork, the average reporting rate is estimated at about 25 per cent. Overall, about 10 per cent of reported rape cases go to court (Shanahan 1992).

Home-based Violence Against Women: Statistics

In 1994, Women's Aid received over 6000 calls to its National Helpline Service (Women's Aid 1995). In the twelve-month period between 1 November 1989 and 31 October 1990, Dublin Gardai responded to approximately 3500 cases of home-based violence (Shanahan 1992), while in a four-month period during 1991, they responded to 1568 calls (O'Connor 1992). More than 5000 cases were reported to the newly-established Garda Domestic Violence and Sexual Assault Investigative Unit in Dublin in its first year of operation (1993–94).[17]

Refuges in Dublin, Cork, Limerick and Galway reported admitting 496 families in 1987 (CSW 1993). In one three-week period in 1991, 55 women with 112 children who sought refuge in Dublin could not be accommodated since all 20 spaces were occupied (Kellegher *et al.* 1992).

In 90 per cent of Dublin-based incidents and 82.4 per cent of incidents outside Dublin, no barring or protection order was in place (Morgan and Fitzgerald 1992).

Bradley *et al.* (1994) surveyed a sample of 335 women attending four separate general practices. They found that about 15 per cent of the eligible women who completed the written *questionnaire* had reported suffering physical abuse from their male partners. No class difference was found in respect of the prevalence of violence. They note that 'one of the striking aspects of [the] study is the apparently low level of identification of the existence of violent relationships by GPs'.

In a pilot study of women admitted to a large Accident and Emergency unit in a Dublin hospital, Cronin and O'Connor (1994) found that of eighty-one women disclosing abuse on at least one admission, forty-six revealed a long history of abuse.[18] In 78 per cent of these cases, the alleged offender was a husband or male partner; 71 per cent of the women listed 'blows' as being the main method of assault, with 'kicks', 'thrown', 'weapon used' and 'shaken' mentioned by the remainder. The descriptions of the consequent injuries show the severity of the assault of women in cases of domestic violence:

> There were 21 incidents of lacerations, 26 fractures including a fractured skull. In 26 of the cases women suffered multiple bruising and in 40 cases the area of injury included blows to the head. In three cases, women were pregnant at the time of the assault'. (O'Connor 1995)

In all cases 'it was clear that women experienced verbal and psychological assault as part of the pattern of physical abuse'. Cronin and O'Connor finally observe that 'tables and figures cannot fully convey the appalling reality of abuse suffered by women' and present several specific examples, among which is the following:

> Woman aged 41, 3 assaults in 1993. In the first assault a hammer was used resulting in fractured skull, multiple bruising and lacerations to the face. Second/third assaults resulted in multiple bruising. Fourth assaults resulted in a fractured cheekbone and nose, multiple bruising and attempted strangulation. With the support of the A & E staff, this woman took criminal charges against her partner. He was given a six months prison sentence. (Cronin and O'Connor 1994)

Physical/Sexual Violence Experienced by Lesbians

No research has yet been published on violence in lesbian relationships in Ireland. None of the existing services make special provision for lesbians who experience violence in intimate relationships although the services do deal with such cases. The 'Lesbian Line' telephone services operating in five locations in Ireland also deal with instances of violence.

Physical/Sexual Violence Experienced by Traveller Women

There are no published data available on the extent and type of violence experienced by Traveller women.[19] At present, both Traveller and sedentary women and their children use the same refuge spaces. The submission of the National Traveller Women's Forum to the National Report for Ireland (UN Fourth World Conference on Women) (1994) observes:

> Some Traveller women, as their sedentary sisters, experience male violence based on concerns to dominate, control and demean, and the abuse of power. Measures need to be taken to develop consciousness and address this violence.

Clearly, there are particular and very sensitive issues for socially marginalised groups such as lesbians and Traveller women in relation to violence. In each case, although for different reasons, women are likely to be especially reluctant to report violence on the basis that such reports will feed homophobia or racism. In the case of lesbians, there is a well-justified fear that reports of violence will be used by irresponsible media to sensationalise lesbians and lesbian sexuality and to further reinforce the construction of lesbians as 'unnatural' and 'deviant'. Traveller women fear that racist stereotyping of Traveller men as 'innately' violent will be reinforced by women's exposure of violence and that this will function to further 'demonise' the whole Traveller community.[20]

Both groups of women, Travellers and lesbians, are reluctanct to publicly name realities which they know from bitter experience will be used against them to maintain their communities in vulnerable, subordinate and marginalised positions. Out-groups have a particular need to assert identity and community and to maintain solidarity, all of which contributes powerfully to making the reporting of violence seem like an act of betrayal. Therefore, until the society as a whole confronts and eradicates its own racism and homophobia, the reticence of Traveller women and of lesbians around violence is likely to persist.

Prostitution

It is estimated that there are anywhere between 100 and 600 women working in prostitution in the Dublin area. No figures or estimates of any kind are available for other parts of the country. It has been suggested that the numbers vary seasonally, with women working at times when money is urgently needed (e.g., before and after Christmas). Women work in a range of settings, including the street, massage parlours, brothels, and escort services. New legislation on prostitution is believed to have driven some women 'underground', making it virtually impossible to establish contact with them (O'Connor 1994).

In a survey of seventeen women working in prostitution in Dublin (O'Connor 1994), fifteen (83 per cent) were critical of Gardai attitudes towards them, and only three (17 per cent) would be willing to go to the Gardai if attacked by a client or pimp. In two of these three instances, the woman had been attacked and had reported the incident. Both women felt the Gardai had taken the matter seriously and treated them well.

The prevalence of rape/assault or other types of violence by the clients/pimps/partners of women working in prostitution is not known, although instances of violence were cited by the women in O'Connor's survey.[21]

Child Sexual Abuse

In Ireland, there are no national statistics on the prevalence of child sexual abuse. However, we know, for example, that in 1993, 64 per cent of all calls (i.e., 1497 calls) to the Dublin Rape Crisis Centre twenty-four hour Crisis Line related to child sexual abuse, and that 58 per cent of clients were counselled for child sexual abuse (DRCC 1993). In every Irish rape crisis centre 'the largest number of clients are adult survivors of child sexual abuse, ranging in age from seventeen to seventy' (Shanahan 1992).

In 1988, an Eastern Health Board report noted that of 990 cases of alleged abuse known to community care teams, 52 per cent were assessed as confirmed abuse, 40 per cent as unconfirmed, and 5 per cent as confirmed non-abuse. Three quarters of the children whose cases were confirmed had been abused more than once, with a quarter suffering abuse for one to three years, and a further quarter had suffered abuse for more than three years (Shanahan 1992).

The caseload of CARI (Children at Risk in Ireland) breaks down into roughly equal numbers of girls and boys, and equal numbers of intra-familial and extra-familial abuse. CARI believe that the incidence of child sexual abuse 'may be as high as 20–25 per cent' but point out that without comprehensive research and statistics, it is impossible to identify the true level of abuse (Geraldine McLaughlin, cit. in Shanahan 1992).

Increases in the Incidence/Reporting of Violence

We are seeing more violence. Everyone is seeing more violence. It is actively difficult to choose not to see it. On 17 January last, an ordinary

Tuesday, I decided to spend an ordinary evening watching TV.[22] I like watching TV. I had a 'choice' of programmes in the 9 to 10 pm slot: a 'thriller' about the so-called aggravated rape and murder of a woman; a 'chiller' about a nurse who fears her husband is a serial killer; a 'drama' about a husband's psychological and physical abuse of his wife and children, and his subsequent murder by his wife; an episode of 'Law and Order' about a young black girl's 'controversial' claim to have been raped by a white policeman. I didn't want to 'choose' any of these, because watching programmes like these makes me more, not less, nervous. I don't want to see fictional representations of how men brutalise women, because they are for all the world (to see) indistinguishable from the 'real thing' I hear about and read about every day of my life. I don't find representations of women as bad or mad, or stupid or victimised at all entertaining. However 'puritanical' it makes me sound, however 'unscientific' my thinking, however unsophisticated and literal my analysis, I can't seem to stop worrying about the relationship between what we see, how we see it and what we do. My alternative 'choice' that evening was a documentary about the history of sport, entitled 'Blood, Sweat and Glory'. Don't tell me I'm paranoid.

Until very recently, there was neither a socio-cultural discourse conducive to recognising and speaking men's violence against women, nor mechanisms for recording its nature and extent. Therefore, in Ireland as elsewhere, it is difficult for organisations such as Women's Aid, the National Refuges Federation, Rape Crisis Centres and others to say definitively whether or not the violence is actually increasing, despite the growth in the numbers of reported instances. However, many women working in service provision believe that both the levels and kinds of violence against women are indeed increasing:

> The level of violence is higher, there are more gang-rapes, the degree of violence used in assaults is higher. The level of violence in society has increased and that spills over into attacks on women'. (Olive Braiden, Director, DRRC, cit. in Shanahan 1992)

In fact, it is difficult to work out with any degree of accuracy the extent to which crime generally and violent crime in particular is increasing in Ireland. It has been suggested that the report of the Garda Commissioner on crime statistics does not reflect the true levels of crime, but only the levels of reported crime (*The Irish Times*, 11 August 1993). In the absence of an overall crime survey it is impossible to determine either the prevalence or patterns of violent crime, nor what proportion of violent crime is perpetrated by men against women and children[23]. In 1991, only seven of the 1,258 female convictions for an indictable offence reported and processed were for crimes of violence against the person. The equivalent figure for men for crimes of violence against the person, as reported and processed in 1991, was 273, almost 40 times greater (*The Irish Times*, 20 July 1993).

The paucity of official data has obvious and profound repercussions on the development of measures for the prevention of men's violent crimes against women. Service providers have repeatedly stressed the urgent need to develop and implement a coherent and comprehensive anti-violence policy (*see*, for example, O'Connor 1995). Piece-meal data mean that there can only ever be a fragmented understanding of the prevalence, nature and degrees of men's violence against women, which produces reactive, *ad hoc* and provisional policy-making. The absence of a comprehensive policy based on a clear and precise understanding of the problem impacts directly on service provision and funding, the development of education and training programmes, transformation of the legal, medical and social welfare systems, the nature and function of the policing of violence and, ironically, the development of research in all of these areas.

But of course the absence of a comprehensive overview is about nothing more or less than the denial of men's violence against women. A problem that does not officially exist requires no official solution.

'Denial' is a linchpin of the forces of conservatism in contemporary Ireland in respect of a range of social issues, all of which call patriarchal forms of social control into question. As we have already seen, there is no divorce law and no legal right to abortion.[24] Yet a conservatively estimated 70,000 married people are actually separated (Ward, 1993), while more than 4,500 Irish women go to Britain for an abortion every year (Smyth 1993). In demanding legal and other solutions to the problems which underscore the realities of their daily lives, women are posing a profound threat to the status quo of traditional gender relations. Issues of sexual and reproductive control are intensely divisive in the upheavals of a society moving itself slowly and painfully towards new values and practices (Smyth 1995a).

3.3   STATING THE CHALLENGE

For all its banality, the truism that change is a slow process, full of checks and balances, contradictions and uncertainties, is nonetheless true, with a particular resonance where men's violence against women is concerned.

On the one (positive) hand, Irish feminists have been persistent and remarkably successful in challenging traditional patriarchal perceptions. At the level of the State, the law now acknowledges men's abuse of women as unacceptable and meriting severe sanction. It is recognised that women and children subjected to abuse require social, psychological, medical and legal support, and that current provision in all of these areas is inadequate.[25] While the State emphasises the joint role of 'statutory and voluntary bodies' in the provision of services, funding has improved, and noticeably so over the past few years. Underlying and propelling these changes is the shift in social attitudes towards men's abuse of women. It is no longer pervasively seen as a 'private, family matter', as 'natural' and 'inevitable', infrequent, or the consequence of pathological tendencies, illness or a-typical deviance. Above all, women themselves are *decreasingly* prepared to 'put up and shut up' as the reporting rates to various services demonstrate.

On the other (negative) hand, while public articulation of the issue marks a crucial social transformation, it is far from being the full picture, as we (feminists) all well know. The very success of feminist activism over the past two decades has provoked a patriarchal counter-attack which is attempting to roll back, delay or dilute women's hard-won and still incomplete rights and freedoms (Smyth 1995b).

The conservative Catholic lobby is vehemently opposed to women's autonomy. Their specific targets are divorce and abortion, expressed in terms of a pro-family, anti-feminist discourse. These are the battle-grounds in their war to retain power: 'Their fundamental aim is control, the control of Irish society' (O'Reilly 1992). The denial of women's rights to independence and to physical integrity produces and maintains the social contexts and structures which 'legitimate' violence against women. Hoff (1994) observes that 'anti-choice arguments usually reflect civic or religious attitudes that implicitly condone or encourage violence against women . . .' The 'Masterminds of the Right' in Ireland have notably *not* spoken out against men's violence against women. Their main concern is the preservation of the sanctity of The Family, that private patriarchal *sanctum* which is such a high-risk space for women and children. Constitutionally, the family based in marriage enjoys 'inalienable rights'. The right of The Family not to be interfered with by the State is *de facto* the right of male family members not to have their rights of 'ownership' of 'their' women interfered with. The State — so reluctant to intervene when women and children are being beaten up and worse — shows no hesitation at all in proscribing women's rights to control their fertility or to leave unhappy and/or abusive marriages. In conservative Catholic ideology and politics, The Family as an abstract ideal is of infinitely higher value than the rights, freedoms and survival of women and children.

The powerful Catholic conservative lobby produces and reinforces a patriarchal ideology which constructs femininity as 'naturally' domestic, dependent and acquiescent, and masculinity as public, dominant and aggressive. But as women increasingly question patriarchal constructions and constraints, and move outside and beyond the spheres of men's control, they threaten the stability and continuity of the patriarchal gender order premised on women's malleability in all domains of personal and collective life. Which means that the lash may be applied all the more ferociously to women's backs. For the 'backlash' is not just a metaphor: it has a concrete, physical reality in women's daily lives. McWilliams and McKiernan quote Yllo's study (1988) of domestic violence in the USA which found that improvements in women's socio-economic status did not necessarily signify a reduction in 'wife abuse', rather the contrary: 'Domestic violence . . . increased in those states in which women's status was highest relative to men's, [indicating] that rapid change towards equality could bring a violent backlash by husbands' (McWilliams and McKiernan 1994). While there is no evidence to indicate, one way or another, whether this is a pattern in Ireland, those working in women's organisations and services maintain that 'Irish society is becoming more violent' and that 'the degree of violence used in assaults is higher' (Shanahan 1992).

3.4 CONTRADICTION AND CHANGE
The judge stated
She drew it on herself,
In a red dress
Up to her ass.
In all fairness he fumed,
Any able-bodied man
Would be hormonally bound
To make a pass.

The unrepentant rapist
Served one hundred hours community service
As assistant caretaker
In the local school.

> The girl withdrew,
> A Valium-addicted
> Wide-eyed
> Frightened fool.
> (Sarah Varian-Barry, 'Raped')

The heightened awareness in Irish society of men's violence against women has not *reduced* its prevalence, nor do the legal measures introduced or strengthened since the 1980s function as an effective or sufficient deterrent. How serious, then, are those in power about stopping the damage, pain and sometimes death of literally *uncounted* women and children in Ireland every year? What I want to do in conclusion is briefly outline some of the complexities and contradictions involved in trying to answer this, because:

> Ireland is nothing if not contradictory and confusing. It is at once a developed industrial society, with increasingly secular tendencies, and a traditionalist 'anachronism' in the Western world. Both dimensions co-exist in a state of volatile tension, which creates particular problems for Irish women who refuse the narrow roles allowed them by tradition, law and practice. (Smyth 1995a)

The State's responses are based on strategies of *containment*. Where a problem is acknowledged, the State (or more correctly, its agents)[26] must now be seen to take action, while at the same time the resolution of the problem must be contained within a framework which ensures that existing power structures, and the interests of the powerful, are not seriously eroded. Thus, one of the most pressing issues for feminist anti-violence activists at the present time in Ireland and elsewhere, centres on the risks involved in negotiating with the State — Government, legislature, judiciary, the police, social welfare and health systems and so on — in order to obtain *necessary* legislative and judicial reforms, service provision, police protection — without being subsumed into and co-opted by the very system feminists set out to challenge and change in the first place (*see* Dobash and Dobash 1993).

Services

Although some institutions are more permeable, or less resistant to change than others, in every instance we can cite there is a built-in containment or 'braking' mechanism designed to ensure that change can go only thus far and no further. So for example, where the operation of services (run almost entirely by women) is concerned, the State (incarnated mainly by the Departments of Health and Social Welfare) now provides the bulk of the funding, but only for a grossly inadequate number of refuge places, or rape crisis centres, or education and training programmes and so on. This ensures that while the principle of support for women and children who have been subjected to violence can be inscribed in State rhetoric, the reality is that large numbers of women and children who are being beaten or raped are *not* in fact being supported by the State. The State tolerates a certain level of violence by *limiting* the number of women it is prepared to support. Further, a considerable proportion of the funding for services is not guaranteed on an on-going basis and requests must be regularly renewed. Women are thus maintained in a subordinate relation to the State as supplicants, dependent on the grace and favour of the powers-that-be. There is a perception that funding is conditional on 'good' (ie, non-subversive, non-radical) behaviour, with consequently de-politicising effects. Persistent underprovision and underfunding mean that women who work in these vital services earn a bare pittance, which functions to maintain them in an economically subordinate position.[27] This in turn is one of the main mechanisms for (re)producing their relative powerlessness in society more generally.

Legislation

The now considerable number of new and amended laws may appear to provide an adequate framework for exposing and sanctioning men's violence against women. However, a number of these laws contain clauses which ensure that their effectiveness is directly controlled by the judiciary (*see* the critiques of Fennell 1993; O'Malley 1993; Leonard 1993). This is particularly marked with regard to rape law, where 'there is a high level of discretion [vested] in trial judges' (O'Malley 1993). For example, the previous sexual experience of a complainant may still be used in a rape trial with the express permission of the trial judge. The judge also retains discretion as to whether the jury should be warned of the dangers of convicting on the uncorroborated evidence of the complainant. The judge now decides if, and to what extent, a woman is to be believed in a rape trial. Further, what is written in the statute books (the 'rhetoric' of the law) is undermined by the procedures and practices of its implementation.

> When new rape law was introduced five years ago, a barrister
> commented that the Criminal Law (Rape) (Amendment) Act 1990
> 'swept away the attitude to rape which partially blames the crime
> on the victim'. However, in practice attitudes have not changed in
> judicial pronouncements. (Bigley 1995)

Inconsistent and lenient sentencing has been a major area of controversy
in rape cases (*see* Shanahan 1992; O'Malley, 1993), culminating in 1992
in public outrage at an especially blatant example of judicial disregard
for women's right to justice. The complainant in the case in question
was a young woman, Lavinia Kerwick, who made a public statement
condemning the trial judge who adjourned sentence for a year on the
young man who had pleaded guilty to raping her. The judge based his
decision on the fact that, *inter alia*, the man had a clean record with good
references from his employer. The young woman's pain, the violation
of her person and of her right to bodily integrity, were apparently of
no consequence to him.

Lavinia Kerwick appealed publicly to the Minister for Justice. She
identified herself (the first time a raped woman had done so) as the victim
of a violent crime perpetrated against her because [of her sex] . . . She
identified herself as the victim of a 'justice' system which denies women
value and status as human beings, entitled to have their rights upheld
and respected by the State and its agents (Smyth 1994). Commenting
shortly after the trial and its aftermath, feminist activist and academic
Ursula Barry observed:

> The broader issue in the Kerwick case is the situation of individual
> women dealing with the courts and having their response to a
> situation determined by the legal system. But also there is the
> fundamental status of women in this society being defined by its
> institutions. (Barry, cit. in Shanahan 1992)

The Criminal Justice Act (1993), introduced on foot of the Kerwick case
and the public controversy it generated, now enables the Courts to take
into account any effect of the offense on the victim when sentencing
a convicted offender, and also provides for a review of unduly lenient
sentences by the DPP (Director of Public Prosecutions). The Kerwick
case provided a clear illustration of the contradictions inherent in a
system which legislates for the punishment of rape as a crime, which
polices infractions of the law, but which ultimately refrains from
imposing the sanctions it has itself determined. It illustrates the State's
simultaneous 'prohibition and promotion' of men's violence against

women: the perpetrator was tried, convicted, but not punished (Hyden and McCarthy 1994). However, the Kerwick case also demonstrated how feminist activism is beginning to affect the construction of gendered power relations: the authority of the State was challenged and at least partly eroded; a change in the law ensued following public outcry.

In 1994, the man accused of the statutory rape of the fourteen-year-old girl at the centre of the notorious 'X' abortion case came to trial (Smyth 1993). He was sentenced to fourteen years' imprisonment for unlawful carnal knowledge (the category of statutory rape does not exist in Irish law). On appeal, his sentence was reduced to four years in March 1995. The man was described by the appeal judge as being 'a hard-working, good family man who lost nearly everything; his reputation, the respect of his community, his livelihood, almost his family'. He had never committed any crime before, had suffered greatly and would never do it again. For these reasons, his sentence should be reduced.

Public outrage was intense following the appeal judgement. A coalition of women's groups, including the National Women's Council of Ireland, Women's Aid, Rape Crisis Centres, the Women's Education Research and Resource Centre and others sharply protested the judgement and demanded the immediate establishment by the Minister for Justice of a Judicial Review Group to report on sentencing in particular and on judicial treatment of cases of men's violence against women in general. Following negotiation with the Minister and considerable media attention, the Judicial Review Group was set up and will report in 1996. The newly-established Courts Commission also has as part of its brief a review of court procedures in respect of cases of violence against women and children. Review groups and commissions do not in and of themselves, of course, 'prove' that official discourse on men's violence against women has been radically transformed, but insofar as they provide mechanisms for furthering the process of change, they indicate the permeability of State institutions to social pressure for change.

3.5   STILL SEEING RED

The State is neither static nor monolithic and may be less coherent or more contradictory than our 'commonsense' way of talking about it indicates (*see* Connell 1987). In at least some of its institutional incarnations in Ireland, the State has begun to shift its practices around violence as a result of unrelenting feminist pressure. However, we need to remind ourselves that it invariably does so only reluctantly, partially and following years of work, persuasion and proofs of 'legitimacy' and 'authenticity' on the part of feminist activists and organisers. And at considerable personal price and pain borne by uncounted numbers of individual women. That makes me see red. And still prepared to stand on barricades.

Text of a speech made outside Dail Eireann (the parliament) following the 'X' Case 'Unlawful Carnal Knowledge' Appeal Judgement (Ailbhe Smyth 16 March 1995).

This judgement is an outrage and a scandal, and we must tell the courts and our legislators that we are outraged — and not to be silenced.

Saying you never did it before isn't enough for any other crime.
    Why should it be so for child sexual abuse or rape?

Saying you didn't really mean it isn't enough for any other crime.

Saying you're sorry isn't enough for any other crime.

Saying you'll never do it again isn't enough for any other crime.
    Why should it be so for child sexual abuse or rape?

The young girl whose life has been devastated by this criminally abusive man knows it's not enough. And so does her family. You know it's not enough and so do I.

We know it's not good enough, not fair enough, not just enough.

And we know that not because we are 'emotional' or 'irrational' or 'vengeful'. No. We know it because it's not JUST.

We know these are most serious acts of criminal violence. The LAW says they are most serious acts of criminal violence. But our COURTS don't seem to know this. The COURTS don't seem to know that one of the most powerful ways men assert their power over women and children is through acts of sexual violence.

And why don't the COURTS know this? Because the COURTS don't want to know. Because the COURTS are manned . . . by men. And they will not point the finger at other men. They don't care enough, because they think, at some level, it's OK.

The COURTS favour 'good family men', in the name of 'justice'. Not women and girls violated by men. No man who rapes is a 'good man' of any kind. Ever. So what do the COURTS mean by 'good'?

They make illogical and insulting distinctions between 'OUT AND OUT'

RAPE and . . . what? IN AND IN RAPE? They say that rape, which is a violent act, is really only a crime when accompanied by 'force' and 'duress'. What bodily evidence do the COURTS want to see? How many times does a girl or a woman have to be hit, punched, bruised, broken? What about the damage and pain the COURTS can't see because they don't want to know?

RAPE IS ALWAYS an ACT OF FORCE. The COURTS, manned by men, don't know that because the COURTS never get raped, out and out or in and in, with force and duress and violence and devastation to their lives.

The courts don't know, so let's tell them again what we have made ourselves hoarse telling them, and the whole system, for years and years and years — MEN DO NOT HAVE THE RIGHT TO RAPE OR ASSAULT OR SEXUALLY ABUSE WOMEN AND CHILDREN. THEY DO NOT OWN WOMEN AND CHILDREN SOCIALLY, SEXUALLY, LEGALLY, JUDICIALLY OR IN ANY WAY WHATSOEVER.

Women and children have rights. Human rights. Rights under our laws. Rights in this State.

So let's tell them again that we will go on telling them again and again and again, until they understand, that men's violence against women is a CRIME. That violent men are CRIMINALS. And that the duty of the JUSTICE system, of our laws, our courts, our judges, IS TO PUNISH CRIMINALS FOR THEIR CRIMES.

We will go on telling them until we have laws, sentencing procedures and JUDGES who understand that MEN WHO ABUSE WOMEN AND CHILDREN ARE CRIMINALS DESERVING OF PUNISHMENT FOR THEIR CRIMES.

And then, maybe, men's violence against women and girls will stop. Because as long as men's violence is condoned by lenient sentences, or none at all, the violence will go on. And will continue to devastate the lives of women and children.

Justice which is not applied equally to everyone is not justice. It is a parody, a farce, a travesty. The travesty must end.

Enough is more than enough.

Notes

1 An earlier version of this paper was delivered to the ROKS Annual Conference, Stockholm, Sweden, in January 1995. I would like to thank Olive Braiden of Dublin Rape Crisis Centre and Monica O'Connor of Women's Aid for taking the time to read and comment on a draft of the paper. And thanks to Denise Charlton and Niamh Wilson of Women's Aid for supplying me with information and documentation.

2 Given that the State is (still) two separate entities in the two parts of Ireland, there are difficulties involved in trying to consider the impact of feminist activism and organisation around violence against women on the island as a whole. This does not mean, of course, that common perspectives and co-operative strategies are not possible, and they are in fact being developed successfully in a number of different ways. For the North of Ireland, see particularly Monica McWilliams and Joan McKiernan's comprehensive study: *Bringing it out in the Open* (1993).

3 A detailed discussion of the role of force in Irish society — all Catholic though it be — in maintaining the subordination of women (*inter alia*), and the (asymmetrical) constructions of masculinity and femininity are beyond my scope for this paper, although I intend to explore them elsewhere in the near future.

4 As far as I am aware, there are no official data available on the total number of women who have contacted Rape Crisis Centres in Ireland since they were set up.

5 In 1995 the Minister for Education announced that a programme of sex education is to be introduced in primary and post-primary schools in September 1995. The 'Stay Safe' pilot programme, which includes material on sex abuse and bullying, will be extended to 2000 more schools. This programme has been virulently opposed by ultra-right Catholic organisations. On the day of the Minister's announcement, in an entirely uncoincidental counter-attack, the anti-abortion organisation 'Human Life International', announced its nationwide survey on 'family planning-type sex education in Catholic schools'. This survey asks parents such supposedly neutral questions as whether they believe safe sex education can lead to promiscuity and the weakening of 'a child's natural modesty' (*The Irish Times* 23 January 1995).

6 The equally common passive voice constructions 'she was raped/abused/battered', 'battered/abused woman' function to produce the same effect of erasure of agency. I rarely use the term 'domestic violence', since the connotations of domesticity function to preclude notions of criminality. However, alternatives such as 'home-based' or 'intimate violence' are not much more satisfactory, while 'battering' or 'battery' (as in North American usage) again invisibilises men's agency. For a brief discussion of the important and vexing problems of terminology, see Dobash and Dobash (1993).

7 In February 1995, Women's Aid ran a 'Zero Tolerance' national awareness campaign, the first of its kind in the Republic of Ireland, to 'try to halt the horror of violent crime against women and children' (Women's Aid Press Release, 27 February 1995).

8 The three ministers referred to specifically in this article are women.

9 As I write, the Republic of Ireland is preparing for a second referendum on divorce. The first referendum, in 1986, upheld the Constitutional prohibition against divorce. Women's Aid is playing an important role in the pro-divorce campaign by highlighting the detrimental effects on women and on children of abusive marital relationships (*see* Roisin McDermott, Chairwoman, Women's Aid, 'The Fate of Children in Abusive Marriages', *The Irish Times*, 18 September 1995).

10 For discussion of the impact of feminism on changing social value systems and social practices in Ireland, *see for example*, Smyth 1994 and 1995a; McWilliams 1995.

11 Discussing domestic violence in Northern Ireland, Monica McWilliams argues that there too, Church and State 'combine to ensure that women remain in the primary role of wife and mother' and that the dominance of 'traditional Catholic and Protestant ideology has affected every facet of women's lives' (McWilliams 1994, p.13).

12 This is the case, broadly speaking, across the entire spectrum of socio-economic, political and cultural issues of relevance to women and to gendered power relations. Research at the Economic and Social Research Institute (ESRI) has been heavily weighted towards the economy, and the Institute has carried out, or published, extraordinarily little research on any aspects of women's social situations and needs. While the Combat Poverty Agency maintains a strong emphasis on gender, its research is primarily, in accordance with its brief, on the causes and effects of poverty. The Oireachteas Committee on Women's Rights has commissioned research on some specific topics over the years, but its budget is small. The Second Commission on the Status of Women, which completed its report in 1992, commissioned chiefly literature reviews and data compilation as it had no funding for in-depth research. Neither the Employment Equality Agency (EEA) nor the Council for Status of Women has regular (or any) funding specifically available for research. None

of the Women's Studies Centres have received Irish funding for research, and there is no council or institute for research on women.

13 The study, which is currently being developed, is entitled *Violence Against Women in Intimate Relationships with Men*. It is being conducted by Kelleher and Associates and Monica O'Connor, Women's Aid (information supplied to the author by Women's Aid).

14 This research was part of the EUROPAP project on health needs in the context of HIV and AIDS. It was carried out by Anne Marie O'Connor of WERRC, commissioned by the EUROPAP co-ordinators in Ireland, the Women's Health Project (Eastern Health Board).

15 The *National Report of Ireland* to the United Nations Fourth World Conference on Women (November, 1994), included *no statistics whatsoever* on the incidence of any form of men's violence against women. In other areas, such as politics, education, employment, housing and households, copious data are presented.

16 The population of the Republic of Ireland is approximately 3.5 million.

17 Information supplied to the author by Women's Aid.

18 This compares with between 22 per cent and 35 per cent of women presenting to A & E units in the USA (cit. Bradley *et al.* 1994).

19 The intense discrimination experienced by Travellers is detailed in the recent Government *Task Force on the Travelling Community* (1995).

20 Anti-Traveller racism and discrimination are very strong in Ireland.

21 Following publication of Anne Marie O'Connor's report (1994), a brief new item appeared in the *Irish Independent*. While the item itself was a neutral account focusing on the reasons why women working in prostitution are reluctant to approach hospitals and health services, the headline read: VICE GIRLS 'DON'T TELL HOSPITALS'.

22 The programmes described are listed in *The Irish Times*, 17 January 1995.

23 In 1988 women were just 2.2 per cent of the total daily average prison population (*The Irish Times*, 20 July 1993).

24 The intricacies of Irish constitutional rulings on the legality of abortion are addressed in Smyth (1993).

25 *See* proceedings of the Conference on Safety for Women, hosted by the Minister for Justice in 1992, with a follow-up seminar in 1993. *See also* Conference organised by the National Federation of Refuges for Abused Women and their Children, hosted by the Minister of State for Social Welfare in 1994.

26 The State, that impersonal abstraction, is neither of these things in its daily and multi-facetted realities. It is incarnated, so to speak, in particular institutions, each with its own rites and rules, each with its own inscription and practice of patriarchy.

27 Reading the financial sections of the annual reports of refuges and rape crisis centres, you wonder how so many workers can be paid out of such relatively tiny budgets.

Section Two

Introduction: Feminist Campaigns and Networking

Chris Corrin

As with other considerations within this work it is hard to separate out some of the issues around violence against women into distinct contexts for analysis. As the works of Hannana Siddiqui and Stella Jegher show, the realities of many minority ethnic women's lives highlight some of these complexities. As Lepa Mladjenović and Rada Boric both demonstrate, the contradictions which feed into refugee women's lives or into 'everyday' domestic situations in times of war are many-layered and complex both to analyse, and respond to, in terms of support and information work from women's groups.

Cooperation amongst women's groups in Central and Eastern European countries has been growing for some time. At the Women's Conference on Security and Cooperation in Europe (CSCE) in Berlin in November 1990, a network was formed of women from Central and Eastern Europe. The text of the declaration sums up some of the injustices facing women across Europe and where the roots of this lie:

> Women from East-Central and East European countries present at the first Women's CSCE came to the conclusion that it is of vital importance to create a network of East-Central and East-European women . . .

Such a network is necessary especially as the newly emerging democracies have proved to be conservative and authoritarian regarding women. They perpetuate and promote male dominance in these societies. The best examples to prove this statement can be found in the tendencies to raise the percentage of unemployed women beyond that of men and to curb or even ban the right of abortion.

It is necessary to develop close relations with women from all other parts of Europe and the world because we share the same problems, even if the manifestations are different — in East Europe increasing nationalism and ethnic conflicts, and in the West racism and xenophobia have similar roots in the patriarchy and have the same disastrous impact on all women . . . (full text in Corrin 1992, pp.251–2)

The concentration in this section is on nationalism and ethnic conflicts and the evidence that across 'Europe' racism and xenophobia have their roots in patriarchal relations of power.

RACISM AND RACIST VIOLENCE

Many women and women's groups are active in resisting racism and racist violence in and across Europe, yet links between local groups and national anti-racist campaigns are not always automatically forged amongst feminist groupings. It is generally Black women and women from minority ethnic communities who still have to 'remind' White feminists of the obvious political links. Within Central and Eastern Europe, Roma (Gypsy) communities are suffering greatly from racism and racist violence, and with various citizenship changes many people from Africa and Asia who now live in any part of Europe not only have less rights to protection in law but are differently placed in terms of the law enforcement and judicial systems. The ethnic tensions apparent in war in the former Yugoslavia have unleashed male violence against women at all levels including systematic rape and femicide. Most countries across Western Europe have been codifying protectionist laws designed to minimize the movement of certain peoples. In the UK in January 1996 up to 13,000 people were facing sudden destitution as the Government planned to remove at least 7,500 asylum seekers, plus their dependants, from the benefits system, pending their appeals against negative immigration decisions. Amongst other changes the Asylum and Immigration Bill includes penalties for employment of illegal immigrants (discrimination in employment will ensue), jail sentences for bogus marriages and helping asylum seekers enter the country by illegal means and a new 'white list' of countries presumed safe in human rights terms, from whom applications will probably be refused. Such countries include Ghana, Pakistan, India and Poland, which produced around 8,000 asylum applications in 1995. The 'numbers game' can be seen at its most bleak when it is noted that in the UK in 1991 only 16 per cent of applications for asylum were refused whereas by 1994 78 per cent were rejected. As the work of Southall Black Sisters has shown, many women face a stark choice between domestic violence or deportation yet this remains a 'hidden' problem: 'Home Office statistics only show that in 1993, 31,100 people were granted settlement after marriage ... 630 were refused permanent settlement ... 555 may have been refused because of marriage breakdown' (Southall Black Sisters 1995). This means that women leaving violent relationships within their first year of entry to the UK face deportation under this one-year rule.

RACISM, ETHNIC NATIONALISM AND FUNDAMENTALISM

Various member states within the European Union have been actively seeking to expand their immigration restrictions for some years. As Avtar Brah has pointed out:

> In the process of its formation the 'New Europe' is insti- tuting a wide variety of measures to keep out immigrants and refugees from the Third World by strengthening its inter- nal controls. Such measures are being introduced via *ad hoc*, secretive bodies and intergovernmental arrangements like the Trevi Group of Ministers, the Schengen Accord and the Ad Hoc group on Immigration. The proceedings of these state agencies are not subject to democratic control. Their attempts at harmonising policies on immigration, terrorism, drugs, public order issues and policing pose serious threats to civil liber- ties and social rights of all minorities. (Ward, *et al.* 1992, p.23)

It is the systematic implementation and enforcement of such restrictive international legislation which serves to reinforce the dangers on a *global scale*. Alongside this expanding 'protectionism' has been the growth of fundamentalism, not only of religious fundamentalism but also the secular varieties. In most European countries endemic racism is a social reality. Recently the growth of organized fascist and neo-nazi parties and organizations (within and outside state structures) has become more apparent. In June 1995 Le Pen's National Front Party won 15 per cent of the vote in French local elections. In Germany, the burning-out of Turkish families from their homes continues to happen. In Turkey, Kurdish villages are obliterated and elected Kurdish representatives are killed and imprisoned. This depressing list of examples could be very long.

FUNDAMENTALISM

Religious fundamentalism clearly poses great dangers for women and various forms of fundamentalism are apparent throughout the world. In their founding statement, the feminist campaigning group 'Women Against Fundamentalism' (WAF) launched in London on 6 May 1989 state that:

> Fundamentalism appears in different and changing forms in religions throughout the world, sometimes as a state project, sometimes in opposition to the state. But at the heart of all fundamentalist agendas is the control of women's minds and bodies. All religious fundamentalists support the patriarchal family as a central agent of such control. They view women as embodying the morals and traditional values of the family and the whole community.
>
> We must resist the increasing control that fundamentalism imposes on all our lives. It means that we must take up issues such as reproductive rights and fight both to safeguard and extend abortion rights and resist enforced sterilisation. We must struggle against religious dogma from whatever source which denies us our right to determine our own sexuality and justifies violence against women. (WAF Founding Statement)

As the excerpts from Ailbhe Smyth's speech outside the Irish Parliament clearly show, religious fundamentalists can and do impose their views and decisions on women, about the rights of women to control their own bodies. Nationalist fundamentalism can generate such violence as 'ethnic cleansing' in which women's bodies become the maps of war territories.

The rise of religious fundamentalism has been apparent internationally in the past decade. In Poland, the March 1993 law on abortion (Family Planning, Foetus Protection and Conditions of Admissibility of Abortion Act, 1993) clearly attacks the rights of women to decide whether or not to give birth to a conceived child. As the Polish Committee of NGOs Report explains:

> The present law justifies abortion exclusively on medical or criminal grounds, to be performed in public hospitals only. On pain of imprisonment no doctor may induce termination of pregnancy for social reasons. Statistics from earlier years show the main reasons women decided to abort were social, mostly to do with difficult family living conditions. In 1980, 98% of pregnancy terminations performed in hospitals were for social reasons, in 1990 94%. Clearly the anti-abortion law mainly affects the poorest women and families with limited knowledge of family planning and often little ability to solve their own problems. (1995, p.45)

In a situation in which there is no guarantee of wide availability of contraceptives, and those on sale are too expensive for many women and are not eligible for the 30 per cent discount which applies to most medications, the 'choices' for women under the restrictions within this Act are evident within Polish society. Women with resources can either find private doctors who will undertake illegal abortions for high fees, or go to agencies specializing in private trips abroad, usually to Russia, where abortion is legal even for foreign women and relatively inexpensive. Some agencies organize trips to western countries such as Germany, Austria and Holland but the costs are a lot higher. Yet, as has been the case throughout time, poor women are being forced to induce miscarriages by using risky methods or by going to non-professional abortionists (ibid. 1995, p.46). The teachings of the Church are an important means by which women's lives are controlled. The help lines of the Federation for Women and Family Planning indicated that many women use no birth control because of religious reasons: 'A significant factor here is the Catholic Church's campaign against abortion and birth control, even extending to the use of condoms to prevent infection from AIDS. It must be emphasized that sterilization is forbidden by law in Poland' (ibid. 1995, p.47). As Ailbhe Smyth notes in Chapter Three the situation in Ireland with regard to Catholic fundamentalism is not disimilar to that in Poland.

Other consequences of the oppressive nature of religious fundamentalism, can be seen in the violent oppression of women's sexuality which is strictly controlled across the globe. Acknowledging women's active sexuality is something that religious fundamentalists undertake in order to control and oppress women. For lesbians in some countries of the world such control can be fatal. The range of abuses lesbians face include: 'torture, including rape and sexual abuse from government officials,

arbitrary imprisonment, 'disappearance' and extrajudicial execution'
(Amnesty 1995, p.110). In Iran, involvement in a lesbian relationship
can cost a woman her life. Lesbianism can be proved by 'four righteous
men who might have observed it' (Amnesty 1995, p.109). In Poland,
until 1991 it was illegal to be involved in lesbian groups and some
lesbians were admitted to psychiatric institutions for 'treatment' (Polish
NGOs Report 1995, p.65). The influence of the Catholic Church plays
an important role in creating prejudice:

> Homosexuality is attacked from the pulpits, on Catholic radio
> stations, on Catholic television programmes, and in the Catholic
> press. The Church because of its dogmatism, lack of tolerance
> towards homosexuality, and enormous influence over Polish society
> represents a direct threat to homosexuals . . . The Church is thus
> implicated in creating many human tragedies for homosexuals in
> Poland. (ibid. 1995, p.66)

As with other areas in which women suffer male violence, the violence
which lesbians experience often remains hidden. In part this is due to the
recognition that by making public the abuse, lesbians will face further
harassment and reprisals. Lack of resources and avenues through which
to call attention to their situation are other factors. As was the situation
with the 'invisibility' of domestic violence in many Western European
countries some years ago — which has changed through feminist public
consideration of this violence — so with anti-lesbian violence, the lack of
documentation leads to a context in which further abuses occur. Again,
violence against lesbians links with migrant women's rights: lesbians
have been refused political asylum on the grounds of their sexuality
because they could not show documentary evidence of abuses against
lesbians in their countries:

> This is partly due to a failure of human rights groups to document
> these abuses, and partly because while many laws are explicit only in
> reference to gay men, in practice they provide the context for abuses
> against lesbians. Lesbians, along with gay men, have historically
> been persecuted through laws that criminalize sexual behaviour
> between consenting adults of the same sex (commonly referred
> to as 'sodomy laws') even when such behaviour occurs in private.
> (Amnesty 1995, pp.110–11)

The irony is not lost here in terms of the associations of 'privacy'. When
men are beating women within a household the issue of privileging a

'private' domestic situation took much political campaigning on the part of feminists — to expose the hypocrisy and use of power against women's interests. 'Domestic violence' is now a public crime in many Western European countries. Yet in terms of lesbian lovemaking, even when it takes place in the privacy of individual bedrooms, this has been publicly illegal for many years. It has again taken much feminist campaigning to bring such injustices onto public agendas to highlight the prejudice against lesbians. As Cheryl Clarke has noted:

> No matter how a woman lives out her lesbianism — in the closet, in the state legislature, in the bedroom, she has rebelled against becoming the slave master's concubine, *viz.* the male-dependent female, the female heterosexual. This rebellion is a dangerous business in patriarchy. Men at all levels of privilege, of all classes and colors have the potential to act out legalistically, moralistically and violently when they cannot colonize women, when they cannot circumscribe our sexual, productive, reproductive, creative prerogatives and energies. (Clarke 1983, p.128)

In many parts of Europe today anti-lesbian violence at the state level and within societies, is still very apparent. In Romania the infamous Article 200 prohibited homosexual acts between both men and women. Proposals for change are currently still under consideration as a direct result of lesbian and gay human rights and pressure groups. As Lepa Mladjenović illustrates in 'Dirty Streets' (Chapter 6 below) violence against lesbians in Belgrade is starkly apparent.

NATIONALIST VIOLENCE AND ETHNIC CLEANSING

Different racialised and ethnicised 'national' political agendas are often projected in terms of 'cultural difference'. Some of the main concerns in this section are with nationalist violence in the form of 'ethnic cleansing' and rape of women in war in the former Yugoslavia.

'Reform' whether in the form of 'democratization' in East-Central Europe or regional cooperation with the European Union, is not gender neutral and women's lives are being affected in so many different ways. Cuts in welfare services which particulary affect women's lives have become quickly apparent in East-Central Europe and in countries like Britain and France. These include declining services in health care and the reduction in state support for child care. Much of the economic change across Europe has had far-reaching negative consequences for particular groups of women, especially women from 'minority' communities, poor women and women migrants. Many women have even less involvement in some of the new political structures. Poverty and insecurity around employment for women are increasing within a context of declining social welfare support. The differentiation between individuals and groups of women is ever increasing. Some women entrepreneurs and professionals have welcomed the changes, whilst many groups, are suffering.

In considering patriarchal relations of power within the framework of the militarism of societies various questions are raised. Patriarchal systems are based on the use of power. Militarist systems are based on violence and its threat. Together these systems can be fatal for women. Why is it that the all-male hierarchies of various religious organizations can decide women's fertility choices and family planning opportunities? Why is it that the war-mongering politicians and military hierarchies in the Balkans are able to pursue plans of genocide, mass rape and ethnic cleansing? Why is it that the international media dictate masculinist anti-women agendas onto so-called 'news' reporting? In this section concentration is on these aspects of male violence as well as on the feminist campaigning and support and information work that is being carried on in different conditions in several countries. In trying to separate out various aspects of male sexual violence for consideration, it becomes clear that they actually intermesh within apparent systemic uses of power.

In certain ways the central organization of societies under the 'partocracies'[1] in Central, Eastern and South-Eastern Europe was a form of militarism of society. This was apparent in the racism towards minority ethnic communities. Roma (Gypsy) peoples have spoken about how their culture was systematically treated as inferior to the dominant cultures. That such open racism has become more apparent within the changed atmospheres and the more market-oriented systems does not serve to cover over the widespread existence of racism before the changes of 1989–90. Yet, in current conditions of poverty and lack of employment opportunities the scapegoating of minority communities has become more visible. In such situations women of minority communities often find it difficult to challenge the gendered oppression within their own communities when they are experiencing oppressive and violent racism from the wider society. In the former Yugoslavia this ethnic violence has emerged violently in many forms.

VIOLENCE IN WAR

Various consequences of the dramatic political changes after 1989 across Central, Eastern and South-Eastern Europe have been noted and connections between the decline of communist regimes and increasing nationalism can be seen. The focus here is on rising ethnic nationalism and some consequences for women's lives. Links are apparent here with the control of women's bodies and women's reproductive health and of creating hierarchies of concern. In Chapter 7 Mica Mladineo Desnica has pointed out in with regard to Croatia:

> Besides, domestic violence, which has always been considered a minor, women's problem (if a problem at all) today has become a woman's patriotic duty. Women are being constantly taught (through the mass media) to feel ashamed to think about such selfish problems when the Nation and our men ('fathers, husbands and sons') are bleeding on the battlefield.

It is viewed as unpatriotic for women for speak out against male violence at home when the 'national interest' is at stake. In terms of declining central organization and potential growth of violent nationalism, Djurdja Knezevic notes that:

> The situation in society in Croatia/former Yugoslavia, particularly concerning women, fits the general pattern of all Eastern European countries since the decline of the communist regimes in these countries. This means: radical decomposition and atomization of societies, loss of any rational social project, accompanied by strong retrograde developments in all spheres of social, economic and psychological life, among which nationalism is at the top of the list. (Knezevic 1993, p.1)

Hierarchical systems of patriarchy are generally based on strict military rules and values. Military values such as physcial strength, aggressiveness, persistence and insensitivity are 'prized' and men are trained and conditioned in these 'values'. Within such systems women are viewed purely from a male perspective with women's sexuality under constant scrutiny and strict control to assure the origin of off-spring. Militarist values are of concern not only in political and security issues but as a major factor in economics, culture and people's everyday lives. Within situations in which social control mechanisms are sanctioned and abused to dominate, subjugate and exploit women, male violence can be analyzed within the context of oppression based on the threat-system of militarism. This ties in with sexualized images of women and their exploitation and oppression, especially within the context of 'ethnic' war. As Cynthia Enloe points out:

> Conquerors' mistresses, wartime rape victims, military prostitutes, cinematic soldier-heroes, pin-up models on patriotic calendars — these are only some of the indications, not only that nationalism is often constructed in militarised settings, but that militarization itself, like nationalist identity, is gendered (Enloe 1993, p.245)

Nationalism is concerned with changing conceptions of femininity and masculinity in everyday lives. As Lepa Mladjenovic and Divna Matijašević pointed out in their talk to the seminar on 'Issues of Violence Against Women' (*see* Chapter 6) within this militarization of relationships in Belgrade boys are often addressed as 'my general', 'my soldier' whilst girls become silent witnesses to boys being given double value — as boys and as army officers. The increasing violence brought home from the front is also a feature of daily life. Women working on the SOS hotline in Belgrade noted the increased incidence of rape, torture and robbery by soldiers who come back to their families.

There is a recognition by policy-makers that as childbearers women are considered 'culture-bearers'. That is, it is often women who pass on their cultural his/herstories and moral outlooks to children. In circumstances in which certain cultural his/herstories and moral values are being denied or re-viewed, it is women who are pressured to fit in with ideological shifts which carry a gendered text — explicitly or implicitly. In her work on *Patriarchy, Language and National Myth* Stasa Zajovic speaks of the ways in which Serbian nationalists brought back to life a symbolic medieval figure — mother Yugovich — 'the long suffering, brave, stoic mother of nine, offering her children up to death in the defence of the fatherland' (*Peace News*, March 1992, p.7). Along with the cult of blood and soil came the cult of motherhood with maternity being viewed as an obligation. Women's fertility is closely monitored and controlled in many countries of Europe. As noted, in Ireland and Poland abortion is illegal and access to sex education and contraception is severely controlled. Linkages between Catholic fundamentalism and state legislation are clear. Poverty is a key link in the chain of women's lack of choices around their general health. In Albania, whilst abortion was legalised in 1992, contraceptives are not a priority for successive government budgets which are in dire straits. Many poor women in Albania are now having to undergo successive abortions under incredibly poor medical conditions (Corrin 1993).

Across much of Europe, Christian coalitions are proposing moral indictments of women who make decisions on termination of pregnancies. In Serbia, Croatia and Bosnia nationalist aspirations intervene in decisions about childbearing as not all children are seen to be equally important. As Milica Antic stresses: 'children are associated with the nation to the extent that they are valued first for the nation, and second as a human being in their own right' (Corrin 1992, p.171). In 1992 slogans were taken up such as 'An unborn Croat is a Croat too'. Ethnic tensions in Kosovo, with Albanian doctors being dismissed, led to many Albanian women having home births in unsafe conditions. The pro-natalist policies of most states in Central and Eastern Europe sat uneasily with the needs for women's labour power. At times when more women workers were needed state policies enabled abortion and eased some child care needs. When labour was more plentiful fears around 'the nation dying out' took over and restrictions were placed on women's family planning. Jolanta Plakwicz notes the swings and roundabouts effects as women activists in Poland: 'learned that the government's decision to abolish rights to reproductive freedom is justified when it is in the 'national interest' such as when the population is declining . . . just as the 1956 abortion bill was meant to keep women from having unwanted children, thus it now turns full circle and they are to be forced to bear unwanted children' (Corrin 1992, p.90). In the creation of Slovenia and Croatia as nation-states Milica Antic points out the need by political organizations to influence 'the family':

> In Slovenia and Croatia the family is a constitutional subject with its own rights. The draft Slovene constitution is written using the male pronoun. Women are mentioned only as mothers, and motherhood is protected by the state'. (Ibid, p.168)

'Moral health' of a particular type becomes important in such contexts so that state policies not only do not recognize other patterns of life as equal — one parent families, childless women, lesbian part`erships — but they are designed to eradicate them. The elements of control here could not be more apparent. Women are being forced into violent situations (enforced abortions, enforced pregnancies, enforced cohabitation with violent men) by the implementation of government policies designed to meet the needs of patriarchal agendas, couched in terms of the 'national interest'. The situations of women being raped in war in the former Yugoslavia have highlighted the implementation of such violent agendas. This violent abuse of women by men within ethnicized and nationalist contexts raises many questions and complexities in terms of how re-created images of 'good' and 'bad' women, ownership and objectification of 'our' or 'other' women, are being violently forced onto communities.

RAPE IN WAR

I do not intend to detail atrocities nor to explain events at length. Rape and sexual assault have been carried out by military and paramilitary men on all 'sides' and of all ethnic groups in the war in the former Yugoslavia. According to information gathered by the United Nations Commission:

> Rape has been reported to have been committed by all sides to the conflict. However, the largest group of reported victims have been Bosnian Muslims and the largest number of alleged perpetrators have been Bosnian Serbs. There are few reports of rape and sexual assault between members of the same ethnic group. (United Nations Report 1995, p.60 Para. 251)

It is telling that the gender of the victims/perpetrators is not explicitly stated here in terms of *women* being raped by *men*. In terms of the ethnic tensions manipulated in the ongoing war, Roy Gutman is explicit in his assertion that:

> The rapes are not exclusive to the Serb forces in Bosnia, and there have been examples on a smaller scale by the other national groups. The distinction made by international relief workers and human rights analysts is that the Serbs set the pattern in 1992 — organizing the conquest to achieve a Greater Serbia, setting up concentration camps, and practising systematic rape. Bosnian Croats in western Herzegovina adopted the pattern starting in spring 1993, as they went on the offensive to create an ethnically pure Croation sector. Forces of the predominantly Muslim government of Bosnia also have been charged with atrocities, but not as a tool of government policy. (Stiglmayer 1994, pp.xi–xii)

In the final report of the Commission of Experts of the United Nations — established to examine and analyse evidence of grave breaches of the Geneva conventions and other violations of international humanitarian law committed in the territory of the former Yugoslavia — it is noted that:

> The practice of so-called 'ethnic cleansing' and rape and sexual assault, in particular, have been carried out by some of the parties so systematically that they strongly appear to be the product of a

policy, which may also be inferred from the consistent failure to prevent the commission of such crimes and to prosecute and punish their perpetrators. (Boutros Boutros-Ghali letter dated 24.5.94 to President of Security Council)

In the Annex to the Final Report of the Commission it is noted that five patterns emerge from the reported cases of rape, regardless of the ethnicity of the perpetrators or the women raped. The first involves individuals or small groups who committed sexual assaults in conjuction with looting and intimidation of the target ethnic group. The second pattern of rape involves individuals or small groups committing sexual assaults in conjunction with fighting in an area, often including the rape of women in public. The population of the village is then transported to camps. The third pattern of rape involves individuals or groups sexually assaulting women in detention because they have access to them. Reports frequently refer to gang rape, while beatings and torture accompany most of the reported rapes.

The fourth pattern involves individuals or groups committing sexual assaults against women for the purpose of terrorizing and humiliating them often as part of the policy of 'ethnic cleansing'. In those camps women are raped frequently, often in front of other internees, usually accompanied by beatings and torture. Some captors stated that they were trying to impregnate women. Pregnant women are detained until it is too late for them to obtain an abortion. The fifth pattern of rape involves detention of women in hotels or similar facilities for the sole purpose of sexually entertaining the soldiers. These women are reported more often killed than exchanged, unlike women in other camps (United Nations Report 1995, pp.58–9).

Within their communities many different aspects come together to further harm women survivors' identities and feelings of self-worth. Vera Folnegovic-Smalc writes of some of the psychological consequences for women raped in Bosnia and Herzegovina and Croatia:

> In our sociocultural community a raped woman does in fact receive a certain amount of sympathy, but rape also evokes a negative reaction. A raped woman is considered defiled; she represents a disgrace to her family and her (national, religious, political) community. (Stiglmayer 1994, p.176)

It is impossible to think through the multiplicity of reactions that women face when they have been kept in rape camps and are turned out heavily pregnant as homeless and often 'stateless' refugees. In at least the fifth pattern it is clear that in these situations the continuum of violence has led to femicide.

Rape is part of the culture of war. From the 'rape and pillage' of the Crusades, the parallels are apparent in the power of forced submission and 'conquering' of the Other. Both Lepa Mladjenović and Rada Boric expand upon the images of Other that have been created in their changing war situations — violence as a means of control and conquest. International feminist campaigns have made some analyses of the abuse of power in rape apparent. Whilst law enforcement and judicial bodies still attempt to place some focus on the 'victims' — the women who are raped — there is legal recognition of the responsibility of the rapist. When (mass) rape in war is carried out, the continuum of violence takes additional forms, and the means of analysis are complicated by ethnic nationalism and ethnic 'cleansing'. Here Lepa Mladjenović in section 4 of Chapter 6 highlights the patriarchal use of power in naming — a situation, a person or a group — as 'unclean'. Again, some children are more important, more 'clean', than others and rape can be concerned with defilement of enemy women, breaking up the social fabric of communities, shaming of men via their women and as a means of breeding the 'right' children. Women become ethnicized as enemy 'Others', and rapists as men representing their national interest. The confusion and complexities here are apparent, with ideas concerning women in war as symbols of the nation — as 'ideal patriotic mothers' or as 'enemy whores'. The 'dying out of the nation' takes on even more sinister connotations in war time. Cynthia Enloe points out that:

> It is precisely because sexuality, reproduction, and child-rearing acquire such strategic importance with the rise of nationalism that many nationalist men become aware of their need to exert control over the women. (Enloe 1993, p.238)

It is clear that nationalist men wish to protect their national interest and ensure the 'survival' of their nations not only by killing the 'enemy' but by breeding the 'right' children. The complexities of rape for impregnation confuse such straightforward 'conceptions'. Do soldiers want Other women to bear their children? How will such mothers and children be able to live — together or apart, in what 'state'? Much information has been used for political propaganda, with women survivors on all sides being 'used' to justify retaliatory violence and violations of human rights. As can be seen, manipulation of information for political aims leads to hatred, revenge and further violence against women.

The first two chapters in this section show that women from a range of situations can come together in varying forms of feminist coalitions to resist violence against women in its many manifestations. Working together in coalition can be difficult and raises complex issues for consideration, as Hannana Siddiqui shows regarding the work of Southall Black Sisters in the UK and Stella Jegher highlights in terms of Swiss and migrant women working together and in the work of feminists in solidarity with women from the former Yugoslavia. In their work both Lepa Mladjenović and Rada Boric consider the layers of complexity that are involved for women living through war, when women's bodies become the maps on which battles are fought. That women make up the vast majority of internally displaced persons who are often unable to go 'home' leaves them vulnerable in the aftermath of ethnic conflict. In terms of where 'home' is and where we belong, Rada Boric sums up a good deal of how many feminists feel in terms of their place in the world:

> As women we are organizing because this is the only way to make our issues visible. We want to be activists, not passive victims. In all this nationalistic euphoria it is easy for me to choose my nationality: Woman. It is not enough to 'look at the world through women's eyes' (as the Beijing Women's Conference says). We must make the world a reflection of women's minds and women's efforts. (Boric 1995, p.13)

The range of work carried out by the feminist groups in all four chapters certainly is breathtaking and indicates the connections that feminist activists are willing to make in their work against violence against women.

Note

1 A partocracy is an authoritarian regime in which The Party is deemed all-powerful.

4

Domestic Violence in Asian Communities: The Experience of Southall Black Sisters

Hannana Siddiqui

I want to consider violence against women, particularly domestic violence for Black and minority women, based on our experience at Southall Black Sisters over the last 16 years. I aim to draw out the issues that have been relevant for us and the challenges we have had to face in dealing with and surviving as an organisation, providing services, making changes and taking on difficult issues at times of great hardship and economic crisis in Britain. In many ways women in Britain are so much better off than women in East and Central Europe, the former Soviet Union and the Third World, but at the same time there are those from some minority communities in Britain who face particular hardships not confronted by those from the majority·community.

Two things have been important for us in assisting women who are experiencing violence. First is the practical day-to-day services for women — giving them advice, help, counselling and support. The other thing is campaigning. I cannot emphasise how important campaigning and policy work are in creating long-term changes, dealing with underlying causes and in making demands on the state, society and on the communities in which women live.

One of the major problems that the women's movement confronted in the early years was whether or not women's groups should take up state or other forms of funding. Women asked, would we lose our independence and grass-roots activism? We argue that it is very important to take up funding because it enables the setting up of centres and provision of services. It is not a question of getting funding, but what is done with that funding, which is so essential. We do not want to lose sight of our commitment, because at the end of the day what makes us successful is our commitment. There are a lot of problems around professionalisation. Many of the women's groups have forgotten the reasons why they set up these organisations and so have become service based. They have become depoliticised — having lost sight of their political commitment around the need to create long-term change. However, funding has enabled us both to pursue a service and to use this as a base for campaigning for long-term change.

DOMESTIC VIOLENCE HAS NO BORDERS

The issue of domestic violence is one that has no boundaries. It cuts across class, race, religion, nationality — it exists all over the world. I agree with a lot of the analyses around patriarchy which argue that domestic violence is a mechanism for control within male dominated societies in order to control women and to exert male power over them. Although there is commonality of experience among women from different classes, races and so forth, we must also recognise some of the differences in order to meet the special needs of particular groups. We are not talking about a homogenous society where all women's needs are the same. There are differences and there is a lot of inequality. There is racism within the feminist movement and the women's movement has not always been able to take into account the needs of ethnic minority or Black women. It is important that we begin to do that if we want to achieve equality and freedom for all women and not just a few.

HISTORY

Southall Black Sisters was set up in 1979 when a group of Asian, African and Caribbean women came together. At the time there was a lot of discussion within the anti-racist movement in Britain about re-founding our identities. As Asians and African-Caribbeans we shared common experiences of colonialism, imperialism and contemporary racism in Britain. We felt that in order to create a strong anti-racist movement in the UK, it was important to re-define ourselves as Black. It is a political term that united us. We recognised that Black had been used against us and was a degrading term but we wanted to turn that concept on its head and say, yes, we are proud to be Black, we are facing discrimination and

we will define ourselves how we want to and make a united movement
against racism.

We are an autonomous, secular organisation. We do not organise
along religious lines. We have women from all racial, religious and
cultural backgrounds coming to us. Secularism is important for us.
There is increasing pressure to define ourselves along religious lines. We
believe this separates people and creates exclusive, segregated identities
based on reactionary notions of religion. We do not see ourselves as
a separatist organisation — we make alliances. When we established
ourselves we felt therefore that we had to take on issues concerning
Black women which were not being taken on by men within our own
community or by outside society. The two main issues we felt we had
to fight were racism and sexual discrimination.

I am mainly talking about South Asian communities because we
are based in Southall in West London which has a very large South
Asian population from the Indian Sub-continent and the diaspora,
although there are significant populations from Africa, the Caribbean
and Ireland living there. The majority of the women who come to us
are therefore South Asian. We find that these Asian communities are
as male-dominated as any other community. It is not in their interest
to take up issues which affect women within the family and the home.
The community is very happy to take up issues around racism, but not
issues which affect women.

Initially, we were a campaigning organisation, we had no funding.
During the early 1980s we managed to get funding from the then Greater
London Council to set up a resource centre for women. We have an
information-advisory centre and we get over a thousand enquiries and
cases every year. Every week we deal with around eight emergencies.
We only have four paid workers and a few volunteers, so the work
load is extremely high. Most of the time we do case work — which
entails providing advice, practical assistance, advocacy, counselling and
crisis intervention. We also do a lot of long-term case work as many
women who come to us live on their own, often as single parents
and are extremely isolated, often do not speak English, and need to
have support structures around them so that they can leave violent
relationships and cope on their own.

Besides the counselling and practical support work, we also do
educational campaigns. We go into schools and speak to young men
and women. We speak to professionals and social workers, teachers,
etc. — as many people as we possibly can. At the same time, we also
have a very high political profile. We feel that it is through these means

that we can get society to seriously think about such issues of violence against women.

Since the early 1980s, our campaigns have been founded on domestic violence. They have centred around very tragic cases of women who have been killed, either women who have killed themselves, having been driven to suicide, or women who had been murdered by their violent husbands. One of the first campaigns was around a local woman in Southall. She hanged herself after years of violence. We picketed the husband's house and we demonstrated through Southall. The campaign was led by Asian women who had gone through domestic violence themselves. Some of them were frightened and had left the area because they were facing violence. But they came to the demonstration and put scarves around their heads so they couldn't be identified. They therefore had a certain measure of security. The idea for that campaign was something we borrowed from the Indian women's movement. What happens in India when a woman has been killed or severely injured is that local women surround the perpetrator's house and basically try to shame him within the community. We were trying to do the same thing — shame the perpetrator. It was not the issue that she had killed herself — for us she had been murdered because she had been driven to kill herself. We were trying to look at some of the religious and cultural traditions that existed in our community. At that time domestic violence in Asian communities was a taboo subject. No one talked about it, women had not organised around it. We wanted to expose it.

We tried to address some very traditional concepts like family honour, for instance, where women are seen as the upholders of the honour of their families. If they leave their husbands or speak up against violence, then they are seen to have shamed that honour. Women get stigmatised and ostracised. This can be a very isolating experience for women who live in tightly-knit minority communities as they are thrown out of those communities without family support. This notion of honour often prevents women from leaving violent situations. We wanted to expose that and turn the concept of honour on its head. We wanted to say that it was not shameful or dishonourable for a woman to leave her family and her husband due to violence. It is more dishonourable for a husband, or a partner or his family, to perpetrate violence against her and therefore the community and society should condemn the perpetrators rather than the women who are subject to their violence. This campaign had a major impact. Since then there has been a growth of the Asian women's movement in Britain. They have established more Asian women's refuges, young Asian women's hostels, and special centres where women can get help.

REACTIONS AND ATTACKS

I now wish to consider the kind of reactions we got when we tried to deal with the question of domestic violence in Asian communities. Obviously the men were very hostile. They felt very threatened. There was a backlash from the right wing. We were accused of being home-wreckers and of destroying families. We were also labelled as a Westernised force, something that was alien to Asian culture. They perpetuated the myth that Black women challenge domestic violence and demand their rights because they have been corrupted by Western values. What people do not recognise is that Asian women in India and elsewhere have been campaigning for years around domestic violence and for the liberation of women. Sexual liberation is not just a Western concept but is something that is a basic human right which women have demanded and developed in both Western and Eastern societies.

The right-wing attacks were predictable. What was interesting was that we had opposition on the left which came largely from sections of the anti-racist movement. They were saying to us that the most important struggle for the minority community in this country is the anti-racist struggle. So if we start talking about problems in our own communities, people will see us as barbaric, backwards it will fuel a racist backlash against us. What was important for us, however, was to continue to fight for the rights of all and not just for a section of society. We felt that we had to take on many struggles simultaneously in order to build a progressive movement. One struggle cannot take priority over another. We cannot create hierarchies of oppression. We must take on the anti-racist struggle, the struggle for women's liberation, the class struggle and so forth, simultaneously. Unless we do that, we make demands for only a section of society and not for everyone.

The attacks on us were quite severe because some of the left-wing, male dominated organisations in Southall petitioned to remove our funding. There was a Labour Party authority in Southall, but they were looking at ways to make budgetary cuts. The attack against us was unsuccessful because we were able to mobilise local women in support of us.

The other widely held view with which we have experienced problems is the notion of multi-culturalism. This view holds that those from the dominant, majority culture have no right to intervene in or criticise minority cultures. To do so would be intolerant or even racist. Unfortunately, this view assumes that minority communities are homogenous entities with no internal power divisions. It therefore ignores the fact that community leaders, who represent the views of the minority community to outside society, do not represent the interest of those with less power and conflicting interests, such as women within these communities. Community leaders, who tend to represent the most conservative, religious and patriarchal forces do not therefore want outside assistance for women within the community. As a result, we often find that outside welfare agencies and policy-makers refuse to help women either because they feel the community solves its own problems or because it would be wrong to criticise minority cultural and religious practices and norms. Women from minority communities are therefore made invisible.

RACISM

For Black women, when we talk about initiatives to deal with domestic violence, we also have to consider the issue of racism. For instance, when discussing police responses to domestic violence, we also have to talk about the policing of Black communities. Some Black women are reluctant to go to the police for help because so many Black men get harassed by the police, and Black communities bear the brunt of police harassment and racism.

Immigration is another issue. Many Black and migrant women who come to us do not have a secure immigration status in Britain. They often come into the country as a bride or a fiancée where their status is completely dependent on their husband, at least for a year. In Britain the 'one year' immigration rule requires an unsettled spouse, married to a settled spouse, to remain within the marriage for at least 12 months before obtaining permanent settlement rights. If she leaves that relationship, she is liable for deportation, back to her country of origin. Many women are frightened to go back because they come from cultures where they know if they go back as a divorced or a separated woman, they will experience stigmatisation and ostracism. Women also experience discrimination and are left destitute, open to economic and sexual exploitation.

Whilst in the UK, they are also, like many other immigrants with an insecure status, unable to make a claim on the welfare state. These women do not even have the legal and welfare rights available to other battered women in Britain. They cannot claim public housing or most social security benefits. They even have problems getting into refuges/shelters because these organisations depend on social security benefits for rental income, on which many survive. Therefore, battered women with immigration problems have nowhere to go. They have a very stark choice: they either stay in a relationship and face violence and even death, or they leave the relationship and face deportation and destitution.

We know there is a high rate of suicide, especially among Asian women. There is a high rate of domestic homicide, generally where violent men kill their partners (both in majority and minority communities). The home is therefore the most dangerous place for women and the safest place for men. We are condemning these women to a life of degradation and violence because these issues are not being taken up by the state. We petitioned the government about the immigration law and said that the one-year rule must be abolished and that other reforms must be instituted. The government refuses to institute reforms to help battered women with immigration problems although they state that they want more effectively to assist women experiencing domestic violence. It is certainly an issue on which we want far more support from the women's movement. One of the things the women's movement has to realize is that their own racism may prevent them from doing so. We were pleased to hear at the Fourth UN World Conference on Women in Beijing in September 1995 of how migrant women in the United States of America successfully obtained the help of the wider women's movement to reform immigration laws to help battered women. We are about to launch a national campaign to abolish the 'one year' rule — a campaign which involves a number of Black women's groups. We are hoping that it will receive widespread support from the anti-racist and women's movements, although both are faced with a challenge as the campaign brings together the issues of race and gender.

MAKING DEMANDS ON THE STATE

It is important to consider the crucial role of campaigning. The determination that women have shown has got us to where we are today. There have been some changes although it is difficult to say how deep those changes go. A number of campaigns in Britain in the last few years have propelled the issue of domestic violence onto the national agenda. The campaigns have received amazing support from all sections of society — from politicians to the media to women's groups from across the political spectrum. These campaigns centre on the cases of abused women who have been driven to kill their violent partners.

We have been involved in the case of a woman called Kiranjit

Ahluwalia, an Asian woman who was sentenced to a mandatory life sentence for the murder of her violent husband. She had experienced ten years of violence and abuse from him. She had attempted to find ways out of the relationship. These included obtaining civil court orders to restrain her husband, but these were not very effective. She had also turned to her family for help, who told her to stay with her husband and make her marriage work to prevent dishonouring the family name. Eventually she got so desperate on the day when her husband had beaten her again and had attempted to burn her face with a hot iron that she poured some petrol on him and set him alight, which later led to his death. She was convicted of murder. There are other women like her in prison, we do not know how many. Women very rarely kill, and when they do they are usually in a situation of domestic violence.

There is another woman called Sara Thornton who stabbed her husband after months of violence. She lost her appeal against her conviction and went on hunger strike after a violent man who killed his wife was not convicted of murder. The judge in the case commented that the woman tried 'the patience of a saint' and that he had been 'provoked' into killing his alcoholic and nagging wife. Sara received massive media coverage and so much support, that she eventually came off hunger strike, having highlighted the injustice of her situation.

We had to fight very hard on two fronts. One was the legal front and the other was the political. At that time (we met Kiranjit in late 1989), there was no widespread debate in Britain around battered women who killed. We then had to construct legal and political arguments not used before in Britain. We looked towards America, Canada and Australia for inspiration because there women had got further in winning their cases and redefining the homicide laws. In some states in America, women received clemency and had actually been released because it was recognised that it did not serve the public interest to keep them in prison. These women were not criminals. They had already been punished with years or months of violence. To lock them up was therefore to subject them to a double punishment. They had rarely committed other crimes, they were unlikely to do so in the future. We adopted and developed these arguments in Britain. We said these women should be released immediately. They are not criminals and they should be reunited with their families.

At the same time, we argued that there should be reforms in the homicide laws in Britain because they discriminated against women. The law on provocation particularly discriminates against women. Under this law, the defendant is not convicted of murder but of manslaughter, which is a lesser offence which often does not entail a prison sentence. Men have been very successful in arguing provocation when they kill their wives by saying that they were provoked by her 'nagging'. Yet here were women who had been through months or years of violence and abuse and were not successful with that plea. First of all the courts are sympathetic to men. Secondly, the law was defined very narrowly and basically required that you have to respond immediately to an act of provocation. It is easier for men to do that because they are physically stronger, they can respond immediately and kill or beat another person of less or roughly equal strength. Women are not in the same position, they are physically weaker. Battered women know that if they respond immediately that they will get beaten or even killed. Women may respond later when a man is temporarily weaker, for example when he is drunk or asleep. We therefore argued that this definition of provocation did not take into account women's experiences. It was assumed if there was a time gap between the provocation and the killing the defendant had time to 'cool off' and to premeditate how to kill. We argued that the cumulative effect of domestic violence could mean that battered women who killed did not necessarily 'cool off' but 'boiled over' in any time gap between the last act of provocation and the act of killing. The long-term effect of domestic violence could therefore not be ignored and thus the law had to recognise this effect in its definition of provocation.

In a very high-profile campaign, we got the UK Parliament to discuss the issue after Members of Parliament introduced bills to reform the law of provocation. Finally, Kiranjit Ahluwalia was released not because of what happened in court, although it was very important to put forward good and imaginative legal arguments, but because of the political arguments and the demands that were made on the state outside of court. I have no doubt in my mind that Kiranjit would not have been released had it not been for the campaign by women. Although Kiranjit was released on the grounds of diminished responsibility (temporary insanity) the legal decision in the case was historic as it recognised that any time gap could indeed be a 'boiling over' period under the law of provocation. We worked in alliance with one particular women's group, Justice for Women, which had formed to support other women who had killed their violent partners. Sara Thornton has been released from prison on bail and is awaiting the date for her second appeal. Other women such as Emma Humphries and Janet Gardner have also been released following campaigning by women. Kiranjit's campaign highlighted an amazing turn around within Asian communities on the issue of domestic violence when men for the first time gave support to our campaign. The same people that had tried to shut us down in the 1980s are now giving lip service to the issue of domestic violence and praising us. I think this is because Asian women have refused to be silent.

CHALLENGES AHEAD

We have made many gains over the last 16 years but I think we have huge challenges before us. One is the whole problem around poverty, unemployment and the cuts in the welfare state which has made it much harder for women to escape to safety. A moral backlash has also emerged. Recently we have witnessed Government ministers and Members of Parliament from the left and right talking about the disintegration of family, and the need to return 'back to basics' and traditional family values. Some people have argued that because of the high rate of single parenthood and the stress that this causes on public housing and the welfare state, that single mothers, especially those who are unmarried, should be denied state benefits or housing and encouraged to return to, or stay within, a traditional family set-up where the male partner is the breadwinner. If this fails, then men, rather than the welfare state, should be forced to support their families. This view fails to recognise that single mothers often act in a very responsible manner in refusing to submit to violence or abuse by leaving a violent partner or by refusing to continue with a very unhappy relationship. In some cases they are abandoned. The main aims of the Conservative government's policies are not to improve the situation of single parents and their children, for they are often blamed for all of society's ills, but to use moral arguments to justify spending cuts within the welfare state, thus penalising single parents rather than acting in their support. There is a backlash against feminism as well. Feminism has been blamed for single parenthood and for encouraging women to get divorced and separated.

Religious fundamentalism poses another problem. Religious fundamentalism is on the rise on an international scale. This development was very noticeable at the Fourth UN World Conference on Women in Beijing held in August/September 1995. The Vatican and Iran particularly were using the conference to put forward their agendas, which essentially worked against women's human rights. At the Non-Governmental conference, Muslim fundamentalists were particularly visible. Secularist anti-fundamentalists, however, did make their presence felt, especially via the activities of women from Algeria, Iran and Afghanistan. At the risk of their own lives these women courageously called for international support for their struggles against fundamentalists, who have used murder, rape and torture to silence dissent in their countries.

Fundamentalism is a very regressive movement and has a very strict interpretation of religious doctrine, where religion is used to achieve certain political ends. It does not allow for different interpretations or dissent. Clearly there is a vacuum and the left socialist movements have failed to provide solutions to the world's problems, and thus fill that vacuum. People are looking for solutions and fundamentalists provide simplistic solutions and a sense of certainty in a world of uncertainty. Fundamentalism poses problems not only for women but for the whole of society because it curbs civil liberties, imposes censorship and creates segregated, exclusive identities where people define themselves along religious lines. Ten years ago we called ourselves Black and gave ourselves secular identities. Now we are under increasing pressure to define ourselves as Sikh, Hindu, Muslim or Christian. It's an identity we are not prepared to take on because we think it is too exclusive and reactionary. The fundamentalists are struggling to control women's hearts, minds and bodies. The maintenance of the traditional family is at the heart of their agenda and women are regarded as the custodians of culture, the transmitters of culture from one generation to the next.

Within minority communities in Britain today, fundamentalists or very conservative forces are attempting to take over or attack institutions which protect women's rights. We now have our first Muslim women's refuge in London which is organised not along the principles that aim to give a woman time and space to make independent choices, but rather to put women under pressure to conform to traditional cultural and religious expectations. This refuge is used as a cooling-off place for women who leave home. They are then rehabilitated back into their families. These women are made to feel extremely guilty as if they have not been good wives or mothers, and are then returned home back into abusive relationships. Another way in which they are attempting to control women is to set up single-sex religious schools. The idea behind this is particularly to control girls by ensuring that they are segregated and indoctrinated at a very young age. An example of how orthodox conservative and patriarchal forces are attacking women's institutions is illustrated by the growth of organised male gangs or networks within Asian communities, particularly in the North and the Midlands of England. These gangs/networks track down women who have left home, intimidate them and force them to return home.

In order to fight fundamentalism we helped to set up a group called Women Against Fundamentalism which comprises of women from all racial, religious and cultural backgrounds. We try to support women in Britain and internationally who are tackling religious fundamentalism.

Our central demand is that there should be a separation between the State and religion. We say that it is only a secular state which can guarantee people's right to worship. A non-secular state will prefer one religion over another. In opposing religious fundamentalism, we face similar issues when addressing domestic violence in Asian communities we have been told by sections of the left and the anti-racist movement, and by the right, that we should not be criticising religious fundamentalism. On the one hand, we have been accused of being a corrupt, racist, westernised force and on the other hand, of fuelling racism. Our stance is the same. That it is possible to pursue a third way, which is neither racist nor fundamentalist, but which is pursued on the principle that many struggles have to be waged simultaneously if we are to demand rights for all, and not just for a few of us.

Note

This chapter is largely based on the talk delivered at the Helsinki Citizens Assembly Women's Commission workshop on *Issues of Violence Against Women* held in Liblice, Czechoslovakia in July/August 1993.

5

Feminist Perspectives in Switzerland

Stella Jegher

INTRODUCTION

Swiss officials like to point out that Switzerland is 'the oldest democracy in the world'. We do not know exactly on which historical facts this assumption is based — but we know that this 'oldest democracy', for us as women, began only in 1971, the year in which women's right to vote was finally accepted by the ruling men, after more than half a century of women's struggles. And today's democracy is still endangered. There is the fact that Switzerland, though standing outside of such international bodies as the United Nations or the European Union, is more and more ruled by the (unwritten) laws of international economy and capital exchange. And there is the fact that 18 per cent of the country's population (15 per cent of the female population) are foreigners who are denied the right to vote.

So our struggle continues to be a double, if not a triple one. To change the situation of women inside the ruling structures, to criticise the latter in solidarity with those who are kept outside, and to change them on the basis of our own experiences, biographies and utopias, diverse as they may be.

In this piece, I concentrate more on the analysis of structural/state violence than on direct experiences of male violence. This is because of the conviction that we have to overcome women's self-portrayal as victims, in order to take a step forward in our analysis of the structural aspects of patriarchal rule. I try not to forget that I am writing from the point of view of a white, unmarried middle-class feminist born in a country which has not experienced war for a long time and which is still one of the richest in the world, although a growing part of its population, and especially of the female one, lives in poverty.

SOME BACKGROUND INFORMATION ON THE SITUATION OF WOMEN IN SWITZERLAND

Apart from the general discrimination between men and women, as it is found everywhere, the situation of women in Switzerland is also shaped by some historical and political characteristics of the country. For example, the fact that Switzerland stayed apart from the two World Wars might have had an influence on the late introduction of women's right to vote, which was, in many other European countries, introduced as a kind of reward for the role women had to play in war times (though this role was important in Switzerland too). Another characteristic factor of Swiss politics which had affected and is still affecting the advancement of women is the direct democracy itself. As a matter of fact, many progressive proposals were rejected in referendums by the (male) people. This is true for the right to vote (which, in one canton, was still rejected in the late 1980s and had finally to be introduced by decree of the Supreme Court). It is also true for several proposals in the field of maternity benefits, abortion rights and women's working conditions.

On the legal level, a constitutional amendment about 'equal rights for men and women in particular in the family, at education and at work' was introduced in 1981. In 1986, a series of laws followed, aiming to improve women's situation. These contain, amongst other items, a revision of the marriage law, in which the man is no longer automatically the head of the family; housework and educational work are considered of equal value as work done to earn a living; and both partners are equally responsible for the livelihood of the family. Other parts of the laws of 1986 concern women's working conditions. As in almost all European countries, women's wages are, the equal rights amendment notwithstanding, still about 30 per cent lower than men's. On the other hand, some 'positive discriminations' in the field of work are in danger today of being given up, for instance, the ban on night and Sunday work for women.

Large inequalities exist especially in the field of pensions for elderly people, where the pensions for women are still dependent on the husband. With the recently-adopted revision of the Swiss pension law, at least the separation of the pensions of married couples as well as a 'bonus' for educational work have been introduced, but Conservative male MPs got through a proposal to raise, at the same time, the pension age for women to sixty-four. For women this had previously been at sixty-two years whereas for men it is at sixty-five years.

As to the political situation, women in Switzerland are represented in Parliament with about 22 per cent on the communal level, about 21 per cent at the cantonal level, and 17 per cent (34 seats of 200) in the national council. On the executive level, the situation is worse of course: only 9 per cent of cantonal executive members are women, and only two women have so far succeeded in entering the Federal Council (national executive). As an answer to this situation, women's election groups have been founded in various cantons to fight for more feminist representatives in Parliament, and in 1995, for the first time, a feminist election campaign was held on the national level.

As to the women's movement, there is on the one hand a range of older, established women's organisations descending from the women's rights movement of the first half of the century. The oldest one is the *Gemeinnützige Frauenverein* (the philanthropic women), founded in 1888. The biggest one the *Bund Schweizerischer Frauenorganisationen* (Association of Swiss Women's Organisations), an umbrella association founded in 1900, with some 400,000 members and 160 member organisations. Other large organisations are the two main confessional ones, namely the Swiss union of Catholic women (founded in 1912) and the Swiss evangelic women's association (1947), as well as the Association of rural women. Most of these older women's organisations are also part of international umbrella organisations like the International Women's Council. They are quite integrated in the institutions of official Swiss politics, but in most social and/or political debates, they often act rather in the sense of bringing in the 'woman and family' aspect than as agents of fundamental social change.

On the other hand, we have a large number of organisations, groups and projects descending from the feminist movement of the 70s and 80s. They are usually more critical, if not deeply hostile towards official institutional politics. Their activities are usually oriented towards political consciousness-raising by different means (demonstrations, publications, leaflets etc.) and/or towards women's self-organised social help. As a general phenomenon, we can say that the broad street struggle of the 70s women's liberation movement has shifted, during the last five to six years, slowly but continuously into a growing specialisation and professionalisation. Especially in the urban centres such as Zurich, Basel, Bern, Geneva, there exist a rising number of feminist non-governmental organisations (NGOs) with ordinary paid staff. Most of them gather their money by private fund-raising, membership and some (not very high) state subsidies.

For the region of Zurich alone, a recently-published handbook counts almost 200 women's organisations and projects. The range goes from specialised information and help services — for women who suffered direct violence, for unemployed women, lesbians, women using drugs, women with AIDS, migrant women, women refugees and so on — to women's groups inside the political parties and political pressure groups such as the women's organisations of different trade-unions, the 'Network against genetic engineering', Peace groups or the 'Women's lobby for town-planning' (a pressure group of feminist architects who try to influence urban structures to make them less dangerous for women); to cultural projects such as the women's music school and feminist theatre projects; and to the projects which deliver very concrete help to women, such as housing for battered women (women's shelters), night sleep-ins for drug-addicted prostitutes, the shelter for abused girls, or the meeting centre for young women.

The main feminist issues of the last years have been: violence against women; trafficking in women; resistance to genetic engineering; the struggle for better social security connected with consciousness-raising about growing poverty among women; the situation of 'migrant' and refugee women and the question of an equal cooperation of the 'Swiss' feminist movement with them.

In this latter field of activity, there exists for instance the *Fraueninformationszentrum Dritte Welt* (Information office for 'Third World' Women), which deals especially with the issue of trafficking in women as well as with consciousness-raising about the social and legal situations of migrant women in Switzerland. Three women from different countries of the South are working as staff members in this project. There is also the FEMIA, a house for refugee and migrant women which offers advice, language courses, computer introductions and cultural activities. Besides these two, there exist a number of groups founded by women of different immigration communities, for instance 'Nosotras' (Latin American women), 'Women of Black Heritage', 'Babaylan' (the Swiss branch of the international network of Filipinas).

While the new 'autonomous' feminist movement of the 70s and 80s was originally not too much interested either in institutional policy nor in international networking and lobbying, a growing number of feminists have developed an active interest in both of these issues during the last decade. Up to now, feminists have participated in local, regional and national Parliamentary elections in seven cantons with their own independent election lists. As to the international dimension of feminist activity, the debates about Switzerland's participation in the European Union, in the GATT agreements, in international security and military structures have led to a growing interest in the analysis of international economy and power structures. Since 1987, the 'Women's Forum on Foreign Policies', of which I am part, has tried to be a voice of feminist thinking and analysis in all these debates.

SOME FEMINIST EVENTS OF THE 1990S IN REVIEW — THE WOMEN'S STRIKE DAY OF JUNE 14, 1991

Women's strikes have a tradition in Switzerland. At the end of the last century, women workers in the textile and in the tobacco industry organised several strikes with hundreds of participants to protest against bad working conditions and unequal pay. During the First World War, women went on hunger demonstrations in the markets to protest against exaggerated prices for food. In 1930–1, the Association of Housewives in the town of Biel called for a boycott of all milk products — a strategy which proved to be successful in reducing the prices. In 1959, women teachers in Basel protested in a one-day strike against the rejection of women's right to vote. By the end of the 1980s, nurses all over Switzerland went to the streets and organised short strikes to reach better wages, especially for nightshifts.

On June 14, 1991, about half a million women participated in the Swiss Women's Strike Day in all parts of the country. The idea for this strike was conceived by a small group of women workers in the watch industry, who wanted to commemorate the tenth anniversary of the Equal Rights amendment, which had been without impact so far. The idea was taken on by the national Federation of Trades Unions and organised within a short time. Although the situation of working women — bad working conditions, unequal pay, unequal access to leading positions, unfair conditions in the pension schemes, the lack of part-time jobs and child-care institutions and so on — was at the centre of the demands, women went on strike not only as workers and employees, but also as consumers, housewives, lovers and mothers. Leaving their jobs for more or less time, refusing to prepare the meals for their families, organising sit-ins in schools, universities, hospitals, offices, having demonstrations and parties in the streets of all bigger cities, they demonstrated to tell everybody that we no longer tolerate any form of discrimination and violence. The strike meant also solidarity with women all over the world who suffer under similar patriarchal systems.

Many women of course publicly expressed their dissent with the women's strike, their will to keep solidarity first of all with their husbands and bosses and their consideration that the strike was a silly action of some frustrated feminists. Some male politicians such as the president of the lower chamber of Parliament did warn women that the strike could be 'counterproductive', as the ruling men would 'no more be ready to support women's demands'. Nevertheless, 14 June, 1991 seemed to many of us like the beginning of a new era for the feminist movement in Switzerland. We dominated the news for weeks. We were visible in our number and in our diversity, we were strong. For one day at least, we felt that 'Switzerland was in the hands of women' as a participant stated in the press. For one day only . . . but one of the key impacts of the women's strike day, was that new women's committees were set up all over Switzerland, especially in the countryside, most of them remaining quite active even now.

THE NON-ELECTION OF CHRISTIANE BRUNNER AS A MEMBER OF THE FEDERAL COUNCIL

Almost two years later, another political event provoked a mass protest of women in the streets of Switzerland: the election of a new member of the Federal Council in March 1993, after the Foreign Minister, a Social Democrat, had announced his retirement from the government. Immediately, an old question was raised: Would a woman finally get into the Swiss Federal Council, this old patriarchal body of seven men? Several attempts had been made in earlier years. In 1984, Elisabeth Kopp, a woman from a conservative party, happened to be the first woman elected as a member of the Federal Council. Five years later, she had to retire because of a political scandal in connection with the activities of her husband. For the next four years, men ruled the Swiss Government on their own again.

In 1993 it was the responsibility of the Social Democratic Party to propose a new candidate. This process is based on the Swiss system of an unchangeable balance of the parties represented in the Government by way of the *Zauberformel* — magic formula. This formula for the composition of government is not written in law but is a conventional rule which is in principle respected by all parties. Christiane Brunner, a

well-known trade unionist who had also co-initiated the Women's Strike
Day of 1991, seemed to stand a good chance. But immediately after she
had been named as one of the two candidates — the other one being
a man — defamation set in. The opponents didn't focus their criticism
on Brunner's political positions (for instance that she had supported
the initiative for the abolition of the Swiss army, or that she had signed
an appeal for free abortion), they attacked her on the grounds of her
patchwork biography, her having divorced two husbands, and raised
sons from different fathers.

The slander seemed to be successful: on March 3, 1993, after
an embarrassing mass media campaign, different political moves
and rising pressure from conservative parties, the male-dominated
parliament elected the male candidate. However, they did not take
the hundreds of thousands of women into account who had started to
identify with Christiane Brunner, a woman who seemed to many of us
'like my neighbour next door'. They did not consider the frustration of
all those women who expected, twelve years after the late introduction
of women's suffrage, that finally they would be represented by at least
one woman in the Federal Council. Hundreds of women gathered on
this early day of Spring on the central square in front of Parliament
House in the Swiss capital Bern to show their solidarity with Christiane
— they now expressed their loud protest against her non-election. The
protest was not in vain: women did succeed in pressuring the elected
candidate to refuse his election!

Yet the women did not win on all counts. One week after the big
rally, another female candidate, Ruth Dreifuss, a trade unionist as well,
was proposed by the Social Democratic Party and was finally elected
instead of Christiane Brunner. A half-baked victory for the Women's
movement — and another starting point for a new era of women's
politics in Switzerland. A few weeks later, district elections in one of
the most conservative areas of the country, the canton of Argovia, led
to a doubling of women's representation in the cantonal Parliament.

THE SOLIDARITY MOVEMENT WITH WOMEN IN THE FORMER YUGOSLAVIA: A CONTROVERSIAL CHALLENGE

Between the two feminist events mentioned above, which relate to
Swiss internal affairs, war broke out in the former Yugoslavia. Media
reports about mass rape of Croatian and Bosnian women shocked the
Swiss public and women in particular. On December 10, 1992, mass
demonstrations were organised by feminist and women's peace groups in
over twenty towns. They gathered a number of women (about 10,000 in

Zurich, some 20,000 overall) who had not been seen on the streets since the peace demonstrations in the early 80s — expect, of course, during the women's strike one and a half years before. There were women who had never ever participated in any street action. The reason for this immense participation may be the high level of identification with the victims of rape, a crime of which everyone among us could become a victim. The demonstrations asked for an immediate end of rape and war, for the recognition of rape as a war crime and — addressed to the Swiss government — for open borders for women refugees from the former Yugoslavia.

The first demand was, as we had to learn later, not a very qualified one: Rape was indeed already defined as a war crime by the Geneva Convention. The problem was more the implementation of this convention in the practice of international war tribunals. For to state the latter as a demand would have led us to the question of how this could work without those interrogations which violate and humiliate the victims of rape again and again, and which we know enough through our home experience in legal processes surrounding allegations of rape. The right consequence of this dilemma seemed to me what one Swiss activist, Elenor Richter-Lyonette, did some months later: she founded a 'Women's advocacy group' with the aim of carrying out a critical observation of how the War Tribunal in The Hague was developing.

As to the second demand, it has to be seen in the general framework of Swiss immigration policy, which is quite restrictive. The Swiss government seemed indeed to give in a little bit under the very big public pressure at the end of the year 1992: they declared that they would admit a contingent of 5000 refugees from the former Yugoslavia. But this promise was never fulfilled. One year later, only some 2000 refugees had come within the frame of this contingent. The official 'explanations' were that 'UNHCR did not ask Switzerland to take more refugees', or that Switzerland 'considers it more important to help inside the country', or that 'Switzerland had already spent more money on refugees in the former Yugoslavia than ever for one single crisis region', and so on. Yet it is true that many thousands of women and men from the former Yugoslavia were still able to find a refuge in Switzerland albeit with very uncertain status, which means that most of them do not get any help from the state, do not know when they will be sent back, and cannot work in our country. One small feminist group in Zurich which has good contact with the Centre for Women Victims of War in Zagreb, still continues to work on the question of refugees. The demand is still to give asylum to more (women) refugees from former Yugoslavia, and to improve the situation for them inside Switzerland. But the conditions are very demotivating — besides the fact that one can ask if it is right to ask for open borders only for one special group of refugees.

At the same time, a fund-raising campaign was started by women's groups, dedicated to helping women war victims, which was extremely successful. As far as I remember, this was the first time ever that financial means amounting to about one million Swiss francs were in the hands of Swiss feminists, to be distributed to women.

Solidarity work with women in the former Yugoslavia started to be a real challenge when we had to notice that it was not for us as women — and especially not for us as Swiss women — to define the pattern of the conflict primarily in terms of gender division, but that we were highly dependent on patterns shaped by the ruling parties of the conflict. Right after the December 1992 demonstrations, Bosnian women living in Switzerland approached the organisers with the question why they had organised the demonstration without them, which meant without the victims. The same claim came from Croatian women in Switzerland. The deeper reason was that we, considering ourselves as 'feminists' with a long tradition of peace activism, wanted to define the issues and demands of the demonstration based on our own standpoints. We were afraid that, leaving the floor to women from different republics from the former Yugoslavia, it would lead to emotional, nationalist statements. This fear was somehow confirmed some weeks later, when Bosnian Committees organised a demonstration asking for weapons and military intervention, wearing Bosnian flags around their shoulders. Not 'our' style . . . but the challenging question was asked: 'What does women's solidarity mean, given the fact that we have completely different identities and experiences in connection with war and peace?'

The conflict continued with the question of how to use the money which had been collected. Should it be given to Bosnian Muslims only, since — as Bosnian women said — it had been collected because of their fate? Should it be given to Croatian feminists, since they were the ones who tried to establish support structures for women war victims and contacts already existed between them and us? Should it be given to the Serbian Women in Black, since they were feminists still trying to speak out against the war? How to share the power we had won with this money in our hands? How to decide criterias?

And another challenging question was asked: Is it possible to act in solidarity if we are bound within a system of 'donors' and 'beneficiaries', 'helpers' and 'victims', instead of being all 'equal' having nothing and suffering the same violence. The question was not new to those of us who had worked in social women's projects for many years. New was the fact not only of our different experiences of violence, but also our different nationalities which made it difficult to exercise real solidarity, even though we did live in the same country. Would we ever be able to free ourselves from the patriarchal patterns shaping our lives, our identities and even our attempts at peace work and solidarity?

PAYING ATTENTION TO OUR DIFFERENCES — 'NEW' ISSUES FOR THE FEMINIST MOVEMENT

While the struggle continues against all forms of violence — battering, rape, sexual harassment, child abuse, trafficking in women and children, discrimination at work, poverty — which affect women in Switzerland as everywhere else, one fact of today's reality of women in our country has become more central in the feminist debate of the last few years: the fact that about one fifth of us are migrant women.

The issue of 'women's rights as human rights' has gained a growing importance in the feminist movement. One of the reasons for this — apart from the events of the Vienna Conference on this issue in 1993 — has been the many changes in immigration and asylum law in Switzerland, which have been enacted during the last decade and which always meant a deterioration of the situation of migrant women. Switzerland's migration politics today are based on a so-called 'three circle system'. Citizens from Western European countries have easy access to the Swiss labour market, while immigrants from Eastern European countries have more difficulties if they are not highly qualified, and those from the South have almost no chance to get work under regular conditions. Migrant women married or divorced are especially affected by these rules, since their visa status is usually dependent on the permit of the husband.

The last development in the field of laws concerning foreigners are the so-called 'coercive measures', accepted by the Swiss people in December 1994 and in place since February 1995. These measures, propagated mainly as a means against illegal drug traffickers, create a twofold legal system. Foreigners without regular visa-status (asylum-seekers, illegals) can be detained for up to three months while the decision for their deportation is being prepared. The 'foreigner police', a special unit of the security forces, decides on detention, for example based on the suspicion that the person concerned will try to avoid deportation. The same police department is also entitled to restrict certain foreigners from entering or leaving a specific territory. Further, the capture of illegal aliens is to be facilitated. It is now possible for the 'foreigner police' to search any building or house upon suspicion that an illegal person is hiding in that place.

All these measures affect women. The last one is particularly threatening with regard to women's shelters and crisis centres which need to guarantee anonymity to their clients in order to remain credible and effective. Since a foreign woman married to a Swiss man is not naturalised automatically anymore (the respective law having been changed some years ago), she has now to be married for at least three years in order to get residency independent of her marital status. Thus, women who leave their husbands during the first three years of marriage or who are abandoned face illegality, departure or deportation. The crisis centres have evidence that the next marriage-law will leave many women with the choice between a violent marriage or the coercion to leave Switzerland.

Women's groups, especially migrant women's groups, have opposed these laws which betray the liberal foundations of our legal system and further discriminate against the migrant communities. A good cooperation and mutual solidarity between 'migrant women' and 'Swiss women' in all fields of women's struggle seems to us one of today's main challenges for the feminist movement in Switzerland. With regard to the Fourth World Conference on Women in Beijing in 1995, a lobbying struggle had to be carried out to make migrant women officially 'acceptable' as Swiss NGOs concerned with the issues of the Conference and having a right to participate in the preparatory work. A liaison-group of feminist NGOs was created, composed of several migrant women's groups and Swiss groups. The proposal to include an NGO representative in the official Swiss delegation to Beijing was unanimously adopted by this co-ordinating committee, but was not accepted by the responsible authorities. Obviously, Swiss officials did not want to include in their delegation a progressive voice concerning migration questions, given the above-mentioned repressive Swiss politics in this area of concern.

PERSPECTIVES FROM BEIJING AND BEYOND

The Fourth World Conference on Women and more specifically the NGO Forum in Huairou has brought some new experiences and impulses to Swiss feminist politics.

About four hundred NGO representatives from our country did participate in the NGO events of the World Conference. They represented a wide range of women's organizations, from the progressive Swiss feminist groups, through to the internationally connected lobby groups which have their seats in Geneva, and up to conservative groups like the anti-abortion campaign 'Right to Life'. On the other hand, a delegation of Tibetan women from Switzerland was not given a visa by the Chinese authorities, which provoked big protests throughout the country, but which could not change the situation.

Among the feminists and some other open-minded Swiss participants in Huairou, a regular exchange of experiences was organized during the forum, which could be based on the coordination work we had previously completed. The contact with Switzerland's official delegation — which was, by the way, one of the smallest delegations of all, comprising only eleven members — went quite well, so that the NGOs in Huairou were informed about what was going on in Beijing at the official level. However, the influence we could have was almost zero.

As others may also have experienced, it is quite impossible to give any 'over-all' results of the NGO Conference. This is of course due first of all to the immense size of the event, and to the 'women's fair' character that it took on in too many respects. On the other hand, we regret deeply the absence of any plenaries or at least open microphones which would have allowed women to make some form of assessment each day or at least at the end of the conference. Against this background, speaking about the experience of Beijing/Huairou is still a puzzling task, in which everyone has her own small piece cut out of the whole.

Nevertheless, some results have started to become familiar amongst the 'Beijing returners' in Switzerland. The first is the deep conviction that the time has come to get much more involved in the institutional level of politics, or in the words of a Philippine participant to Beijing: 'to take over'. In less utopian words — we have to go on fighting on all possible levels of politics, in finding ways of institutionalised exchange between the different levels of politics in which feminists are involved, in asking for accountability, and of course in lobbying our government and those women who work in the public administration. This is not new, yet I think that both the preparatory process for Beijing in our country and the discussions at the Conference itself have given us a big push in this direction. Some discussions in Beijing amongst feminist politicians from different countries with different political systems have brought important results concerning — amongst others — systems of both vertical and horizontal experience. By this I mean exchanges between women in politics, as well as the question of independent candidacy for elections and/or including feminist candidates moving into traditional parties. In Europe there is the hope that a network of independent feminist election lists and several Women's parties will soon be started.

A second conclusion of the Beijing experience concerns the field of economics. Feminist analysis of both macro- and micro-economics was one of the discussion themes which gained most interest by participants from all over the world. This might show that the effects of structural adjustment and male-biased economic concepts do not affect only women in the so-called 'Third World' any more. Female poverty, due to structural changes, has become a problem which concerns a growing number of women in the more industrialised countries too. The discussion about common strategies against structural adjustment is one of today's most important issues of solidarity between women in the North and the South. The same seems to be true for the theme of 'counting women's work' which, if we think it through, means nothing more than the fact that what women work at is not their *contribution* to economics, but *our* economics.

Not by accident, all demands of the NGOs which questioned the ruling economic paradigms were not accepted by the official platform for action. Everyone knows, on the other hand, that the implementation of this platform will never be realised if there is not a fundamental change in economic thinking, since the thousands of billions which its implementation would cost would never be afforded. Even more, our struggle for an approach to economics which would not be a gendered one has to be improved on all levels. This is especially the case in all of our struggles at the national economic level and in social politics. This is, I think, a conviction which most Swiss feminists share today.

A third impression from Beijing is the issue of diversity and common struggles. Some of us felt that this Conference was too much about 'self-service': the Conference in which every woman could choose the specific issues she is interested in, without being obliged to find common positions in urgent problems of today's world. Sometimes, it was also like a competition among the different minority groups or groups of women to project themselves. So, one of questions for the future might be: How do we find, from the important acknowledgment of our different identities, a common strength and common strategies?

This is a question that we also have to resolve on a national level. In Switzerland, as I have described above, there are lots of projects, groups and organizations but no common structure and strategies within the feminist movement on a national level. This is why one of the most important areas of follow-up work after Beijing will be the process of creating a national structure which would give the feminist movement a common voice to express and implement the growing strength that we feel we have.

6

SOS Belgrade July 1993–1995: Dirty Streets

Lepa Mladjenović and Divna Matijašević

6.1 WORKING IN CONDITIONS OF MISERY, INCREASED VIOLENCE AND DESPAIR. A PAPER DELIVERED AT THE HELSINKI CITIZENS ASSEMBLY WORKSHOP ON 'ISSUES OF VIOLENCE AGAINST WOMEN' IN LIBLICE, CZECHOSLOVAKIA IN SEPTEMBER 1993

As of the summer of 1993, there are four million refugees from the former Yugoslavia, half a million dead, a couple of million injured, and thousands of women raped in war.

In Serbia, about 300,000 Albanians left Kosovo because of political pressure, about 100,000 young men left the country to escape military duties and became deserters, about 600,000 refugees came to Serbia, 80 per cent of whom are women and children.

The terrors of war, war rapes, the embargo, rapid inflation, a repressive regime and ethnic violence have completely changed the conditions of women's lives here. The average salary is less than the cost of one abortion, or one pack of heart medicine, two kilos of meat or half of one shoe. In the meantime, the kids are playing war games and the TV is showing old sex-and-violence movies, constantly shaping a reality which does not reflect the one in which we live.

Women are in different ways subjected to violence constantly. Their lives are shaped by this violent reality that is most of the time taken as a way of life, and therefore passes as socially invisible. In Serbia, the constitution guarantees women general human rights, but the reality is different because:

> women's work is never done and is underpaid and what we look like is more important than what we do and if we get raped it's our fault . . . (NUS Women's Campaign)

The 'SOS Telephone for Women and Children Victims of Violence' was opened by the feminists in Belgrade in March 1990, precisely because male violence against women affects every woman's life and is highly invisible. We believe that violence has a gender, and that male violence against women, like the institution of compulsory heterosexuality, is the basis of women's oppression. In our work, our first task is to identify, name and reveal this violence. After that, together with each woman, we search for ways to confront it and eliminate it. The SOS Telephone is a non-government, non-nationalist women's group made up of volunteers, organized through non-hierarchical structures to support women and children victims of violence.

Facts about SOS Belgrade

In three and a half years of work, we have received about 5000 phone calls from women and children, organised six training programmes for new women volunteers, and supported the opening of two other SOS Hotlines in Kraljevo and Nis. More than 150 women have been working on the Hotline for at least two months. Usually, there are twenty to thirty active volunteers/experts. More than 100 women have been met personally outside the SOS. About fifteen self-help workshops have been held for the volunteers. A self-defence course has been organised by an American expert. A seminar on social work and violence against women has been held by experts from Germany. Four SOS Bulletins have been published. Official contacts have been established with more than twenty institutions in Belgrade, including community social work centres, Red Cross, UNHCR, police, lawyers, some medical and mental health institutions, city government, and different faculties of Belgrade University. Public discussions and lectures in different institutions have been organised about six times a year.

Organisation of Our Work

The main scope of the SOS Hotline's activity is talking with women on the phone, and creating a relationship of mutual trust and belief which will eventually inspire women's strength and courage to resist violence. The other work is based on the principle of co-ordinating certain jobs at certain times.

The war has increased violence against women and created new terrors and new types of violence that women are subjected to: first of all, rapes in war and second, women refugees. This new reality has changed the nature of the SOS group which, at the beginning of the war was the only women's group in Belgrade that worked with women victims of violence. At the moment, apart from the basic phone work, we have formed three SOS sub-groups:

1. Group for women raped in war.

This group was formed in January 1993 and will be the founder of the Rape Crisis Centre which should open in October. The group has worked until now with women from Bosnia who are survivors of sexual violence in war. The future Centre will deal with women survivors of all different kinds of sexual violence, besides war-rape: incest, rape in marriage, acquaintance rape, sexual harassment.

2. Group for women refugees.

This includes organising workshops, taking care of the health needs of women, making contacts between women and the rest of their families, organising funding for medicine and other needs, like clothes or school equipment for children.

3. Group for out-services.

This is a group of two women formed in May 1993. The women are responsible for making personal contacts with women who call SOS in desperate situations and therefore require immediate support. They also act as support persons when women need to go to institutions like social work centres and courts.

Having international solidarity money for SOS work has undoubtedly created many more possibilities, but has also introduced problems: which work will remain voluntary and which will be paid? One decision has been made, that daily phone duties from 6 p.m. to 10 p.m., will always remain voluntary work. In the meantime a permanent paid workplace has been opened for administration and co-ordination work, daily from 11am–6pm in the SOS office. We also have part-time workers for public relations work, refugee women work, treasurer, out-services work, research, etc.

Effects of the War

As we have already mentioned, the war in Croatia and Bosnia has changed everyday reality, women's lives and our work on the SOS Hotline. Our main conclusion after two years of war is: Violence against women and war against women exists at all times and everywhere; during war it intensifies and increases. The war has indeed proved that women calling the hotlines already know most forms of war-violence. One woman recently said to us: 'I am not afraid of war, living with my husband, I am already 20 years in war.'

Nonetheless, all types of violence have increased and some have specific modes. The summary of our experience is as follows:

Firstly the militarization of relationships. The hierarchy of everyday values has changed, and therefore events and deeds in connection to war have become very important. In line with this the presence of weapons in families has increased. Women who call SOS report that their partners threaten them with weapons in 40 per cent of cases. The police say that about 200,000 weapons are legally in Belgrade, a city of a million and a half inhabitants, and they estimate that there are two or three times more guns in the city. This comes to every second adult now having at least one gun.

Secondly, rape, torture and robbery by soldiers who come back to their families. Men who return from the front very often continue the same behaviour they developed in the war. Women who call have reported being surprised by the attitudes of the men they knew. Wives report being raped in the middle of the night, sisters report being robbed of money or objects of value by their brothers (soldiers), mothers report being harassed, tortured mentally and/or physically by their sons (soldiers). There has also been a marked increase of rape and other military behaviour among adolescent boys. Nowadays, parents more often address boys as: 'my general', 'my soldier', 'my commander'. Girls are only the silent witnesses to boys being given double values — once as boys and second as army officers. Boys most often play war games, and some dress in war uniforms. Having a need to rehearse their future role of conquerors, adolescent boys are already starting to rape girls. Girls are more often reporting rape at the ages of sixteen, seventeen and eighteen.

Thirdly, there has been an increase of reported rapes and prostitution. SOS has noted that, even though a very small number of rapes are reported because of the taboo, women reported rapes twice as often over the last year. This includes refugee women who are raped in new families, incest, rapes by friends, acquaintance rapes and marriage rapes by partners who come back from the war zones and others. SOS has also noted that in Belgrade and surrounding cities, new night bars have been opened with 'entertainment girls'. Some of them are mostly for ex-soldiers and some of them are for the UN soldiers. This phenomenon will be investigated more in the future.

Finally, the group for women raped in war has worked with women coming from the war zones. All of the women we contacted until now had only sought medical assistance, either for an abortion or for giving birth. Our main aim is to create a relationship of trust and solidarity with them since they still do not ask for help. We are now trying to satisfy their primary needs. Since we have money for the survivors of war, we can supply them with clothes, bus or air tickets (if they go out of the country), medicine, food, etc. The Rape Crisis Centre will develop a special programme for long-term work with rape survivors.

We have two main policies concerning war rapes:

1. *Any and every rape is a violation of human rights. We have to work to change the legal system so that every perpetrator will be punished.*

2. *War rapes should be explicitly made war crimes. The Geneva Convention should give this crime its full name. A War Crimes Tribunal should punish all the soldiers who are perpetrators of rape. State institutions and the general public should know that this is a crime to be punished.*

Meanwhile, we are witnessing thousands of Muslim women being subjected to systematic rapes, death and deportations as a part of the genocidal military tactics of the Serbian Army. (Though instances of genocide have recently been recorded on all three sides in the war.)

Refugees

Refugees who have come into families have changed the dynamics and balance among the members of these families. This imbalance is most often reflected in violence by frustrated men against women.

Women refugees in the refugee settlements are mostly left in very passive conditions, with lots of leisure time which then is filled with grief for the missing ones, loneliness and self pity. SOS groups have until now supported women from Bosnia who wanted to go to foreign countries, along with a few families in some Bosnian towns, refugees of Muslim origin in Belgrade connected with Mosques, and women and children in a few settlements. Future plans include developing twinning projects where some women from foreign countries will pay the cost of living for some refugee women, and introducing self-help projects in two particular refugee settlements.

Economic Misery

War and the economic embargo have drastically lowered the standard of living of the citizens of Serbia. According to official data (June 1993), more than 70 per cent of the population lives below the poverty line, which is 5 or 10 DM per month. During the month of July, the inflation rate was 800 per cent. (This means that a salary by the end of the month was eight times less valuable.) Misery, in all its forms, has affected violence against women. Women's means of surviving at all have decreased. In the hospitals there is the lack of medicine and the lack of food for children and husbands. Women are always the last to ask for medical help, especially if they know it costs money. Women are under twenty-four hour mental pressure — how to feed the family and what to give them for dinner the next day. Women cannot pay lawyers. Women have to work an extra job for a whole month if they are to pay for an abortion (which once upon a time was free). Women are the ones who are going to be slapped in the face by men who are frustrated by the new poverty. Women take care of the old and the sick. Women take care of their relatives and friends in the war zones. Women are in despair when they cannot buy school books and other equipment for their children. Women are remembering how their mothers or grandmothers cooked without oil or meat, and how they washed without detergent. They are the first ones who breathe and sleep with the burdens of war and the last ones allowed to fall into depression or despair, because then the whole family is shattered.

Many of our days are filled with activities that deal with war. We search for candles and food cans for packages to be sent to Sarajevo. We run to find bus drivers going to certain Bosnian towns in order to leave them our plastic bags with batteries and yeast and a few words, which we are never sure will reach their destination. We write letters to our Bosnian sisters in war zones or out in Denmark, Sweden, Holland . . . exchange their letters, read them aloud, cry together. And when the night comes and the sound of the wind brings back the fear of the war out there, some of us try to fight helplessness by thinking, what else we can do?

In the end, we are left with two major tasks: how to spread women's solidarity in times when every woman has to fight for her own life, and when violence, thefts and lies are becoming the main mechanisms of survival (of the state, families, and individuals). And secondly, how to transform our own and other women's depression and despair into language and action for women. The war has brought death and torture into our lives much faster and much closer to us than we expected. It is the solidarity of women from other countries who write to us, come here and send us support that often inspires us again and again — they are our sources of hope so seriously threatened by men in war. And it is definitely our women's activities that give life to our optimism and joy that lay under the shadow of the pessimism of our minds and the daily news.

6.2 AUGUST 1995
Network of Violence Against Women

In the last two years new groups have appeared in Belgrade to deal with violence against women. The Autonomous Women's Centre Against Sexual Violence was opened in 1993 by the Group for Women Raped in War with the idea of becoming the Rape Crisis Centre. The reality the Centre works with women with refugee status and with women survivors of domestic and sexual violence. In these two years the Centre has become the women's space where many different ideas originated and many activities started, concerning rape in war, rape in marriage, abortion law, breaking incest taboos, supporting women's human rights, lesbian rights, e-mail communication and printing feminist notebooks.

Volunteers of the SOS Hotline for Women and Children Victims of Violence had become the central resource for developing other women's groups: the Centre for Girls, Safe Houses for battered women along with Shelters and Communes and Second Hand Shops.

The network of autonomous women's groups in Belgrade also includes, apart from the above-mentioned groups, Women in Black Against War, LABRIS Lesbian group, the Women's Law Group, the Women's Studies Centre and '94' — the Women's Publishing House. All these groups share the policy of independence and non-nationalism, and are basically grounded on feminist principles. The war and nationalism have given various forms to all of these groups and many women fight inner energies between despair and rage. Usually the joint actions of all of them are concerned with organizing the Eighth of March (International Women's Day) street actions or the anti-war demonstrations.

There are always some problems in these groups, but the women's groups everywhere in the world are full of everyday disconnections and discontinuities — there are probably many different flowers which we could water in each other's souls in order to keep feminist passionate politics in harmony and action.

Today, 7 August 1995, more than 180,000 people are walking along the roads of Bosnia in a 200km long line towards Belgrade. With the last bags of their own belongings, on tractors, horses, buses, kamions, cars, on foot; with their exhausted bodies and their proper names that determine their destiny. These are the people who from now on will be called refugees, they will never go back home, and many of us will still cry together their tragedy. This time they are of Serb ethnic origin and they come from the state of Croatia.

These old women, old people and children are walking with the urgency of survival. The hole of sadness has opened in their hearts. They will never be the same. Just a month ago the same survival walking marked some other roads of Bosnia. Then, it was the many thousands of people of Muslim names cleansed from Srebrenica and Zepa.

This is the fifth year that the images on front pages are filled with people with their last suitcases leaving their homes. What some of us fear now is that we will end up in the ethnically clean states, that fascist policy, the dead and the expelled will be the soil of the future falsified democracy in our states.

Women in Black

In the first days of August 1995 the fourth Women in Black International Meeting was taking place in the small village in Vojvodina — at the same time that the Croatian army very efficiently produced an exodus of people with Serb names from Krajina. There were approximately 150 women participating from twelve countries. The meeting passed in different layers: in the evening we were listening to the news that we were breathing during the day; during the day we discussed our realities and pain in the workshops ('ethnic cleansing', 'reality of the war', 'state and fear', 'women's disobedience') where we also cried at the latest news. At the same time from the beginning, the Serbian authorities were constantly producing obstacles to Women in Black. So, the Yugoslav Embassy in Madrid did not give visas to twenty-two activists from Spain. Then the local authority made pressure on the scout organization who wanted to support us by giving us tents and blankets — the tents were never received by us. Then, on the day of the meeting the bus with fifteen Italian peace activists was not allowed to enter the country, after being kept for thirty hours at the Hungarian border. The next day, whilst Italian pacifists were finally settled in a town in Hungary, seven of us from the meeting went to meet them. The same day, on the way back, the police on the border stopped two of us who they had on the list as 'Women in Black chiefs'. The investigation lasted four hours, and they already knew a lot about us. In the meantime some of the foreign participants were also questioned by the local police.

Still, on the last evening the beautiful group of women prepared for us The Anti-War Cabaret. We expected some very heavy subjects again — Mother Courage or Daughter of Tbilisi — but in the midst of our expectations the group started to imitate the daily problems in the camp during the meeting: waiting for the only shower, waking up in the sleeping bags, photographers during the vigil and so on. So, we ended this encounter with fantastic laughing together and lots of dancing.

Women in Black is now in its fifth year on the streets of Belgrade. This is the only permanent visible protest against the war, militarization, violence and the involvement of the Serbian regime in war crimes. Apart from the street vigils and issuing public statements, Women in Black also work on publishing: it issues a journal three times a year, the women's peace agenda and a calendar. From 1993 Women in Black has also been involved in the work with refugees in three different refugee camps.

At the beginning of 1995 the state did not give permission to the Group for their work in refugee camps. In one of the camps in June 1995 the director called the police to throw the Women in Black activists out of the camp. In the others, activists still go, anarchically.

6.3 DIRTY STREETS

Physical and sexual abuse are part of the global process of disempowering the people. This is the systematic strategy to bring women and children into a state of powerlessness so that they can be better controlled. If she has been beaten up over the last twenty-five years and cannot tell that to anybody, if she lives with broken bones and a broken soul, where will her intelligence end up, the autonomous initiative of this woman? If she is plunged into shame and guilt how are we expecting her to become the subject of her life? Violence against women produces hate, fear and loss of control. 'I amount to zero' a woman said to us on the SOS Hotline.

The war has made many more silent victims. It has shown us the common ground between war violence and the violence that women suffer in everyday life. The similarities can be seen in the logic of the oppressors, and persecution, which renders difference to the state of Otherness to be hated, abused and annihilated. We have also seen the commonality in experience between women abused because of their gender or because of their ethnicity. We have learned that traumatic experiences produce the feeling of hate of oneself and of the others, feelings of guilt, isolation, loss of control of where one comes from or where one should go to.

The logic of war and the logic of violence against women have many common strategies. One aspect of the common logic is the control of the territory of the Other by means of fear and violence. The Other is a country of the 'enemy' or the body of a woman. We know that not all women have been raped but all women live in fear of rape, just as not all people in war are dead but all of them live in fear of death.

200,000 people left Krajina in two days, only fear could produce such an exodus. Fear is the tool.

The second aspect of this common logic is in the principle of pride and revenge. And revenge usually means torture or death. SOS Hotlines around the world show that generally a husband revenges his anger on his wife. It can be any anger ranging from the wrong meal or the wrong political situation. Revenge and violence in the family perpetuate the order of patriarchy. On the other hand after four years of war we see that nation-states dwell on the exclusive principle of blood and soil which serves to separate people and establish the dynamic of domination. Thus the constitutions declare there is a constitutive nationality and a minority nationality. Thus one has been 'ours' and the Other, 'theirs', and an immediate dichotomy is established — better and worse, the powerful and the disempowered. In nation-states the ethnic minority is used to define the superiority of the ethnic majority, through violence and hate if necessary. 'History gives us a right to shoot first in defence' say the nationalist leaders on the Serbian media. The pride of the blood and soil has to be controlled. In the family the 'constitutive minority population' or the disempowered, are the women and they become the Other to be controlled. 'Beat up your wife every morning, if you don't know why, she will know' says an old proverb. Therefore, the laws that ensure pure family and pure nation, become the whip which threatens any dirtiness: individuals of the other national origins, mixed heterosexual marriages, children of mixed parents, refugees, lesbian or gay families, anti-militarists, those disloyal to husbands and other patriarchal figures. When the local gang in my neighbourhood beat me up because I am a lesbian one of them said: 'You are dirtying my street'. Cleansing becomes the value, not human life.

This logic of control and revenge one can see not only in wars, but in the conflicts of nationalist parties, in Hollywood movies, in every history textbook. So, when the husband has come back home and said in anger: 'You bitch', and hits his wife against the wall, that's it. That is the end. Shoot first in defence. He is marking his soil. He is controlling the body of the woman. He has taken her body as if it is his property. He is crossing his limits, he is entering into ours. That is how the war starts. He is the same soldier who will pick up a gun and kill, because he has never learnt that his body and a woman's body are two different entities. The social order ensures that the oppressed are always available to the oppressors, the father can enter into his daughter's vagina, even without pain and forever ruin her body's boundaries and forever make her lose the feelings for the parent and the home. The soldier enters the nearly captured town, marking out his property. The psychiatrist is entering the room of the patient without knocking, as do many mothers. The parents who beat up children are entering into their bodies without blinking an eye, some of them even say: 'Take off those pants' and then start hitting them with a belt. If the girl's sexuality is ruined in this way, we call it incest. The integrity of the child's body has been violated.

The victims of violence fear authority and are easily made obedient. If the married woman says 'This is killing me twenty-four hours a day' what kind of political decisions for this society can she make? If fear is her basic existential state, if she uses her entire energy just to survive — does it not satisfy her husband as well as her politicians? If the perpetrators are never accused and if survivors cannot make decisions for themselves, what kind of democracy can we talk about? If the state cannot guarantee safe public space in which all victims of violence can speak aloud their testimonies in the knowledge that the perpetrators will be brought to justice — what basic human rights can that state guarantee?

Didn't we ask ourselves so many times how can a man in war rape a woman he hates so much? How can he literally enter her body, because we thought that if you hate someone you cannot even touch her. We were wrong. Because in those moments we have forgotten the stories, of incest and rape in marriage — were these women talking about love? Or did they feel hate and betrayal? 'He robbed my soul and my body' one of them said. Many men have forever learned that there are no limits to entering the body of those who are less powerful than they are. So, the army with more weapons enter the 'enemy' country. So, the man enters and rapes a woman. And when they have killed and made the others homeless, the conquerors can hammer up the plates with their names on at the city halls. They won the revenge — they can spread their names on the new territory. They have already hammered up the plates with their names on against the family doors. Whose last name do you have? It is still very few of our mothers who have been disobedient to the rule of the father. And the fathers — didn't they learn how to conquer territory from the beginning of this civilization? The state gives them that right. To stamp their names on women's bodies, to rape them, to beat them, to kill them. Every state in this world legitimates violence against women and views women as men's property. Patriarchy will perpetuate wars forever.

If we want to get out of the logic of war we need to understand that violence produces the circuit of hatred: the oppressed are left alone and isolated 'frozen in time and paralyzed with rage' said one incest survivor.

The oppresseds' lives are closed inside, hate and anger without the means to overcome the pain. The oppressor hates, but he has the power and the means; he tried to overcome his pain by taking revenge. So we need to break such circuits, we need victims of violence to have permanent safe space in public in order to be able to talk. To get out of the shell of shame and guilt, and we will believe them. We need to unblock on the personal, social and legal levels, the life stories of abuse so that the logic of revenge and control can be eliminated. Otherwise the circuit is eternal: women take revenge on children and on themselves. Men take revenge on women and children or the ethnic Other. And then everybody enters the logic of war. Some, in the emotions of victims, others as the minds of aggressors. And some as both victims and aggressors.

We need to transform the silence of the anger and revenge of victims into a language of survivors and positive public actions. We need to start with ourselves — remembering all the violence we have ever experienced. Remember and come out with stories of pain and anger that we hide. Who do we humiliate when we are angry?

We need to break the circuit of violence by breaking the family secrets, family taboos, family values that hid the victims in deep holes of darkness and silence. Children and women then will be able to rise up from the 'enormous woundedness all around' and talk and we will be stunned by what they are saying. And if all the children said all of their incest stories and if all of the women speak their pain of male violence and if all the people of Other ethnic names speak of their persecution — only then we will have the possibility to begin to stop the wars and to start to transform the power of patriarchy that controls, into forms of individual strength and new types of social relationships that are not based on domination.

6.4   LETTER FOR WOMEN IN SARAJEVO

On 9, 10 and 11 of April 1995 a group of opposition activists from Belgrade visited Sarajevo. The trip was organized by peace organizations from Belgrade: LIVING IN SARAJEVO and the ASSO-CIATION OF SERBS in Sarajevo. After 1,000 days of the war, this was the first time people got from Serbia permission from the Bosnian authorities for such a trip. There were thirty-eight of us, out of which eighteen were women. Most of the activists were from the peace groups, independent media journalists, human rights and women's groups. To arrive in Sarajevo meant crossing four borders, changing five buses, and forty-two hours of travelling. Rain, clouds, winds and snow was an ordinary weather report of the early spring in Sarajevo. But in the war the weather has a special meaning and determines more destiny to pure life existence than usual. War is something else.

Dear our sisters from Sarajevo

The eighteen of us who were three days among you, we wish to tell you that we came back. We wish to tell you that after leaving Sarajevo we passed the Adriatic coast, it was a beautiful sunshine day. Some of us had a desire, a crazy fantasy to transfer all the people from Sarajevo — babies and women and men and those with injuries and those who are silent and the oldest — to transfer all of you to the sea, at least for six days, for five days, so that you can all lay on the beaches without fear, without the look of the other that kills now or later, without sounds that destroy soul and bones. So that we can cherish you with warmth. You all enjoy yourselves on the coast, and we who come from the other, from the third side we prepared for you to sleep, to eat, drink and smoke.

Yes, after your words from the occupied town, your faces which do not say about pain under the pain, after seeing injured men carried near us to the tunnel, after bullet storms that kill, after having to climb up the mountain Igman on the snow and mud . . . the next day the bus has taken us to the sea in the sun. It was an experience of freedom; tranquillity and the wideness of the breath. There is no justice. Some of us looked at the sea with tears or pain in the chest, and from the sea images rose of your swollen hands from the cold water, of graves in the yards, hills that watch us, hallways where girls play with gum, the big spot of the blood on the corner of the streets Kralja Tomislava and Marsala Tita where on the 10th of April 1995 Maja Djokic lost her breath. She was eighteen, coming back from volleyball. And a little bit further the spot of Munevera Selimovic, killed the same day. On the television news of Bosnia and Herzegovina there was Maja's picture from childhood, she was moving a pencil through her hair and smiling. There is no justice.

We are writing to you in the knowledge of the complexity of the facts of where each one of us came back to and where each of us came from. It is extremely difficult not to feel wrath against those on the other side of injustice: where each of us sleeps tonight. And we didn't feel this wrath in you. But we did feel, from the tears to the laughter, the power of each of your individual commitment to overcome the lethal belief in the proper name, proper land and blood. Maybe, in fact, we couldn't really experience the horrible danger caused by this commitment: you say 'we want solidarity' and they kill, you say 'we want to live together' and they kill, you say 'we only want to breathe and listen to the music' and they kill. And so it goes every day and night on each voice of life. It is now more than 1000 days.

We came back changed more than ever. We are full of traces of your testimonies and our deep feelings that life is far more difficult for you than you wanted to show to us. We are full of anticipation of what you haven't said, of what is not sayable, of what is caught in the tear which did not fall, or in the tram that didn't pass. Women will remember.

We have seen that you have remained different among yourselves even though the killers from the hills want to reduce you to mere carriers of water, of mere counters of the bullets, to invalids or names inscribed in the books of dead. They have not succeeded. They have not reduced you to one thought, even though you all share one condition of cellars, darkness and bullets. We have seen your different women's groups, we have taken your papers, books, statements. We have seen you in the theatre, in newspapers, on the radio, on the television, on the streets: you are of all different names. We are fascinated. We have felt your decisions to defend the right of the politics of difference and your wish to live together, and we are supporting you totally and ceaselessly in that politics.

We will talk and write and speak about you.

We will repeat ten thousand times how you are courageous and how much we love you.

We will come to you again, as soon as possible.

Drinking coffee with you in Sarajevo touches our souls.

20 April 1995
from women in Belgrade
Lepa Mladjenović
Jadranka Milicevic

Note

Section 6.1 written jointly by Lepa Mladjenović and Divna Matijašević.
Sections 6.2 and 6.3 written by Lepa Mladjenović.

7

Croatia: Three Years After

Rada Boric and Mica Mladineo Desnica

7.1   A PAPER DELIVERED BY MICA MLADINEO DESNICA, AT THE HELSINKI CITIZENS ASSEMBLY WOMEN'S COMMISSION WORKSHOP ON 'ISSUES OF VIOLENCE AGAINST WOMEN' IN LIBLICE, CZECHOSLOVAKIA IN SEPTEMBER 1993

The general picture of Croatia today is more or less similar to those of all East and Central European post-socialist countries. All you have to do is add war and approximately half a million displaced persons and refugees. We are facing a disastrous economic situation. Two thirds of Croatia are reduced to twelve hours of electricity a day. There are enormous expenses stemming from the war, an inflation rate of 30 per cent a month, a high unemployment rate (55 per cent women), and high costs of living. In a few months, we may be living under sanctions. This is our physical life. Our souls are governed by a right-wing conservative party ruling the country not with an economic programme but rather with a national-populist programme, by the huge influence of the Catholic Church which seems to be making up for fifty years of socialism, and by a militarization of all segments of life. Insupportable war propaganda is facilitated by state-controlled mass media which gives us regular portions of hate and looks for 'traitors of the nation' on every corner.

Although it sounds quite awful, somehow I have a vague feeling that we are just at the beginning. We are witnessing and participating (some willingly and some not) in the labour pains of a nation. Of course, women are very important in this process, but only women who are safely placed within the family. The family was given a special privileged status in Croatia's new Constitution as the pillar of society and the only guarantee of preserving Croatia's newly won independence (a dream we have all dreamt for a thousand years, they say). Paradoxically or not, there has been a boom of women's organizations and groups during the past two years of war — twenty-two and maybe more — compared to five or six during the pre-war period. Only five of them declare themselves as feminist, and others can be considered as women's organizations, not because they are women oriented or have women and women's problems as the focus of their activities and concerns, but primarily because their membership consists of women. Mostly they call themselves 'non-governmental, non-profit, non-party, humanitarian organizations'. Their common concern is: displaced persons and refugees, children and disabled people, war invalids, families of fallen soldiers, reuniting families, collecting and distributing humanitarian aid. In brief, a grand background front of women (which is exactly the name of one organization, the Croatian Background Front). While men are waging war, women are trying to cure the by-products of war and to put together the pieces of their civilian lives. Their work is mainly on a voluntary basis; it is free, unpaid, anonymous and taken for granted. The consciousness of women's specific position and their problems in the time of war does not exist. Even less are they aware of the long-term negative consequences that will affect mainly women.

Women Organizing During Times of War

For further discussion and future research, there are several questions which must be answered. First, what kind of psychological mechanisms are at work during wartime (which is quite obviously an anti-women time) that motivate women to organize themselves? Is it the sense of being jeopardized, if so jeopardized by whom/what? Is it an external enemy, an 'aggressor' or rather the extreme male principle, the concentration of anti-femininity? Is it the need to overcome the sense of uselessness while 'our fathers, husbands, sons' are being killed on the battlefield? Is it an excessive quantity of human misery and suffering that activates women's 'genetic wish to help, cure and heal'?

Second, why is the State so tolerant towards women's self-organizing in war-time while during peace-time it is seen as subversive activity?

Could it be that in war-time the State, having more important business to do (like waging war, controlling the population, and other 'high-level' activity), happily lets women take over (of course, for free) lower, less profitable but more painful functions?

And third, what will happen to all these groups and organizations once the war is over? Will they disappear or will they eventually discover women's specific concerns?

As described above, the general stand of almost all women's groups/organizations is that discussing so-called 'normal' women's issues (such as reproductive rights) would be a shameful thing to do at this tragic moment (one of the conclusions of a women's conference held in Zagreb in April 1993).

Domestic Violence in Times of War

This could explain the attitude towards domestic violence as well. It has never been so invisible and hidden as it is today. (The same thing has happened to women themselves — they are visible only as victims, and even then only when they serve a particular purpose, and, of course, when they are not behaving well. Let me just remind you of the media attacks against prominent feminists and some other well-known women in Croatia who tried to speak in their own voices, refusing to use the prescribed patriotic discourse.)

This lack of visibility makes it difficult to determine whether the war caused the escalation of domestic violence against women. All facts and common sense (if we still have any) indicate that it must be so, but there is no evidence of this. There are no figures which could help us prove it. Social work statistics cannot be used. Their offices are almost impossible to reach because they are overcrowded with displaced persons, refugees and the local impoverished population seeking social aid. The police also have a more important job to do because the crime rate is constantly increasing (the black market in arms and other goods, explosions, shootings, robberies, prostitution, and drug dealing).

And finally, the experience of Women's Aid Now and the Autonomous Women's House, two women's organizations dealing with violence against women, cannot be a solid indicator. Women's Aid Now has expanded its activity by opening its SOS phone line to all victims of war violence. The Autonomous Women's House, a refuge for abused women, cannot provide reliable figures due to its limited capacity (ten women with children). Besides, domestic violence, which has always been considered a minor, women's problem (if a problem at all), today has become a woman's patriotic duty. Women are being constantly taught (through the mass media) to feel ashamed to think about such self problems when the Nation and our men ('fathers, husbands, and sons') are bleeding on the battlefield. Their duty is to make the pains of 'our soldiers' easier, to be understanding and patient — in other words to be again in the background front.

Yet the experiences of the women's refuge show that the forms and means of violence have undoubtedly changed. No more wooden sticks, shoes and other 'classic' instruments of violence, but guns, bombs, etc. Soldiers bring weapons with them when returning from the front. Others can buy them easily on the black market. Everybody has weapons. Further, in the last few months more women sought refuge — ten women had to be refused in the last two weeks. We are entering the third year of war. Day-to-day living is getting harder and harder. Supplies of patriotism are nearly exhausted and the national duty has become too heavy a burden to carry.

We live in a transition period, or rather a period of legislative void. Old socialist laws are still in vigour but the shift in social policy is noticeable. The attitude of social workers toward women who report domestic violence and seek refuge has been very negative. Divorce procedures last longer than they used to — reconciliation procedures have become social workers' greatest concern. Some procedures that used to be just a formality, such as battered women getting a 'temporary measure' for child custody until a divorce is over, are much more difficult.

When a woman presses charges for criminal assault (heavy bodily harm) with required certificates, at court these heavy injuries are often re-named as light bodily injuries (it is the court expert's right of discretion) and the charges are dropped. Whenever it is a matter of terminology, interpretation or application of the law, it is done to women's disadvantage.

What I have described is just a tiny segment of women's reality. I have said nothing about the anti-abortion campaign, the demographic policy and other conservative trends which affect our lives. And I have said nothing about the violence and traumas women have been subjected to during this war. I am tired. After six years of activism in the field of women's rights, I feel as if I am nowhere. It happened again — we must start all over again.

7.2   THE CENTRE AND THE CIRCUMSTANCES WE WORK IN

During the whole period of the work of The Centre for Women War Victims, Croatia has been and still is weakly balancing between peace and war. The war option was once again chosen — Croatian military actions in Western Slavonia earlier in the Spring of 1995 and 'Krajina' this Summer faced us again with the reality of war. The action was the result of an unwillingness on both sides to develop peaceful solutions to the crisis in this area. And we still face the threat of a continuation of the war.

The war option brought again new deaths, family tragedies, new refugees, new waves of material destruction — looting and deliberate burning of properties, violation of human rights. The result is that whole areas were ethnically cleansed and any hope for building democracy fell apart once again. Preconditions for assuring civil society (institutions and legal systems do not work) are lost too. War has always been a good excuse to defend the malfunctioning and manipulation of laws and legislation.

Apart from war, this country has been generally struggling with all the problems common to countries with an economy in 'transition' (privatisation, unemployment, changing value systems and beliefs, decline of health care system, education system). At the same time the consequences of war are visible and also invisible: the economy is malfunctioning, parts of the country suffered heavy destruction, part is still not under governmental control. The rise of nationalism and right-wing tendencies in society as part of governmental policy are, unfortunately, our reality.

The local population is poorer and poorer and the psychological consequences of war are serious. Rapid legal, administrative, political and social changes pushed through are often taking away certainty, control and even the right to feel positive about past lives (during the previous, now discredited regime). For the majority the standard of living has also rapidly decreased: the average monthly salary is equal to the average rent of an apartment, basic living costs are equal to those in Europe.

Croatia had and still has a large displaced and refugee population. At the end of 1994 there were 380,000 displaced persons and refugees according to the data of Office for Displaced Persons and Refugees (ODPR) of the Government of the Republic of Croatia. This is roughly 9 per cent of the pre-war population of Croatia. Most of the refugees and displaced persons have been in exile between one and four years. According to the United Nations High Commission for Refugees (UNHCR) 80 per cent of refugees are women and children. In the Zagreb region they are mainly accommodated in private lodgings (mostly in expensive, rented flats, which do not meet basic needs of relatively decent housing). Many of these qualify as slums. Refugees may live in very cramped conditions in private flats — such as seven to a room. Obviously this exacerbates any physical and psychological problems.

At the end of 1995 we noticed some changes in the number of displaced persons and refugees mainly 'thanks to' new political and military actions undertaken in Croatia and Bosnia. While military action 'Storm' (performed in August 1995) formed preconditions for the return of a few thousands displaced Croats to their homes, formally ending their four year long suffering, at the same time the Croatian Government lost the chance for peaceful re-integration of their citizens. Serbs, inhabitants of former Krajina, out of fear (based on Croatian political blindness concerning their own Serbian citizens) and long lasting 'own' propaganda and manipulation, left the country. As the last Serbs were leaving, the counter hunt began — the expulsion of Croats from Vojvodina (Serbia) and Bosnia, as well as Muslims from Bosnia. All those actions are inseparably linked and the future does not promise much more than a huge displacement of people and forming ethnically cleansed states on nearly the whole of the territories of earlier multi-ethnic societies. One Croatian journalist recently wrote that there was a doubtful willingness of a state which was happy to lose 200,000 citizens as Croatia did.

Because of four years of war in Croatia, and three in Bosnia, hundreds of thousands of people have been killed, 4,000,000 have been expelled, material and cultural wealth has been destroyed and the feeling of security within our multinational community has been shattered and radically endangered. The war conducted here has, unfortunately, taught people that there is no other solution. Although women are more aware of the roots and causes of such a situation and they do see a solution more acceptable than 'war games', their voices are hardly heard and their roles — in peace processes, contribution to social and material reconstruction, support to displaced and refugee people — are not even recognised.

The Centre is one of the first organisations linked to the feminist and anti-war network (women were co-founders and are still a majority of many of them) which continues to provide political support, psychological, humanitarian, and financial help to displaced and refugee women, as well as giving referrals on different topics important for refugee and displaced women (health care, humanitarian organisations, resettlement information). In spite of non-visible global influence on the whole scale we have managed to establish strong grassroots networks as important bases for long term society changes and keeping positive values, energies and beliefs.

Women working in the Centre for almost three years are more confident and assertive about the work they do and its significance in re-building civil society. When we established the Centre we knew what would be its aim. To empower women — those who lost their security, loved ones, property, their memories, their identity — to empower them to regain control over their lives, to recognise and oppose the male dominant structures that does not care for the Others. Women belong to the Others. They are victims of every war, or more, they are those who are victimised, in their names the crimes are made. Their bodies are used as symbolic battle fields. In spite of their non-participation in decisive political processes that lead to wars, women are forced to bear war's consequences.

When the mass rapes of women in Bosnia became known in the summer of 1992, feminist groups from Zagreb and Belgrade working with the survivors of male violence started to organise to do something about it. With the support of women's groups from around the world, centres based on feminist principles were opened in Zagreb, Zenica and Belgrade to work with women war survivors. No militaristic tactic of hatred could eliminate the desire of women from the former Yugoslavia to stay in contact and to work on women's solidarity. We share the experience that war is an extreme pattern of patriarchal social structure, and that civil violence against women and war violence have things in common. War crimes against women have two dimensions: that of ethnic cleansing (mass rapes in Bosnia performed mostly by Serbian military troops) and of crimes against gender. This latter side is minimised and silenced and that of 'strategic rape' often manipulated for political reasons. Soon the entire issue of rape in war was forgotten by the official state politics, too often misused by media (to the proportion of pornography). Only women's groups are still trying to press the issue of rape, to open trials, to have access to a War Tribunal so that charges against rapists would be undertaken and rape treated as a war crime against gender and by every means as a crime against humanity.

Women are surviving this war in many different ways — as victims of sexual violence, as refugees, as targets of political harassment, as widows or single mothers, and as victims of intensified domestic violence as the consequence of war and militarism (men are returning home from the battle fields armed and every day newspapers are full with 'tragic events' in which women were killed and the killing justified by war and 'his trauma').

Women are also activists, organisers of humanitarian aid and a help to those who suffered war losses and atrocities. At the same time they have to struggle for everyday survival, finding food for the family, fighting poverty the way they know, to make ends meet on low salaries (if they did not already lose their job — because women are the first to go when there is a lack of posts). Aside from them a parallel society is run — patriarchal structures are deciding their fates for them. War proved to be a good excuse for sending women not only back to the kitchen but to the bedrooms. Human losses in war are turned into politics of national renewal — the task is for new (preferably male) Croats to be born. National became more important than civil, and women are fit only for the role of motherhood. The homeland mother is a role created by the new Democratic Movement. Reproductive rights are no longer women's rights. Attempts of women from feminist groups (collecting signatures, defending women's right to free choice was undertaken in June in some towns of Croatia and 20,000 signatures were collected) to change the political scene and to make women and their issues more visible, are hardly recognised by the official press and totally neglected by official politics.

Women have not been able to have any participation in decision making or in the peace negotiations. There has been no place for women's voices to be heard. Whenever they have managed to subversively do any action they are pronounced 'national traitors', 'witches', 'lesbians' and so on. The same nationalistic patriarchal structure is aware that women took their share of war work seriously and with an aim (or wish) to help in healing the war wounds and trying to rebuild the lost values of secure and peaceful lives, yet it is simply neglecting them (unless women's work can be used for their own national and political goals).

Women from the Centre are aware of the circumstances they live and work in and are taking initiatives and being actively involved in the design and implementation of many new activities and projects which try both to be an answer to the situation emerging from the continuation of the war and to move with human lives. Immediately after Croatian military actions in Western Slavonia in May 1995, we began to work with the local population in the Pakrac area, finding women there fearful and traumatised. Croatian women were resentful of Serbian women. We started with individual counselling, then we formed self-help groups in women's houses. Our facilitators hope to bring women from both ethnic groups together in mixed groups later this year giving them time to cope with the new situation. Our intention is to help real and meaningful re-integration of both sides.

The level of our own secondary trauma (no-one stayed untouched by this war) is visible but we are managing to cope with it through psychological supervision, careful attention to our own needs and the support of international women's groups. The feelings of helplessness and hopelessness are very hard to fight, and there are numerous occasions when activists can do nothing, just sit and look at women struggling with problems beyond their control.

Despite the hard work the turnover of women working in the Centre is smaller than one might expect. This means that by September 1995 we had twenty-five full-time staff, including activists, office workers, administrators and a driver, and five part-time staff — our cleaners and psychologists.

We started to think of our future in a systematic fashion, not any more operating only on a crisis level. Many women participated in new sub-projects: the training sub-project (we will continue to organise ongoing training for the Centre, as well as train other groups in need on a range of issues), the income generating sub-project (we have to find ways to secure some income for women we are working with), the women's health sub-project (we have started health education for refugee women and displaced women, doing basic education and preventative work) and the in-depth counselling sub-project (some women in the Centre will be trained for that).

The Women We Work With

For the majority of refugees and displaced the first phase of relief passed. They settled down, and found their always changing way towards humanitarian and sometimes financial aid. Because the vast majority of them do not work (practically, it is illegal for refugees to work) they are almost completely dependent on such aid. They have to endure the day to day struggle to survive since the quantity and quality of humanitarian aid is diminishing, refugee camps are relocated from the Zagreb area and relatives or friends with whom refugees and displaced persons used to live cannot sustain them any more, their savings (if they had any) are spent and they are in serious financial troubles. Circumstances were more stable two years or even one year ago but are again changing. In early 1995 displaced persons, and refugees made up 11.9 per cent of the pre-war population in Croatia. For the majority the first phase of relief passed but there is an overwhelming inability to control their own lives due to various factors: war traumatization, economic dependency on financial and humanitarian aid, uprooting, disappearance of social connections and an incapacity to build new ones. The long duration of exile and a realisation that no one can predict the end of the war, produce despair and depression. All of the factors mentioned above influence women's self-esteem, self-confidence and their images of themselves.

Lots of humanitarian organisations have left the country (to Bosnia or closed down the project in the whole region) and the official politics concerning refugees is very unstable. Whenever some territory in Bosnia is freed, the Government takes away the refugee status for the refugees from that area (which means losing a symbolic (25DM) financial aid per month). In late September 1995 the decision to abolish refugee status for 100,000 refugees from Bosnia was made. We reacted promptly demanding that they reconsider their decision bearing in mind that such a decision is a direct violation of refugee human rights. In reality it means that they would have to leave Croatia and return to Bosnia, but there is hardly any place in Bosnia which is really safe for one to return. Even if there is a possibility of housing there is no infrastructure (electricity, water, services, jobs) and there are over 10,000,000 land mines in the region and fights still going on. It's as though it is forgotten that the majority of refugees are women, children and the elderly whose very lives would be endangered once again.

Even if the situation was much safer, women would be faced with a new trauma of resettlement — returning home. As one women in our self-help group said 'When we were running away from all this horror we were happy just to get out, now we have to go back and face the disaster, and try to patch all the wounds'.

Many women live alone with their children (without spouse) and a significant number of them have to take care of elderly relatives as well. Their psychological condition is influenced by numerous factors such as disruption of nearly all relationships and social connections, loss of close friends and relatives, inadequate information about them or missing family members, loss of property, no possibility to return, constant insecurity, permanent war clashes in their own villages and fear both of serious illness and new conflict in Croatia and Bosnia. Resocializing in the Zagreb community is hard because the local population is, in general, hostile with prejudices. Some of the refugees do not know ways of functioning in an urban environment having their whole identity rooted in rural peasant values and history. Their children usually have problems in school (e.g. being labelled as refugees with negative connotations).

All of the factors mentioned above influence women's self-esteem, self-confidence and images of themselves. They find it hard to endure the complete dependence on external help and the impossibility to provide normal living conditions for their dependants and themselves.

Women try to start or to rebuild their social network, some succeed, some do not. Those living in refugee camps are more likely to rebuild social connections having an opportunity that emerges from living together in rather small and crowded areas. For the majority of women scattered all around the town it is harder. The building up of social networks is a hard task because of ruined confidence. It takes time, and requires a secure, controlled situation.

Newcomers to Zagreb are on the whole, people who are badly traumatised as until this moment they have been living in war areas. They suffer great disillusion on arriving in Zagreb, as they have held it in their head as a kind of paradise where no problems will exist and everything will be provided for. However, after their arrival they face new but still difficult circumstances, trying to find ways to survive, realising that for most of them resettlement to a third country is not an option, coming up against bureaucracy, not being entitled to refugee status and therefore not being entitled to free care. Unable to cope with these new struggles and uncertainties some choose to go back to Bosnia. This paradox shows the hard times faced by refugees — that they choose to go back to conflict areas rather than stay in Zagreb.

Although the circumstances are very hard, women find creative ways to survive by themselves or are encouraged by others — they consider themselves survivors. They pride themselves on being able to cope with everything that comes along and think that they deserve recognition, sometimes asking for it for the first time in their lives. We are supporting them in all their efforts to stay strong and we appreciate their strength.

Self-help Groups

During the period of three years we have been regularly working with more than 1000 women in self-help groups. We closed thirty-five old groups where women were no longer in such need and opened thirty new ones in refugee camps, along with our premises in Zagreb. We have opened this summer four groups in the Pakrac area and we are just establishing the first groups in Petrinja area (earlier occupied by the paramilitary Serbian army). More than 500 women were resettled to third countries with the help of the Centre (contacts, visas, technical and material support).

The goal of the project of psycho-social help for refugees and displaced women through self-help groups are: to help women to resocialize in their new communities, to maintain or improve their present psychological status, to fight dependency on external help, to provide women with information, to raise an awareness in members of self-help groups of their own needs, to maintain and strengthen tolerance towards differences, to work in the local community raising awareness of refugee problems and to try and counter prejudice against refugees.

We have continued to work with women of different nationalities, different ages and different backgrounds. Because the Centre is adapted to the needs of refugee women we are working more with women living in private accommodation, because we have discovered that refugee women living in refugee camps have kept their own micro community. We tended to close groups in the refugee camps due to two reasons. Firstly the Governmental Office for displaced persons and refugees removed many refugees who used to live in so called 'illegal' camps in Zagreb and its suburbs to legal ones in Gasinci and Varazdin (with actually worse living conditions). Hence some women we used to work with are no longer in Zagreb. Secondly, women living in the refugee camps are better off (if one dares to compare), having organized shelter and paid meals if nothing else, than women living in private accommodation.

Although the principles of work are the same in the refugee camp setting, and in our premises, there are some differences that are notable. The crises are the same but women with different living situations cope with them differently; the current challenges of life are different for them and this is reflected in the groups. The work with women from private accommodation tends to be quicker in building up trust between members as they do not have the situation of living daily together. Women in the refugee camps are more reluctant to open themselves because of the fear of gossiping. And they tend to look a lot for possibilities to be alone, since day to day living in the overcrowded camp atmosphere is hard, without real possibilities to be physically alone (although psychological isolation can be prevalent). By contrast, women in private accommodation are socially isolated, especially if they are newcomers to town. They have a greater need for rebuilding their social connections over any need to be alone (if they live in an overcrowded place, which is usual, then they may end up isolated but not alone).

As the Centre's activists become more and more experienced and gain more practical knowledge (ongoing training and facilitation of groups and work supervision) they are capable of structuring group meetings in a way that is open for immediate changes according to the needs of women. The self-help groups run differently according to the personalities of women in the groups as well as the personalities of mediators (we work in pairs). But more or less the same pattern is noticeable in all the groups — the first three months are usually spent in trust building (less in the groups in the Centre, more in the refugee camps). Women just check how serious the mediators are and then how serious other women in the group are. They use that time to re-tell and compare their experiences. They start from facts and over a period of time end up on feelings. Practically at the same time they try to solve their communal problems on the camp or try to get more information on humanitarian aid and different agencies if they live on their own.

The issues outlined above are discussed for the whole period of group meetings. Besides the trust building, groups also deal with the range of emotions such as fear, anger, grief. Grieving is the most common, probably at the root of all other feelings and the hardest one to cope with. All of the group members (including mediators) grieve for something. Allowing women to show their grief is sometimes revealing, and sometimes encouraging in a way of giving permission to be sad and to show one's feelings. Low self-esteem is another problem groups have to deal with. Feelings of inadequacy and dependency are predominant. Women need a lot of mutual encouragement, as well as encouragement by mediators, pointing out their achievements (which are remarkable when you look at them from different angles) to regain the feeling of self respect.

The solidarity shown is on different levels depending on the women in the groups. This is never easy to judge from a 'normal' position. It is hard to show solidarity if you have nothing or very little and when you have lost everything. But, nevertheless, some examples of solidarity are amazing, for example, the whole group collecting money for a woman in great need who had to pay rent immediately, otherwise she would be thrown out.

An important factor in regaining control and building self-esteem, as well as developing solidarity, is the way in which we distribute humanitarian aid. The group is asked to distribute such aid by themselves for themselves without mediators interfering in the process. It gives women a sense of control and capability as well as a dignity because they are part of the decision-making process.

These are just some examples of our work in the groups, which goes on including all the things we used to do before, like giving referrals, discussing everyday problems, helping women to get their relatives out of Bosnia and helping them to resettle.

Humanitarian Aid

We do consider humanitarian aid as a vital part of the Centre, although we are not a purely humanitarian organisation. Humanitarian aid is very important to women we are working with because they live on it. As our general policy is to act according to the need of women we collected and distributed around 15,000 kg of aid. We routinely check women's needs and make our requests for humanitarian aid to givers based on the women's own specifications, and we distribute the aid in the groups together with the women themselves. This is always a good way to exercise women's solidarity, and sometimes to bring out sources of conflict. That gives us the opportunity to teach women to solve conflicts in a non-violent way.

Rosa House

Six women and six children moved into the Rosa House — a house for women and child refugees — in January and now there are eight women and eleven children living there. The house is in a small town close to Zagreb and one of the women living there said at her second house meeting 'the house really smells like home'. We have managed to furnish it and to get some supplies for the women while working with them to develop training in work/business skills. Activists there are working separately with their children and are counselling women. They are currently planting the garden and are enjoying their first 'own products'.

Other Activities

We have set an appropriate time where ex-group members can casually come and socialise weekly. The women and ourselves find it very useful. They do not feel alone again, they have their space and time to be together, to strengthen their friendships and to meet women from other ex-groups so widening their network of social support. We have established the habit of inviting members of our groups to meet again as groups every few months and women are more than enthusiastic to share their experiences and to be with each other. We have organised an Art Workshop once a week so that women can develop their creativity and share ideas. In one of our premises training is going on for eighteen women, where a refugee trainer is teaching women how to sew. The idea is to enable women to learn new skills and to do some basic work for themselves.

Activists continue to help women to start reintegration of women into the local community through outside visits such as to the theatre, cinema, coffee shops, parks. Women find excursions to the nearby mountain very helpful. Most of them are of rural origin and they feel revived in the woods. Autumn chestnut picking was a big success.

Our information exchange continues to take place through activists passing on their experience and knowledge to each other at our regular Monday meetings of activist teams. Much of this information is derived from women they are working with or by personal enquiries. This ensures that our referrals are based on up-to-date knowledge. A young sociologist from the Centre is preparing a special report based on data about women we worked with during this three years.

We published a book about our work early this year, and a group of women from Valencia published a book about their training with us.

Training

Training for the members of the Centre is on-going and it became more diverse in the last six months period. During three years all the activists and office members passed through more than twenty training programmes and workshops (last year there was one training per month). They covered various issues (from counselling skills to stress management), lasting from two days to two weeks. Funds for training were assured by different sources. Training was given as a support to the Centre — trainers funded themselves and women in the Centre offered their hospitality.

Our members attended different workshops, such as the one organized by Dublin Rape Crisis Centre, for example, improving their skills and sharing their experiences and sometimes their disagreements with other people working in the same field. The Centre was co-organizer for the Dublin Rape Crisis Centre workshop in Tucepi for women from Zenica, Tuzla, Sarajevo and Split.

The Centre has its own Educational Team able to give workshops and trainings on different issues, especially on facilitation of self-help groups. The most exciting event was the request by Oxfam UK for us to train women working with their programme in Tuzla, Bosnia and Hercegovina. Three of our activists went there on two separate occasions to lead a fourteen day workshop on the basics of group mediating. Four others did training for women from women's groups in Split and one for social workers from the Federation of the International Red Cross and Red Crescent on 'Non-violent Communication and Conflict Resolution'. As more requests are coming in we are preparing ourselves to become trainers that can train on a variety of issues.

Other Activities for the Centre

We have broadened our international advocacy work on refugee issues through attendance at various conferences particularly those in preparation for the UN Fourth World Conference on Women. We took an active role in the Vienna ECE region preparatory conference, the Cairo Conference on Population and Development, the Geneva NGO working group conference, and the New York Commission on the Status of Women. We have been holding consultations to try and ensure that a broad range of views on issues of violence against women, women in conflict situations and the needs of women refugees are included in conference documents. We were able to attend these due to the generosity of the Population Institute from Washington D.C. and individual donors and friends in these countries, who gave us accommodation and helped us with costs. Four members of our Centre were able to be present at the Fourth UN Conference on Women and took an active role in various workshops held there on issues concerning refugee women as well as peace and war topics.

We continue our work in supporting journalists, film crews and NGO's with information and interviews concerning the situation of women refugees. Some of this work in 1995 included hosting a Canadian film crew who were doing a documentary on our work to be shown on the Women's Channel, working with Swedish journalists, RA1 5 TV crew and Japanese journalists and supervising a promotional video of our work made by American film students. This has already been shown on a Benefit evening for the Centre in New York, where our friend and supporter, playwright Eve Pusler, did a performance for us as she had in Dublin on our fund raising tour.

We continue to talk with aid givers and financiers lobbying to ensure that their long-term support of NGOs in this region continues and to provide them with details of our experience of working both with women refugees and with international and national agencies.

We feel strengthened by the unexpected recognition awarded to us by International Women in Black in the shape of their 1994 Peace Prize. We share this prize with our sisters — other members of Zagreb Women's Lobby, Women in Black Belgrade and Medica Zenica. This is the second peace prize (the first was in 1993 from Barcelona) that our Centre has won in recognition for working with women regardless of their nationality. We have continued with all our regular fund-raising attempts, contact work and hosting visitors. We have been financially supported by many women's groups as well as different international agencies. Many foreign women showed their solidarity, supporting us in our work. Many women from the Centre attended different meetings and conferences at home and abroad. They did fund-raising and political tours, participated in different workshops and women's camps, meeting women and sharing experience and love.

Some Quotations by Women We Work with and Activists Themselves

'The only thing keeping me together is the possibility of returning home.'   Suada

'I would more gladly sleep on the barren land in my village (in Bosnia) than be here in Zagreb.'   Woman in Katarina's group

'They have taken away everything from me but they can't take away hope.'   Katarina

'They took everything from me. If I would not have my group I would feel more miserable.'   Woman in Rada's group

'I am not feeling safe in my home in Zagreb — just as women in my groups situation changed overnight so could mine.'   Danijela

'The differences in the groups are very helpful. It is fantastic that there are differences.'   Tanja

'My life is divided only into two: before the war and after it. The war changed me totally — it took away my self confidence, courage. Now, facilitating self-help groups is my therapy.'   Branka

'During this war period we passed through metamorphosis. Due to the work process at the Centre old values have been changed.'
                                                                    Maja

'When I first came to work at the Centre my barometer of self respect was a long way below zero. Now between humanitarian aid and metaphysics I find a purpose in life.'   Danijela

'Every day I am angrier at the situation, at this war, and its consequences.'   Goga

'Before I needed gentleness. Now I dare show it . . . we were put in a shell not of our own request, now it is splitting and like new-born babies we are needing lots of care.'	Biba

'People say that you are refugees and worth less than the others.'	Tanja

'I believe the third world war is coming and it has already started.'	Tanja

'My Tears are a reflection not only of my own sorrows but of all the other's sorrows too.'	Katarina

'In all this crazy situation, work in the Centre seems like living in the oasis, I am privileged.'	Rada

'Women say I am lucky to be here in the territory of the former Yugoslavia, to work as part of the Centre. I say some days it feels more like a curse. How can I ever live a normal life again?'	Rachel

'All the troubles paid off. The work in the Centre, nevertheless, has some sense.'	Martina

Note

This is written for all the women at the Centre for Women War Victims — with the help from many separate reports by Rachel Wareham and Martina Belic, Vesna Kesic and support from Nela and Paula Novak.
Section 7.1 written by Mica Mladineo Desnica.
Section 7.2 written by Rada Boric.

Section Three

Introduction: Policy Implementation and Education for Change

Chris Corrin

As the chapters within this volume show, feminist grassroots campaigns and organizations have developed many services and initiatives for women and children who have suffered male violence, including refuges/shelters, as well as support, advice, information and counselling services, and educational and training initiatives. Different governmental approaches are apparent across countries. The two chapters in this section consider both governmental, judicial and police responses in terms of 'street-level bureaucrats' in Spain and the intermeshing of women's campaigns and analyses in this area of work. It is clear that one of the major contributions that feminists have made has been in making visible male sexual violence and in raising awareness, both within societies and across state structures, of the need for changes in both attitudes and legislation/policy initiatives. As is apparent in the case of the Zero Tolerance campaigns, these were designed with clear goals, both in terms of making the issues of power around domestic violence, rape and sexual abuse publicly visible and thereby less acceptable and in giving politicians a more sensitized awareness of how policy can be effected and implemented to reduce violence against women. Making demands on the state in this area has been a difficult and dangerous but very necessary project in which feminist groups and campaigns have been involved throughout many countries in Western Europe. Similar demands are now beginning to be made through women's campaigns in some of the Central and Eastern European countries. The feminist awareness of women involved in Women's Aid Networks and those involved in establishing the Zero Tolerance campaigns, gave direction and clarity to the projects within which they have been involved. Similar campaigns take on different resonances depending sometimes on which community groups or government officials are implementing them. In the case of the Zero Tolerance campaigns in Scotland and England it was a surprise for feminists involved in the campaigns in Scotland when London boroughs took up the campaign in very different ways, concentrating on violent men and custodial sentences — rather than women survivors — with posters stating 'There are no words for domestic violence, only sentences' under the picture of a man behind prison bars. Not only did some of the London campaigns appear to swerve the focus from women survivors but it seemed to give an unrealistic impression of the likely outcomes, as so few perpetrators do go to prison.

This section considers the interface between feminist grassroots campaigning and developments within state structures and policy-making with regard to male sexual violence. The possibilities of 'education' in its broadest sense are considered in terms of 'changing people's minds' away from myths about male sexual violence and towards the possibilities for creating change for the better for women and children.

LEGAL RESPONSES TO DOMESTIC VIOLENCE

In connection with male violence within households, some governments' legal responses take a largely welfare approach (stressing mediation and therapy); others propose criminal sanctions in all situations; whilst others occupy a position between the two in which a mixture of responses are proposed.

Most Western European governments, when deciding how to tackle male violence against women, have viewed the problem[s] as requiring legal solution[s] so have opted for the criminal justice approach. It is an important point, to be discussed, that the lack of a systematic approach on the part of most governments and legislators means not only that the linkages between sexual violence and women's oppression are not recognized, but that law-making and service provision remain fragmented and of less value in changing women and children's situations for the better. That 'domestic' violence, sexual assault, sexual harassment are generally treated within legal practice as very different crimes means that the true nature of male sexual violence is not apparent. It is in this regard that arguments regarding a 'feminist jurisprudence' arise.

It is apparent in both law-making and law-enforcement, that the law is not a neutral force in any society, reflecting as it does the interests of the dominant forces. The views and interests of such powerholders in the societies which we are considering throughout Europe are basically patriarchal and can often be racist. In this connection, Pragna Patel has noted with regard to the work of Southall Black Sisters that:

> In our work with women and violence, this question crops up with predictable regularity: how to afford safety and protection to women and children by making demands of the police, the judiciary and the welfare system, but at the same time recognise that these very institutions have been in the forefront of attacks against black people in this country since the 1950s. This tension has been prevalent throughout our work and has in fact been central to our thinking. (Patel 1990, p. 43)

In the areas of policy-making and law reform, feminists are actively making challenges both to prevent any reinforcement of male control and racist control, and to ensure that any measures incorporate and reflect the needs and interests of all women. Despite the importance of feminist innovative legal initiatives, it is well to note that these have not yet provided solutions and in those European countries where they have been initiated they remain a background frame within which other measures can be developed.

As always, remembering the specific socio-economic and cultural contexts in which legislation is being promoted and implemented is vital. As we see from the Spanish case feminists are initiating changes in the way legislation is being promoted. Campaigning groups in the UK such as Justice for Women and Southall Black Sisters are developing feminist responses to certain legal issues such as suitable defences for women who kill violent partners. They are working on a defence of self-preservation which would be more suited to the situations in which women are experiencing male sexual violence, than the current defences of self-defence or diminished responsibility. It is apparent too that in certain countries such as Albania and Romania male sexual violence is not necessarily recognized as a crime. Even if the crime of assault is recognized in law the social barriers against a woman being able to follow through on a complaint, court case and subsequent sentencing (or lack of punishment) are powerful deterrents for women in countries where there are no clear government responses to counter male sexual violence. As we have seen in the case of Hungary and Russia hostile attitudes on the part of the police coupled with 'woman blaming' creates a climate in which women often decide not to report crimes of violence against them. In her report on the situation in Romania Laura Grunberg notes that:

> Domestic violence has increased and the family has become less and less a shelter against the adversities of the outside world. More and more the home has become a place for venting emotional tensions. Certainly fear, embarrassment, ignorance and mistrust of the legal instruments prevent many women from lodging complaints against the aggressions they have experienced. Hence the actual number of acts of violence is far greater than the figures reveal. (hCa 3, pp. 62–63)

In breaking this circle of the hidden nature of domestic violence it is clear that both public awareness and attitudes need to be developed within a feminist framework and appropriate legislation, enforcement and implementation be enacted.

Two important general points are highlighted by Jane Connors in her work on *Government Measures to Confront Violence Against Women*, in terms of legal measures with regard to male sexual violence:

> First, in most countries (except where sexual abuses are concerned) such violence receives no special treatment in law, meaning that women have to rely on the general law. Second, most legal systems have not displayed a synthetic approach to the problem. (Connors 1994, p. 183)

By a synthetic approach Connors is referring to the fact that legislation in most countries deals with manifestations of violence against women separately, as if they have no uniform or related structural cause. As the Spanish Chapter 8 shows, this means that laws concerning different forms of such violence are found in different legal solutions and different forms. Writing about the situation in Moscow in 1993 Elvira Novikova noted that violence against women and children within the home is considered normal behaviour:

> Domestic abuse, drunkenness, rudeness and the beating of women
> and children are unfortunately not rare phenomena in our chaotic
> life. It is sad that this is often viewed as usual, **normal** behaviour.
> Legal practice reinforces this view. For example, if a woman is hit
> by an unknown man in the street, it is considered a crime against an
> individual citizen with all the subsequent legal consequences. Yet
> it is a completely different story if she was beaten by her husband.
> This is considered an internal family issue. Such behaviour by men
> is often forgiven. (hCa 3, p. 69)

From a theoretical perspective, links across the range of male sexual
violence are not made and this results in a general lack of awareness
in linking 'the various manifestations of violence against women
to subordination of and discrimination against women generally'
(Connors 1994, p. 184). This failure within legal discourse to recognize
the systematic nature of women's oppression has had consequences
for service provision and other strategies, which have developed in
fragmented ways. Policies to combat violence against women in
law-making, and the approaches that people within legal systems
have pursued when trying to deal with these issues, have clearly not
been uniform within individual countries let alone across Europe or
internationally.

LAWS AND LAW ENFORCEMENT CONCERNED WITH DOMESTIC VIOLENCE

All European countries have general laws concerned with assault and
in theory these laws can be applied to women assaulted at home.
Yet, in many countries these general criminal laws are not applied
unless the situation is extreme. In Albania, for example, women had
to prove their injuries to a certain level of bruising before their situation
could be considered sufficient to take out a prosecution for assault.
General criminal laws are not responsive to the specific issues arising
from cases of women experiencing violence within the home. Certain
special laws taken up to deal with domestic violence include approaches
developed from breach of the peace and the injunction. Various levels of
sophistication based on these approaches are apparent in the context of
'protection orders' which can be issued to protect women from violent
men. Yet enforcement is an area which is often insufficiently resourced
so that if breached, women are again at risk of violence and often the

women are expected to return to court to have another order placed. This is not a remedy which is generally responsive to women's needs.

In recognition of the need for police enforcement of laws regarding domestic assault many countries throughout Europe have clarified laws relating to police powers of entry, arrest, and bail procedures. Police training in issues concerned with domestic violence is a more common feature throughout Western European countries, as are special 'mother and child' units which deal primarily with cases of male sexual violence. Yet as the Spanish example shows, an effective legal and enforcement response requires that all agencies and authorities recognize the root of the problem and have the will to implement initiatives for change so that an effective legal response can be given. Such a response would include recognition of the dynamics of domestic violence and a consistent response at all levels of the legal system, judiciary and law enforcement bodies. Offenders would receive appropriate disposition and treatment at each stage and victims and their families would receive appropriate services (Connors 1994, p. 187). It is clear that unless there are changes in attitudes, and the will to implement policies to change women and children's situations for the better, there cannot be an integrated response in terms of the law, provision of services and training, nor in educational measures.

SEXUAL HARASSMENT AND SEXUAL ASSAULT

The range of legal approaches to sexual harassment vary both according to how and where the harassment takes place — in the street, workplace, public venue — and the type of harassment. Often legislation applies only in cases of rape, sexual assault, indecent assault or common assault which happen outside the workplace. Across Western Europe the range of legal measures in place which recognize sexual harassment within workplaces and educational institutions differ markedly in their scope and powers. Within many of the proposals for legislation at the European Union level the focus on women's equality does not focus on power imbalances and is often geared towards increased efficiency in the workplace. Such studies as *The Inventory of Positive Action in Europe* from the European Commission does not mention sexual harassment but offers generalised guidelines such as 'respect for the dignity of women at the workplace'. Again, the need for a synthetic approach is important. Most countries within the European Union now have Sex Discrimination and Equal Opportunities statutes — in the UK the Equal Opportunities Commission was established by the Sex Discrimination Act of 1975. Despite legal definitions — of workplace harassment amounting to less favourable treatment on the basis of gender — it is in the area of enforcement and implementation that a myriad problems can and do arise.

For women within Central and Eastern European countries sexual harassment issues are very likely to be the butt of many jokes against women and against feminists 'with no sense of humour . . .'. As Jirina Siklova and Jana Hardlikova point out within the situation existing in Czechoslovakia in 1992:

> Sexual harassment, about which so much is written in the West, is not discussed very often; most women do not know what it is. Obscene comments about women, women being criticized due to their looks, various 'playful' smacks, and pseudo-flattery are routine in most workplaces. . . .
>
> But just as we encountered the term 'sexual harassment' which can be translated as sexual bothering and unwanted sexual attention, some comedian twisted this term into 'sexual rattling' (playing on the Czech word 'haraseni' which sounds like 'harassment' but has a different meaning) and the whole issue had its back-bone broken. (hCa 3 1993, p. 52)

Whilst there are clear differences here in terms of the lack of state legislation and enforcement bodies, the reality for many women working within Western European countries lies in the knowledge that many men do use their power to sexually harass women at work often in situations where it is one person's (more powerful) word against another. It is in such areas that the Zero Tolerance campaigns aim to focus publicly (on buses, billboards and within workplaces) on men's attitudes towards women and on how men use their power against women. Legislation alone cannot create effective social change as attitudes have also to change so that effective implementation of legislation is possible.

Almost all countries in the world have laws regarding crimes of sexual assault against women. Offences include rape, indecent assault, abduction, procuration, defilement and unlawful detention for immoral purposes. From the mid-1980s there has been discussion about reforming both the substantive and procedural law covering these offences. As Jane Connors (1995, p. 192) points out the areas of debate are:

> the scope of the offence
> whether sexual assault in marriage is a crime
> the question of the consent of the victim
> the related issue of the accused's perception

of the complainant's consent
evidentiary requirements, including the law of fresh complaint, the
introduction of evidence as to the victim's past sexual history, and
corroboration
amelioration of court procedures
sentencing
the treatment of sexual assault complainant

Many countries have widened their definition of serious sexual assaults
beyond penetration of the vagina and the anus, including for example
forced oral intercourse. It is interesting to note (Connors 1995, p. 192)
that some countries have removed the word 'rape' or its translation from
the statute books, being of the opinion that use of this word militates
against the acquisition of conviction.

Laws concerning rape or unwanted sexual contact within marriage
have also been implemented unevenly across Western Europe and are
only very slowly being considered within many Central and Eastern
European countries. In connection with rape or unwanted sexual contact
within marriage Julie Mertus points out that:

> In the US, the Federal Bureau of Investigation has estimated that
> a woman is beaten every 18 seconds. And in most regions of the
> world, including many states in the US, husbands are free to rape
> their wives without fear of legal reprisal. (Mertus 1995, p. 141)

Within this context laws concerning safe, legal abortion are important.
Certainly in Romania and Albania during the pro-natalist policies of
Ceauşescu and Hoxha stark violations of women's rights regarding
their bodies and their decision-making around conception and delivery
of children were apparent. The consequences of abortion becoming
legalized within an environment lacking sexual education and cheap,
safe and available contaception can be catastrophic for women's health
as in the recent past in Romania:

> Initially regarding abortion only as a sign of newly won freedom,
> as an act of release and not as a dangerous act of necessity, women
> had an amazingly high number of abortions between 1990–1991
> (about 2.5 million). At present, the high cost of abortion and more
> education about contraceptives may return people to common
> sense. (hCa 3, p. 64)

In this context, feminist campaigns regarding reproductive health can
be seen to vary in scope and in the context of the struggle. In most

European countries there is recognition that it is through their governments, courts, legislation and policy-making that women can have their reproductive autonomy challenged. State forces intervene in women's rights to control their bodies. Whereas for women in the South activism has largely centred on resisting programmes and technologies imported from the North. Yet as the work of Stella Jegher and Hannana Siddiqui shows there are poor women, minority ethnic women and Other women within Northern countries for whom choices are structured differently. Evidence of different needs and strategies were apparent at the NGO Forum of the UN Conference on Population and Development which took place in Cairo in September 1994. For her part, Nira Yuval-Davis notes that whilst there appeared to be two sides to debates on reproductive rights as human rights — imperialism represented by various international aid agencies and world religions, particularly Catholicism and Islam — there is the aspect of what women do regarding these two poles:

> Women reproduce biologically, culturally and symbolically their ethnic and national collectivities, as well as the work force, their families and citizenship of the state. National and ethnic conflict and projects fulfil a very important role in understanding the issues of women's reproductive rights. Although imperialism and religion play a role in ethnic and national conflict, it's very important to understand that they cannot be reduced to this. (Yuval-Davis 1995, p. 13)

Here we are reminded that women are members of collectivities and that reproductive rights campaigns need to take account of the multiplicity and many dimensions of identities, so that we do not loose sight of the differences in power within these different collectivities.

For feminists North and South the emphasis is on the need for women-centred approaches recognizing the range of women's health needs and highlighting choice, safety and services across this range. In her work on the *Impact of Violence Against Women on Reproductive Rights*, Lori Heise emphasizes that an enemy of choice exists that does not appear in official discussions of reproductive choice — male violence:

> Violence in the form of rape, sexual abuse, or battering affects women's ability to protect themselves from unwanted pregnancy and sexually transmitted diseases (STDs), including AIDS. Even where violence is not used to control women's behaviour, the possibility of violence helps ensure female deference to male decision making regarding sexual behaviour and contraceptive use.

These interpersonal barriers to women's reproductive autonomy can be as significant as government policy, if not more so. (Heise 1995, p. 239)

This has relevance for the rapes in war in the former Yugoslavia.
 As Rada Boric points out in Chapter 7:

When the mass rapes of women in Bosnia became known in the summer of 1992, feminist groups from Zagreb and Belgrade, working with the survivors of male violence, started to organise to do something about it.

In her work Ailbhe Smyth has noted that denying Irish women rights to abortion [and divorce] reflects 'men's appropriation and regulation of women's sexuality, reproduction and labour and of the use of force to ensure their subordination'. In order to change individual men's behaviour, structural injustices, legislation, policy-making and social attitudes in combatting male sexual violence there are strong arguments in favour of public awareness campaigns, educational projects and consciousness-raising with regard to the extent and scope of the violence women daily experience.

EDUCATION TOWARDS CHANGE

As can be seen from the work of the Zero Tolerance campaigners, (aimed at gaining 'zero' public tolerance of men's violence against women) public awareness at both the state-structural and the societal level regarding issues of violence is at a relatively low level within the UK and there is no evidence to suggest that this is not the case in many other European countries. Feminist campaigners have long been involved in education projects to change awareness of women's different situations within societies and to highlight the injustices and dangers that many women suffer throughout the world. Much of the awareness-raising with regard to male sexual violence has been in the form of public educational campaigns designed to work within community contexts and to show women that they are not alone in living with the threat and reality of violence in their lives and that this can be altered in certain ways. This type of organisation, carried out in small groups, role-playing, using theatre and discussion groups, has implications far beyond its immediate aims, as often such work directly challenges more traditional notions of political organizing and popular education. In her handbook on popular education workshops (Davies 1995, p. 224) *On Our Feet, Taking Steps to Challenge Women's Oppression* Liz Mackenzie outlines that popular education is a type of education which:

takes place within a democratic framework
is based on what learners are concerned about
poses questions and problems
examines unequal power relations in society
encourages everyone to learn and everyone to teach
involves high levels of participation
includes people's emotions, actions, intellects and
creativity
uses varied activities

Popular education also follows a cycle which:

begins with people's own experiences
moves from experience to analysis
moves from analysis to encouraging collective action to change
oppressive systems
reflects and evaluates its own process

Feminist projects throughout the world work on educational campaigns combining many aspects of the above. The aims of much of this work in the area of male sexual violence are to let women know they are not alone, to help women to gain power and confidence to challenge unequal gender relations and be able to resist male sexual violence and in some instances to campaign to stop it.

A whole network of feminist groups throughout the UK and Ireland focus on working with individual women and groups of women in both the areas of support, information, counselling and case-work and in developing environments in which women can question and challenge some of the widely-held views regarding the unequal and gendered distribution of power in our societies. Those groups are part of the Women's Aid federations and have developed their services over the last twenty-five years. Networking is important within and between these groups, as Sue Goldsack points out:

Networking with other Women's Aid groups is an important aspect of the way we work. For instance, Glasgow Women's Aid is a semi-autonomous group within a national Scottish network of 37 Women's Aid groups. Women's Aid groups in England, Wales and Ireland are also part of national networks. We all work towards the same aims and objectives. In this way we increase the service we provide to women, share information, tactics and campaigns, and new groups are assisted in getting started. Together we are a more powerful political force. (hCa 3, pp. 84–5)

Part of the work of Women's Aid groups, Rape Crisis Centres, Women's Counselling and Resource Centres and similar networks throughout Western European countries is to carry out educational work both with individual women and groups of women who have experienced male sexual violence and with other agencies voluntary and public, such as other women's organizations like Lesbian Lines and Incest Survivors groups and with police, health and social services and local and regional councils.

It was from within the local and regional councils that the Zero Tolerance campaigns in Edinburgh, Strathclyde, Central region and elsewhere in Scotland, England, Wales and Ireland were developed. These campaigns centre on the need to make male sexual violence visible and to engender public discussion, not only on the prevalence and extent of the range of this violence, but also on ways in which the conditions in which male sexual violence is condoned and perpetuated, can be countered and altered. The Women's Support Project in Glasgow was established specifically to bridge the gap between crisis work, such as that of feminist activists in Rape Crisis Centres and Women's Aid groups, and the professionals responsible for handling cases of child sexual abuse and other forms of violence against women. In their work this group provide information, training and education in the west of Scotland. In describing their work Jan Macleod, Patricia Bell and Janette Foreman explain that from their feminist analysis of male violence the group has been prepared to make wider links in order to get their views across:

> For example, people can easily persuade themselves that domestic violence is a private, family matter and that battered women choose to stay in a violent relationship. We often have to point out that domestic violence abuses children, too, before people will take the issue seriously. We build on discussions of domestic violence before talking about incest and child sexual abuse. This is partly to minimize the mother-blaming which goes on whenever child sexual abuse is raised, but also to give workers a social and political framework within which to make sense of the day-to-day problems which women face. (McLeod, Bell and Foreman 1995, p. 248)

As domestic violence is more familiar to many people than child sexual abuse, discussion of the two areas together enables links to be drawn between them in challenging male power. The workers within this project stress that through their experience it is not just clear guidelines and procedures that are required but more importantly changes in attitudes need to take place so that people believe in what they are being asked to implement.

In assessing the needs for varying responses, from the state structures and from community-based campaigns, it is clear from Chapters 8 and 9 that there are many interlinking areas for consideration in terms of state structures — responses and responsibilities — and social groups and organizations, in terms of research and resistance. Feminist groups are at the forefront of making demands of the state in terms of action against male sexual violence.

8

Partial Achievements of Central-State Public Policies Against Violence Against Women in Post-Authoritarian Spain (1975–1995)

Celia Valiente

THE ROLE OF STREET-LEVEL BUREAUCRATS IN THE IMPLEMENTATION OF PUBLIC POLICIES[1]

In the last two decades central-state policies against violence against women (AVAW policies in what follows) have been similar in Spain to in other European Union member states. Such measures have mainly been of four types: legal reforms, in order to declare violent actions against women unlawful acts which are punishable; diffusion of information about women's rights among the population; promotion of research about the phenomenon of violence against women and elaboration of statistics; and social services for victims of violence, for instance, refuges for battered women. Nevertheless, AVAW policies have been formulated and implemented with some delay in Spain in comparison with other Western countries. This delay was due in part to the fact that since the mid-1930s to 1975 Spain was governed by a right-wing authoritarian regime, which was notably anti-feminist.

In Spain, as in many other industrial countries, AVAW policies have reached in the last two decades only partial achievements, mainly because of problems of implementation. This chapter argues that this implementation deficit can be partially explained cross-nationally by the characteristics of this policy area. The implementation of most AVAW policies is the responsibility of a high number of street-level bureaucrats: judges, prosecutors, police, staff in hospitals, forensic surgeons (*médicos forenses*), and social workers, to name just a few. All of these bureaucrats treat directly with 'clients' (whether the alleged perpetrators of violence or their victims). These bureaucrats can easily jeopardize the implementation of most AVAW policies due to the fact that they have a high degree of discretion and autonomy to perform their jobs, and are not subjected to strict supervision by the people who occupy higher positions in the organizations for which they work.

The first section of this chapter describes the main AVAW policies in Spain. The second section contains a description of the peculiarities of this policy area, which in all countries have hindered to variable degrees the implementation of most AVAW policies. The final section focuses on the role played by different social and political actors (chiefly feminists, state feminists,[2] and state officials) in the policy-making process in Spain since 1975.[3]

POLICIES AGAINST VIOLENCE AGAINST WOMEN IN SPAIN[4]

A broad definition of the phenomenon of violence against women 'includes any act of verbal or physical force, coercion or life-threatening deprivation, directed at an individual woman or girl that causes physical or psychological harm, humiliation or arbitrary deprivation of liberty and that perpetuates female subordination' (Heise *et al.* 1994, p. 1165). Nevertheless, for reasons of economy of space, time and research resources, this chapter focuses on the study of policies directed at the following violent behaviour against adult women: rape and any other form of sexual attack, and domestic violence, that is, violence perpetrated in the family sphere. Other violent behaviour, such as forced prostitution, sexual harassment at work, genital mutilation and abuse of female children are not considered in this chapter.

As noted, the main AVAW policies in Spain are chiefly of four types: (i) legal reforms, (ii) actions to diffuse information about women's rights among the population, (iii) promotion of research about the phenomenon of violence against women and elaboration of statistics; (iv) social services for female victims of violence.

With regard to legal reforms, they are the most important AVAW policies in Spain. In the penal code (*Código Penal*), the different violent acts perpetrated against women are defined as either misdemeanours (*faltas*) or offences (*delitos*), and each of them is assigned a punishment (*pena*), which is lower for misdemeanours than for offences. From 1975 to 1989, sexual attacks against women were still listed as before under the title 'offences against purity' (*delitos contra la honestidad*). Specifically, most sexual attacks against adult women different from rape were still called 'indecent abuses' (*abusos deshonestos*). This terminology was not an anecdote but a very telling aspect of the legal definition of such attacks, because it reflected the fact that when it was formulated, it was considered that perpetrators committed them against the purity, decency or chastity of women, and not against women's freedom to decide whether to engage or not in sexual relations.[5] Besides, rape was defined in a very restricted way, because it referred only to heterosexual vaginal coitus, and not to anal or oral coitus, and because it was established that only men could rape women. Furthermore, in all cases of sexual attacks against women (including rape), if the victim 'forgave' the perpetrator, no prosecution could take place.

It is important to note that divorce was established in Spain in 1981 (Act Number 30 of July 7).[6] This meant that if the executor of violent acts against a woman was her husband, she could not until 1981 obtain a divorce, remaining therefore legally married (although perhaps separated) to the violent husband. A relevant reform of the penal code took place in 1983 (organic[7] Act Number 8 of June 25), which established that even when victims of rape (not of other types of sexual attacks) forgave the perpetrators, they should still be punished according to the law.

It should be noted that until 1985 abortion was a crime in Spain in all circumstances, penalized in most cases with a period of imprisonment which ranged from six months to six years, plus the prohibition on health professionals against performing their professions in private and public centres. Therefore, if a woman had been raped and became pregnant, according to the penal code, she had to give birth to the baby. Organic Act Number 9 of July 5 1985, however, allows abortion in three circumstances: when the woman has been raped, when pregnancy seriously endangers the life of the mother, and when the fetus has malformations.

The most important reform of the penal code regarding violence against women took place in 1989 (organic Act Number 3 of June 21), which instituted changes that had already taken place in other countries. Sexual attacks were no longer called 'offences against purity' but 'offences against sexual freedom' (*delitos contra la libertad sexual*). By the same token, some sexual attacks different from rape were no longer called indecent abuses but sexual aggression (*agresiones sexuales*). Besides this, the concept of rape was expanded to include not only vaginal, but also anal and oral coitus. Nevertheless, penetration with the penis is required in order to legally define an assault as rape. Two consequences follow immediately from this requirement: a sexual assault with penetration of foreign objects is not considered a rape; and men can rape women and men, but women can only rape men (Bustos 1991, p. 115; Cabo 1993, p. 261). Rape, like homicide, is punished in Spain with a period of imprisonment which ranges from twelve to twenty years, and sexual aggression with a period of imprisonment which ranges from six months to twelve years. In both cases the perpetrator has to compensate the victim financially, although this sum of money is only very rarely paid to the victim (Rodríguez *et al.* 1988, p. 151). Another point should also be remembered: rape and other sexual aggression are offences defined in the laws independently from the marital or professional status of victims, for instance, irrespectively of whether the perpetrator is the husband of the victim, or whether she works as a prostitute (Bustos 1991, p. 115). Finally, the 'forgiveness' of the victims of any offence against sexual freedom (and not only in the case of rape, as established in 1983), did not cancel the punishment for such behaviour.

The 1989 reformed Article 425 of the Penal Code classified repeated physical domestic violence against women perpetrated by husbands or cohabiting partners as an offence, and not as a misdemeanour, as it had been legally defined in the past. 'Repeated' (*habitual*) here means violence which has been perpetrated at least three times (Bustos 1991, p. 65; Cabo 1993, p. 229). The offence of repeated physical domestic violence is punished with a period of imprisonment which ranges from one to six months.

Finally, since the 1989 reform, state officials (for instance, prison guards) who take advantage of the power and influence over their clients that their jobs confer, to ask for sexual favours of their clients or their relatives, are punished more severely than before (López 1992, pp. 317–23).

In relation to the diffusion of information about women's rights, such diffusion is important because only when women are aware of their legal rights — among them, that nobody has the prerogative to treat them violently — can women efficiently defend themselves against assaults. It is also useful that women know which social services and other resources are available for them in case of being victims of violence. In this regard, the main state feminist institution of the central state, the Institute of the Woman (*Instituto de la Mujer*) —

hereafter IW — created in 1983, has set up and administered women's rights information centres (*centros de información de los derechos de la mujer*) in some cities, where citizens can obtain information about women's rights, through an enquiry made in person, by phone or by mail.[8] As well, a free-of-charge women's rights information phone line was set up in 1991, with the main purpose of reaching women who do not live in cities. In addition to these general information services, the IW has organized several information campaigns related to the specific issue of violence against women (Gutiérrez, 1990, p. 125; Threlfall 1985, p. 63).

With respect to the promotion of research about the phenomenon of violence against women, it should be highlighted that up to 1983, when the IW was set up, very little research on women's issues existed in Spain, when compared with other Western countries. The IW has since published books and periodicals, given grants to researchers, awarded books and articles, commissioned pieces of research, and established a documentation centre in Madrid to provide bibliographies and information to all citizens. A significant part of these research activities focuses on the phenomenon of violence against women (*Instituto de la Mujer* 1985, p. 29).

A paramount dimension of research activities has been the collection of statistics of reported cases of violent attacks on women, statistics which, for instance, in the case of domestic violence, hardly existed in Spain until 1983. Feminists (and femocrats since the creation of the IW) have urged the police and civil guard — police who work chiefly in rural areas — to collect data of reported cases of aggression in which victims have been women (Gutiérrez 1990, p. 129). However, it is necessary to bear in mind that the Spanish statistics on this issue, as is the case with the statistics of many other countries, only deal with reported cases.[9] In Spain, as in many other countries (Kornblit 1994, p. 1181), underreporting is a common phenomenon, in such a way that estimations about the real number of cases are only tentative. Nevertheless, the judiciary was urged to collect data about court decisions (*sentencias*) regarding cases of violence against women (Gutiérrez 1989, p. 9), and the same happened with the personnel who work in social services, such as refuges for battered women (Spanish Senate 1989, pp. 12185–7). It should be noted that these statistics are in many cases incomplete and hardly comparable (Rodríguez *et al.* 1988, pp. 35–7).

Finally, as for social services for female victims of violence, these have been set up later and are currently less comprehensive in Spain than in other countries, as happens with social services in general.

The state does not always provide directly all these social services for victims of violence, but in many cases it subsidizes non-governmental non-profit women's organizations which provide them. The best known social services of this type are battered women's refuges (*casas de acogida de mujeres maltratadas*) (*Instituto de la Mujer* 1986, p. 22; Scanlon 1990, p. 99). The first refuges were set up in 1984, and in 1993, fifty-one refuges existed in Spain (*Instituto de la Mujer* 1994, p. 99).[10] As in other countries, these refuges are mainly temporary safe accommodation for female victims of violence and their children. In addition, women receive there other services which range from legal advice to psychological support and vocational training, with the aim of helping them to initiate a new type of life away from perpetrators of violence. Finally, it should be stressed that in Spain, in contrast with certain other countries, there are very few programmes for male perpetrators of violence against women: only some treatment in prisons for rapists and executors of sexual aggression, and hardly any for batterers.

DISTINCTIVE FEATURES OF POLICY-MAKING IN THE POLICY AREA OF MEASURES AGAINST VIOLENCE AGAINST WOMEN

Jane Caputi (1992, pp. 204–5), among other authors, has conceptualized violent acts against women as a necessary means to the maintenance of patriarchy (the dominance of women by men which exists in all societies). From this premise, it can be deduced that violence against women will be a permanent characteristic in our societies, which would have to be transformed radically in order to eradicate it. It can also be deduced that currently, AVAW policies are mainly inefficient because they do not substantially undermine the source of the phenomenon of violence against women: male domination. Amy R. Elman and Maud L. Eduards (1991, p. 420), while examining the assistance that battered women receive in Sweden, conclude that such assistance is basically insufficient, although not negligible, chiefly because in the policy-making process in the area of gender equality, 'progress in women's conditions is defined exclusively in terms of gainful employment and shared parenthood rather than in terms of sexuality.' This definition of the improvement of women's status systematically deflects policy-makers' attention away from the phenomenon of violence against women. In contrast with the propositions of Caputi, Elman and Eduards, this chapter claims that in most Western countries AVAW policies have been difficult to formulate and implement not because of the presumed necessity of violence as a means to maintain patriarchal domination, or because of the definition of the betterment of women's lives formulated by policy-makers, but partly due to the peculiar characteristics of this policy area. These singular features refer to problem definition and policy formulation, but especially to policy implementation.

With regard to problem definition, it is a crucial stage in the policy-making process because for a policy to exist, a situation must be conceptualized as a 'problem', about which state officials are willing to do something. In all countries, it has been very hard for feminists, state feminists and state officials to define violent behaviour against women as a social problem, because they had to counter-argue against those (among the general population and the political elite) who believed that no one could be seriously speaking about a problem which affects the whole society but rather about isolated episodes of violence committed by deviant or mentally disturbed men who live at the margins of society. Furthermore, these problem 'definers' had to break the assumption that violent acts against women pertain to the sphere of individual privacy, a realm where the state must refrain from intervening (Connors 1989, p. 49). Finally, they also had to disclaim the argument that violence is a normal — if regrettable — means to solve disputes and disagreements among people, that is, an ordinary component in human relations, and subsequently, that violent actions against women are not truly a problem but 'things of life'.

In relation to policy formulation, one of the most important difficulties has been the high number of policy actors involved at this stage of the policy-making process. This obstacle can be clarified with the example of the several measures which deal with rape victims. As shown above, legal reforms have been passed in Spain by parliamentarians in order to expand the definition of rape to include not only vaginal, but also anal and oral intercourse, and also to permit rape victims who become pregnant to have an abortion. Nevertheless, policy formulation does not finish with the works of parliamentarians since rape victims need to be examined and treated by health professionals as soon as possible. Therefore, the Ministry of Health should give instructions to personnel employed in health centres to perform such tasks correctly. The Ministry of Health also has to organize the provision of abortions in health centres, and some social services such as therapy or psychological support have to be set up to help rape victims overcome such experiences and reconstitute their lives. As has been said, most of the provider organizations are non-governmental, non-profit associations, which receive some financial help from the state. Therefore, some state units, such as the Ministry of Social Affairs or the IW, have to formulate a policy of subsidizing social movements. If many executives are involved, concerted action among them is required in order to formulate a coherent set of measures. But such concerted action is difficult to establish since each political executive has its own priorities which might not coincide with the priorities of the other state units. Moreover, generally speaking, the different state units (for instance, Ministries), are not used to working closely with each other but loosely, or worse, independently.

However, if difficulties exist with regard to the definition of the problem and policy formulation, the chief obstacles for establishing most AVAW policies appear at the implementation level. This feature has been pointed out by other scholars. For example, Jill Radford (1992, p. 255), while examining the treatment of domestic killing by the legal system in England, claims that 'discretion dominates every stage of the process — from the decision to act on reports in the first place to the appropriate punishment for the crime at the final stages.' The Spanish case confirms Radford's proposition, since the main problem at the implementation stage (which frequently has been an insurmountable obstacle) has been the enormous number of 'street-level bureaucrats' who held disparate views on the same problem. Street-level bureaucrats are state officials who interact directly with citizens and 'have considerable discretion in determining the nature, amount, and quality of benefits and sanctions provided by their agencies' (Lipsky 1980, p. 3). As Michael Lipsky has clearly explained, several reasons account for this high degree of discretion, for example, that these bureaucrats are professionals, in the sense that they are expected to use their own knowledge and *savoir-faire* to solve problems, which are quite complex and not easily remedied by the implementation of routinized procedures. In addition, the population expect from such bureaucrats not only impartiality but also flexibility and responsiveness to unique circumstances. Furthermore, the number of rules which in theory street-level bureaucrats have to follow is almost infinite and these change constantly. No wonder, then that such state officials adhere only to the most basic rules and exercise discretion in the remaining aspects of their work, without being *de facto* closely supervised by anybody above them. Moreover, street-level bureaucrats' priorities can be different from the goals of the high-rank managers of the institutions and agencies for which they are working. As a result, although the basic guidelines of any policy are set up by legislators, or by policy-makers and high-level bureaucrats, street-level bureaucrats can actually modify and distort such basic guidelines in accordance with their own priorities and views. Finally, civil service provisions, originally established to guarantee non-arbitrary hiring and promotion, actually confer a high degree of autonomy on civil servants, since it is very costly for their superiors to fire them or to reduce their rank (Lipsky 1980, pp. 13–24).

The numerous street-level bureaucrats involved in most AVAW policies can easily obstruct the implementation process, since they enjoy a high degree of discretion. It is important to remember that in Spain the main AVAW policies have been legal reforms, precisely the measures in whose implementation the highest number of executives involved. An example might be useful to illustrate this point. In Spain, repeated domestic violence against women committed by their husbands or cohabiting partners is defined by the penal code since 1989 as an offence, and is punishable accordingly. For this law to be in fact applied, the police and civil guards have to know it, and be willing to receive and adequately handle the complaints. Moreover, personnel who work in health centres and/or forensic surgeons have to be prepared to examine the victims rapidly. If both health centre personnel and/or forensic surgeons perform their tasks with delay, injuries might be partially or totally healed, and the victims of violence might be deprived of some of the most important incriminating evidence. In addition, it could be the case that victims of domestic violence have to leave the family domicile, where violent acts are repeatedly committed against them, and can therefore be repeated in the near future. If victims do not have enough economic resources to afford other accommodation, and have no relatives who can lodge them, they might have to go to a refuge, if vacancies exist. In some cases refuges are full, and their personnel (or social workers who work for state agencies) have to decide rapidly which potential clients are to be given preference, and which others have to be dismissed (or sent to other social services which provide accommodation to their clients). As for the legal system, judges and prosecutors first investigate the cases, and then convoke a trial where the alleged perpetrator of violence is judged. Judges and prosecutors have to know the special characteristics of the offence of repeated domestic violence, among other things, that it normally takes place in the domicile, without witnesses except the victims (or their children), and that proofs (injuries in most cases) might have already disappeared. Due to these and other characteristics of domestic assaults, judges and prosecutors have to be guided by the purpose of trying harder than in other (easier) cases to elucidate cases of domestic violence in order to punish the offenders. The coordination of the performance of all these and any others involved is required in order to effectively apply the 1989 legal reform in its explicit goal of protecting victims of domestic violence. Such coordination is difficult to attain for multiple reasons, some of which are illustrated in the following section, which examines the role played by different social and political agents in the policy-making process related to AVAW measures in Spain since 1975.

SOCIAL AND POLITICAL AGENTS IN THE POLICY AREA OF MEASURES AGAINST VIOLENCE AGAINST WOMEN IN SPAIN SINCE 1975

Generally speaking, in Spain the issue of violence against women had not been a priority for activists in the women's movement up to the late 1970s or early 1980s, when certain feminists 'discovered' the problem of violence against women in some cases accidentally (Threlfall 1985, pp. 62–3). For instance, feminists from the Separated and Divorced Women's Association (*Asociación de Mujeres Separadas y Divorciadas*) who provided counselling and legal advice to women who wanted to initiate separation and/or divorce proceedings, found that the main purpose of many of their clients was to escape from a situation of high levels of domestic violence. By the same token, some activists who worked in health centres as physicians or psychologists were shocked by the high number of female victims of violence who turn to these centres for help. Such professionals started to suspect that the number of victims (from all social and economic backgrounds) who did not ask for help, due to their lack of awareness of their rights, or simply their fear of being more violently treated by their aggressors if they dared to report their cases, was very high.

The next step taken by feminists was to 'open the eyes' of state officials and of the population in general, in order to develop zero tolerance towards violence against women. Women's advocates also posed demands to policy-makers to intervene in this area, organizing services for the relief and help of the victims, and reforming the legal system in order to effectively protect women against aggressors. It should be borne in mind that in those years only very few statistics existed which counted the number of violent assaults on women (none which were reliable existed in the case of domestic violence). Therefore, it was extremely hard for feminists to argue convincingly before policy-makers that violence against women was a serious social problem (in many cases, a life-or-death matter for victims) which deserved state attention and solutions.

One of the first means used by feminists to call attention to the magnitude of the phenomenon of violence against women and to demand the first state measures was the organization of sporadic but highly visible mass mobilizations against sexual attacks against women, mobilizations which also dated from the late 1970s and early

1980s. Demonstrations generally happened after violent assaults against female citizens (generally rapes) had taken place in a city or town. These first mass mobilizations were organized not only by feminists or members of other social movements (such as neighbours' associations — *asociaciónes de vecinos*), but also by political parties and trades unions. Not only the organizers participated in these demonstrations, but also many other people who were not normally very active politically, but who felt concerned about the violence perpetrated on women who lived in their towns or cities.

In 1982, a group of women who provided direct assistance to victims of violence constituted the Commission to Investigate the Ill-Treatment of Women (*Comisión para la Investigación de los Malos Tratos a las Mujeres*). This commission was composed mainly of social workers, psychologists and lawyers and they started to pressurize policy-makers with regard to the formulation of more AVAW measures, and to the implementation of those which already existed. For instance, they requested the Ministry of the Interior (*Ministerio del Interior*), on which the police and the civil guard depended, to remind police agents of their obligation to receive complaints of all cases of violent acts against women and to report them to the judicial institutions. Members of this commission also urged this Ministry to order agents to prepare statistics (Gutiérrez 1990, p. 124; Threlfall 1985, p. 62).

Activists in the women's movement rapidly found an important ally in state feminists. Since its establishment, one of the IW's priorities has been the issue of violence against women (Gutiérrez, 1990, p. 124).[11] Approximately 10–15 per cent of the IW's budget has been devoted to subsidize women's organizations. The emblematic services provided by feminists to female victims of violence — refuges — have been financed with the subsidies of the IW (and of other state units). The times of feminist activism based exclusively on goodwill, altruism and absolute lack of financial resources were over; high-cost services such as refuges could be instituted partly because of the existence of subsidies.[12] In addition, the IW, like the majority of state feminist institutions in the Western world, has neither the competence nor the budget to formulate and implement most gender equality policies, but does have the explicit task of trying to convince other state units to set themselves such policies.

Feminist organizations which 'specialized' in the issue of violence against women were created mainly since the mid-1980s, including the Association of Assistance to Raped Women (*Asociación de Asistencia a Mujeres Violadas*) or the Anti-Aggression Commission (*Comisión Anti-Agresiones*), but also others. In the mid-1980s then, two actors (state feminists and feminists) were already in motion defining the different dimensions of the problem of violence against women and pressurizing policy-makers to do something (or many things) to deal with such issues. They were not the only ones in the years to come. For instance, on November 5, 1986 a unit (*ponencia del Senado de investigación de malos tratos a mujeres*) of the Senate liaison with the Ombudsman and human rights committee (*Comisión de relaciones con el Defensor del Pueblo y de los derechos humanos del Senado*) was formed with the aim of collecting information about domestic violence against women in Spain, analyzing it and giving advice to the Ministries of Interior, Justice and Education about potential measures to be taken (Gutiérre, 1990, p. 124). The unit was headed by a female senator from the social-democratic party (*Partido Socialista Obrero Espanõl*, PSOE), and its other members were two male PSOE senators, one male senator from the conservative party (*Partido Popular*), and one male senator from the mixed group (*Grupo Mixto*). The unit finished its works in Spring 1989. Its analyses and recommendations were very similar to those elaborated by many feminist groups and femocrats (Spanish Senate 1989).

The concerted efforts of feminists and femocrats have been in the origins of the formulation of many AVAW policies described in the first section of the chapter. Nevertheless, state feminists and members of the women's movement found with dismay that, if it was hard to formulate AVAW measures (for instance, legal reforms), the implementation of them was not at all automatic. In fact, feminists and femocrats discovered that pressure had to be exercised constantly on state officials for programmes to become more than rhetorical declarations. In 1995 the IW can show a positive record in having implicated other state units in the formulation of equality policies (AVAW measures, among them), which would probably not have been set up in the absence of the IW. In contrast, the IW has hardly intervened in the implementation of such policies, mainly due to the lack of personnel and material resources. As a consequence, feminists have been those who have insistently put pressure on street-level bureaucrats for programmes to be adequately implemented (or just put in practice). In the following paragraphs I describe the three main professional groups on which feminists have concentrated their lobbying efforts: the police and civil guard; personnel of health centers; and members of the judicial system. Needless to say, the prominence of these groups with regard to the implementation of

AVAW policies is not specific to the Spanish case. On the contrary, this is a common phenomenon in many other Western countries.

With regard to the police and civil guard, an increasing number of agents have performed their duties impeccably while dealing with female victims of violence, but others have not. In fact, feminists have continuously complained about the insufficient protection given by the police and civil guard on some occasions to female victims especially in the case of domestic violence. Sometimes they have come too late when called precisely because violent acts being perpetrated were against women (Cova and Arozena 1985, p. 36). Moreover, they have not given proper protection to women who have been repeatedly victims of violent attacks. Some of these women have finally died or become severely injured.

Feminists have also denounced the fact that, especially in the case of domestic violence, when women have gone to report violent attacks against them, the police and civil guards have sometimes tried hard to convince victims not to sign a complaint 'in their own benefit', and have acted as mediators in an effort to reconcile the two partners. In other cases these agents have not informed female victims that they had the right to be attended by police-women or female civil guards if they have been victims of violent assaults. Finally, when female victims of violence are prostitutes, police and civil guards have not always performed their duties as diligently as in the case of other women.

Activists in the women's movement have thought that one of the reasons to explain the lack of professionalism and low interest with which some police agents and civil guards can treat cases of violent assaults of women (especially if they are committed in the domestic sphere), lies in the fact that a significant number of them still think that they should not be involved in such cases, because they belong to the sphere of the privacy of the individual, where the state should not intervene, or should intervene but has no adequate means to do it. Other agents simply do not believe the account given by some women while reporting episodes of domestic violence, and still others think that some women 'have asked for it'. Without denying the centrality of these sort of convictions, it is necessary to emphasize that police and civil guards can easily translate attitudes of indifference towards the phenomenon of violence against women into inaction or omission, since they are street-level bureaucrats with a high degree of discretion. In fact, Lipsky (1980, p. 13) identifies the police as one of the emblematic examples of such bureaucrats, who daily 'decide who to arrest and whose behaviour to overlook'.

To overcome attitudes of indifference and weak performance of some police and civil guards, feminists have pressurized those authorities on which the police and civil guard depend to supervise their subordinates in order to make agents more active in matters of violent attacks against women. For instance, in part as a result of such pressures, several circulars have been sent to police stations explaining the laws regarding the punishment of violent acts against women, ordering the police to be diligent in the performance of their duties in this matter and to collect statistics of reported cases (*Ministerio del Interior and Instituto de la Mujer* 1991, p. 110). In addition, since 1988 a police station dedicated exclusively to cases of violence against women, staffed only by policewomen, exists in Barcelona. In other cities, units specialized in such cases, where some policewomen work, but which are not police stations but departments within them, have also been set up. Furthermore, since the mid-1980s, courses and seminars about violence against women have been delivered to the police and civil guard (Gutiérrez 1990, p. 129; *Instituto de la Mujer* 1986, pp. 15–16). Nowadays then, after more than a decade of feminists' mobilizations, some female victims of violence have been attended in stations by policewomen (or by policemen knowledgeable about the issue), some victims have been truly protected from their aggressors, and some statistics have been collected. Nevertheless, these cases are still not the absolute majority. Therefore, there is still a lot to be done with regard to the police and civil guard in this policy area.

In relation to personnel in health services, feminists have insistently denounced these street-level bureaucrats for not always examining the victims of violence as soon as they had to. Moreover, such examinations have not always been as exhaustive as they are supposed to be (Gutiérrez 1989, pp. 26–7). In addition, the privacy and intimacy of the victim has not always been sufficiently protected while being examined. Feminists and femocrats have then pressurized the appropriate authorities to order such professionals to be more diligent in their assistance to the victims. As a result, some professionals are currently more responsive to the needs of female victims of violence, but again, they are not the majority. As it has been noted (Heise *et al.* 1994, p. 1172), people who work in the health system are crucial, because 'as one of the few institutions that see women throughout their lives, the health sector is particularly well placed to identify and refer victims to available services'.

The third area of feminists' concern related to the implementation of AVAW policies has been the functioning of the judiciary. In fact, some have identified it as the biggest obstacle for the successful implementation of measures against perpetrators of violent attacks against women (Gutiérrez 1989, pp. 42–3; Threlfall 1985, p. 61). Women's advocates have insistently complained about the slowness and superficiality which has characterized the examination of victims by some forensic surgeons (*Asociación Española de Mujeres Separadas y Divorciadas* 1985, p. 23; Gutiérrez 1989, pp. 25–6). In addition, feminists have objected about the relevant number of complaints of violent attacks against women (especially in the case of domestic violence) which are classified by judges of the lower courts as misdemeanours instead of offences, and have therefore been punished accordingly in the subsequent trial.

Feminists have also denounced several practices that regularly occur in trials, practices which hinder the explicit aim of the laws of effectively protecting the victims and punishing the perpetrators of violence. First of all, as it has been explained by Allison and Wrightsman (1993, pp. 171–94) for rape trials in the USA context, and by Sue Lees (1992) for murder trials in Great Britain, on many occasions a trial of violent acts against women becomes a trial of the victims. They frequently have to answer questions related to their style of living or to their past sexual activities, under the suspicion that some women (for instance, those who go out alone at night, or who frequent bars, or who do not have a permanent domicile or a stable partner, or wear certain types of clothes, or are conceptualized as promiscuous) put themselves in danger of being treated violently, since they might indirectly induce men to behave in such a way. Feminists have demanded with vehemence that judges, prosecutors and lawyers do not investigate the private life of the victims unless it is strictly necessary, since what is to be judged in a trial of this type is the violent behaviour of the presumed perpetrator, and not the intimate life of the victim (*Instituto de la Mujer* 1985, pp. 71–2). A decision of the Supreme Court of Justice (*Tribunal Supremo*), that is, the highest judicial unit in all matters except those related to constitutional guarantees, in 1990, corroborated feminists' arguments, declaring that the sexual life of a victim of rape before rape takes place is irrelevant in the trial (*El País*, November 5 1990, p. 29). Nevertheless, even now some judges, prosecutors and lawyers make investigations about the previous sexual life of the victim, investigations which are not at all necessary for the elucidation of the cases.

The feminist movement has also complained that in cases of insufficient proof, prosecutors very often are not active enough in the investigation of violent acts against women before the trial takes place, and do not subsequently maintain charges against presumed perpetrators of violence (Baiges 1985, p. 11; Cova and Arozena 1985,

p. 36). This alleged deficit in maintaining charges by prosecutors is very important, because when judges write court decisions they punish perpetrators of violence with a punishment equal or lower than the punishment demanded by prosecutors.

Another battlefront of feminists' struggles has been the investigation during the trial of the reactions of female victims of violence, especially in cases of rape. The penal code does not say anything about this matter, but in Spain, as in many other countries, it has been a widespread requirement in trials that rape victims prove that they had very actively resisted their aggressors. This *de facto* requirement is paradoxical, since victims of other offences or misdemeanours, for instance, robbery, did not have to prove that they had resisted the thieves. After numerous decisions by the Supreme Court of Justice which made reference to the high degree of resistance of rape victims, the Supreme Court of Justice affirmed in a decision of 1987 that rape victims do not have to prove that they have 'heroically' resisted rapists, and that it was enough to show that they have been intimidated or threatened, for instance, with a knife (*El País*, October 8 1987, p. 29). While the matter seemed theoretically to have been set, feminists have complained that in many trials victims are still asked to prove that their degree of resistance to rapists was high. As a consequence of this and the investigation of the degree of the resistance, victims have had to answer humiliating and embarrassing questions. For instance, in 1989, in a rape trial, the presumed victim was asked if the day of the rape she wore underpants. According to the president of the court, the question was necessary in order to calibrate how the alleged rapist had acted (and the victim resisted), taking in mind that he had a knife in one hand, and with the other he had to take some clothes off the victim, a task which would have been harder or easier depending on her resistance (*El País*, June 27 1989, p. 24; June 28 1989, p. 31).

Finally, the unfairness of several punishments given to perpetrators of violent attacks on women committed in the domestic sphere has been denounced, especially economic sanctions and house arrest (*arresto domiciliario*) (Baiges 1985, p. 10). With respect to economic sanctions, it should be borne in mind that the most common marital property regime in Spain is community property (*gananciales*). Under this regime each spouse is the owner of half of common properties, that is, of all properties and income obtained by any of the two spouses since they marry. When in this situation a violent husband has a fine imposed on him, he normally pays it with common properties, half of which belong to his wife. Therefore, this fine damages the financial position of his spouse, who might have been herself the victim of violence.

With regard to house arrest, it is in many cases a counterproductive punishment for the obvious reason that in the common situation in which the perpetrator and the victim are husband and wife and live together, it is the latter who finally might suffer the consequences of the punishment, since the perpetrator might behave more violently while under house arrest.

Feminists have found several allies in their demands on the judiciary. For example, a minority sector of judges and prosecutors is sensitive to women's demands and has supported them while pressing charges and writing court decisions under criteria that sometimes have gone far in the interpretation of the laws. For instance, in one case the judge considered that a woman had been raped in a case of anal coitus, at a time when, according to the law, rape could only take place in cases of vaginal coitus (*El País*, January 19 1989, p. 32). Feminists and their allies have pressurized policy-makers in high positions to set up guidelines to make the judicial system an efficient mechanism to punish violent attacks. Several superior organs of the judiciary, like the attorney-general of the state (*Fiscal General del Estado*), that is, the supreme organ of the prosecutors, or the Ministry of Justice, have sent circulars asking prosecutors to be more active in the defence of female victims of violent acts and in the investigation of cases, and to collect data (Gutiérrez 1989, pp. 10–13). As a result of these and other efforts, some trials now take place without irregularities, but not all of them. It should be stressed that judges and prosecutors are also street-level bureaucrats with a high degree of autonomy. The former have also been identified by Lipsky (1980, p. 13) as another emblematic example of such bureaucrats, who 'decide who shall receive a suspended sentence and who shall receive maximum punishment'. In fact, the attorney-general of the state can dictate mandatory norms about how prosecutors have to perform their duties. By contrast, judges are independent, meaning by this independence that no state unit exists with capacity to give mandatory instructions to them, and that they write court decisions only in accordance with the constitution and Spanish laws, but not to any other type of instruction (Gutiérrez 1989, pp. 9–11).

CONCLUSION

This chapter has described the main policies against violence against women established in Spain after 1975. It has also been argued that if many difficulties arise when AVAW policies are formulated, the stage which is full of (sometimes insurmountable) obstacles is the implementation phase. This is due not to the patriarchal necessity of violence as a means to maintain the domination of women by men, nor to the definition that in some countries policy-makers (and feminists) make about the betterment of women's conditions (mainly in terms of access to waged labour outside the home, a definition which turns attention away from the phenomenon of violence against women, as several scholars have argued). The difficulties in the implementation stage of AVAW policies arise chiefly because of the high number of street-level bureaucrats involved in the implementation of most AVAW policies, including: judges, prosecutors, lawyers, police, civil guards, forensic surgeons and personnel in health centres, among others. Characteristic of these street-level bureaucrats is direct dealing with 'clients', and the high degree of discretion and autonomy that they have while performing their jobs. Therefore, each of these bureaucrats is in a key position to jeopardize the implementation of any AVAW programme. For a policy to be implemented, the concerted action of all these bureaucrats is necessary. Such concerted action is difficult to organize, because, among other reasons, each has priorities and ways of working, which might probably be different from those of other bureaucrats. In addition, obvious as it might be, since violent acts against women are perpetrated everywhere, the implementation of AVAW policies is a very decentralized process. As a consequence, for a successful implementation in any single village, town or city, all these street-level bureaucrats have to be willing and prepared to assist victims of violence. Furthermore, when so many agents are involved, the question of 'who does what' remains in some cases permanently unsettled. The interviews conducted for the preparation of this chapter show the existence of some disagreements among several agents in this regard, for instance, in some cases, between personnel who work in health centres and forensic surgeons.

Two or three decades ago feminists realized in all countries that women live in a violent world. An increasing number of activists have subsequently thought that effective resistance to the phenomenon of violence against women across countries should involve not only the women's movement but also the state (Heise *et al.* 1994, p. 1174). Nevertheless, the findings of this paper remind us that it is important for feminists to concentrate their pressure on the state not only with regard to the formulation of new AVAW measures but also to the implementation of those which already exist. Besides, due to the high degree of decentralization of the implementation of AVAW policies and the high degree of autonomy of street-level bureaucrats, feminists have to put pressure not only on the superiors of these bureaucrats, but also on each single bureaucrat of this type. As a consequence, activists in the women's movement accurately sense that they have to fight on numerous fronts, and that battles are fought but never completely won.

If the description of the characteristics and dynamics of this policy area made in this chapter is accurate, it might be concluded that feminists' provision of direct help to the victims of violence is still going to be useful and irreplaceable in the following years. Feminists' direct assistance to victims is sometimes an easier task than the lobbying activities to state units, since such assistance can in some cases be organized by feminists alone, or by feminists and femocrats without resorting to a high number of street-level bureaucrats. This has been in fact the strategy pursued by women's advocates in Spain in the last two decades. It is not only that the supply of direct assistance to victims (and programmes for the population in general) has never been abandoned, but also that such programmes have flourished in the last years.

In the past two decades the main AVAW policies have been legal reforms, characterized by the many difficulties in their implementation, due to the fact that it is precisely in this type of measure where the highest number of street-level bureaucrats are involved, some of whom (for instance, judges) perform their task with the highest degree of autonomy. Nevertheless, generally speaking, obstacles for the implementation of AVAW programmes might be tempered in the near future since it is highly possible that the importance of other AVAW policies different from legal reforms (for instance, social services) will increase. It is also encouraging to bear in mind that the issue of violence against women, together with abortion, are still unifying motives for the different branches of the Spanish feminist movement to engage in joint activities, even though the movement, in relation to other issues, has usually been very fragmented.

Notes

1 I would like to thank Angel J. Sánchez for his help provided in the collection of secondary sources and Roberto Garvía for his priceless comments on an earlier version of this chapter.
2 Since the 1960s, institutions with the concrete purpose of promoting gender equality have been set up, developed (and sometimes even dismantled) in most industrial countries. In social science literature such institutions have been called 'state feminist' institutions or bureaucracies. The people who work in them are described as 'femocrats' or 'state feminists'.
3 This chapter is largely based on an analysis of secondary literature, legislation, published and unpublished political documents and seventeen in-depth personal interviews with four members of women's organizations, one judge, one police agent, three civil guards (police agents mainly for the rural areas), one social worker, two members of the personnel who work in a battered women's refuge, one female victim of violence, one forensic surgeon,

one physician specialist in the examination of female victims of violence, and two lawyers specialist in AVAW legal measures, conducted in Madrid in March 1995. In order to maintain the anonymity of the interviewed, their names do not appear in this chapter.

4 I will concentrate on the central-state policies considered most relevant, that is, those which affect a large number of women, and/or are financed with a significant amount of public resources, and/or are specially innovative. The description of the programmes made here is by no means exhaustive.

5 This type of terminology also enjoyed certain currency in other Roman law countries. For instance, in Italy, sexual violence was listed in the penal code under the title 'crimes against public morality and right living' (Addis 1989, p. 2). In France, sexual assaults were prosecuted according to an article of the penal code which dealt with 'assaults on morals' (Stetson 1987, p. 163).

6 Divorce had also existed during the II Republic (1931–6), but it was abolished by the subsequent dictatorship.

7 According to article 81 of the 1978 Constitution, an organic Act (*Ley organica*) regulates, among other matters, fundamental rights and public liberties. An absolute majority of the Low Chamber, in a final vote of the whole project is necessary for the approval, modification or derogation of an organic Act. For an ordinary — not organic — Act, only a simple majority is required.

8 These information centres were not an original creation of the IW, because the former *Subdirección General de la Mujer* dependent on the Ministry of Culture, had already set up three centres, which the IW inherited. The number of centres increased steadily. Whereas in 1984 there were only three, from 1987 on there are eleven.

9 The number of reported rapes has been in Spain: 1,723 in 1989; 1,789 in 1990; 1,936 in 1991; and 1,599 in 1992. The number of reported sexual aggressions has been: 2,502 in 1989; 2,277 in 1990; 2,282 in 1991; and 2,335 in 1992. Finally, the number of reported cases of domestic violence against women has been: 13,705 in 1984; 15,681 in 1986; 15,230 in 1987; 13,644 in 1988; 17,738 in 1989; 15,654 in 1990; 15,462 in 1991; and 15,184 in 1992 (*Instituto de la Mujer*, 1994, pp. 92–3).

10 The first battered women's refuge was set up in 1971 in Great Britain (Connors, 1989, p. 34) and in 1974 in the USA (Stout 1992, p. 134).

11 The establishment and characteristics of the IW, its effects on policy-making and the relationships between state feminists and activists in the women's movement are described in Valiente (1995).

12 The IW's policy of subsidizing the women's movement is described in Valiente (1995).

9

No Man Has the Right

Katie Cosgrove

'Has woman a right to herself? It is very little to me to have the right to vote, to own property, etc. if I may not keep my body and its uses in my absolute right.'

Lucy Stone in a letter to Antoinette Brown, 11 July 1885.

Feminists have long since been aware of the extent of male violence against women, and understood its significance in our continuing subordination. Locating this abuse within the context of structural inequality, we have identified its role as a key mechanism in the exercise of male power and control over women.

In recent years there has been an increasing awareness of the scale of the problem. The UK Government in its response to the Home Affairs Committee stated that:

Domestic violence is pervasive. Throughout society, many people, predominantly women, are at risk of attack in their homes from their spouses and partners, both current and former. The Government is entirely convinced that domestic violence must be tackled vigorously and that it must be treated as a crime. (Government Reply to the Third Report from the Home Affairs Select Committee June 1993.)

Research on the prevalence of this violence has shown consistently high levels of abuse. The National Working Party Report on Domestic Violence observed that this is more common than violence in the street, pub, or workplace (National Inter-Agency Working Party Report on Domestic Violence July 1992). Accompanying this is the recognition that violence against women is a grossly under-reported crime. A local survey in Glasgow in 1989 by the Women's Support Project and the local newspaper found that 52 per cent of the 1,503 respondents had experienced some form of male abuse, and that relatively few had reported this officially (Women's Support Project, Evening Times Violence Against Women Survey March 1990).[1]

As the body of empirical evidence on this violence grows, there is a parallel acknowledgement of the interrelationship between the different ways in which men abuse, and the realisation that this can only make sense if we understand the continuum of male violence it represents and why it occurs.

Accepting this, however, means accepting its concomitant: that women are more likely to be abused by men known to them than by strangers. Against all the received wisdom on the risks we face in relation to our personal safety we have to confront the reality that the home is the least safe place for women, not the streets. This is more difficult to address, for it means that our safety is not dependent on obeying exhortations to restrict our freedom of movement, lifestyle, dress code. It also means that we have to look more searchingly at the relationships we have built with men, and the specious notion of protection which these have afforded us.

Whilst there is undoubtedly more information, it persists in being a largely hidden problem. Thousands of women continue to experience abuse in silence. Against a backdrop of political indifference, cultural acceptance, and social legitimacy it is still marginalised and dismissed. In recent years the Zero Tolerance campaign has made a major contribution to the process of changing this in Scotland. Its high profile and unswerving commitment to highlighting this issue has created a forum for discussion and debate, and a focus around which initiatives to tackle the problem can coalesce. It has been, and still is, a catalyst for action. Borne from consultation with women's groups and organisations, it has established the parameters for the debate on male violence within a feminist ideological and philosophical framework, yet has done so also from within the framework of local authority structures and priorities.

The success of the Zero Tolerance campaign is the focus for this chapter. In the space of three years it has been launched by thirteen councils/local authorities. It has achieved international acclaim, and has recently been adopted by the Health Authority in South East Australia. In looking at its content and implementation in Strathclyde I hope to explore the context within which this has occurred, and how this success can be understood as a paradigm for future campaigns and initiatives on male violence.

BACKGROUND TO THE CAMPAIGN

The Zero Tolerance campaign is essentially a crime prevention initiative which tackles the issue of male violence against women. It was first launched in November 1992 by Edinburgh District Council's Women's Committee. Initially designed to highlight the nature and extent of this abuse, it used a series of four posters to focus on its most common forms — domestic violence, rape/sexual assault and child sexual abuse — and to link these with the unifying theme that no man, irrespective of his relationship with a woman or child, has the right to abuse them. It sent out a clear and unequivocal message that there is no acceptable level of male violence.

The campaign was created by two women: Evelyn Gillan, then Women's Officer at Edinburgh District Council, and Franki Raffles, a freelance photographer and designer. The impetus for the campaign came from the results of a consultation exercise carried out with women in the city during which they identified the threat of male violence as an issue of concern. Coupled with this were the findings of research conducted in Edinburgh schools which sought to clarify the perceptions and views of adolescent students towards this problem in society, and which showed that:

> Boys, some as young as twelve years old, were more accepting of violence against women than girls.
> Boys and girls found violence more acceptable if the perpetrator was married to the victim.
> The majority of young people interviewed expressed some likelihood of using violence in future relationships.

AIMS AND OBJECTIVES

The primary objectives of the first stage of the campaign were identified as:-

1   Informing people of the scale of the problem

2   Dispelling many of the myths surrounding this issue
3   Emphasising the criminality and unacceptability of this vio-
    lence.

From the outset the designers were clear about the way in which the
campaign should proceed. They wanted to change societal attitudes
towards male violence by making it socially unacceptable, and by
challenging the norms, beliefs and values which give rise to, and
sustain it. They were equally clear, however, that a public awareness
campaign could not, in itself, eradicate male violence. They did not
present a simplistic espousal of public education as the sole means for
political and social transformation, but stressed that this could be only
one component of an overall strategy for change.

They derived some inspiration from the approach of the Canadian
Government which had implemented a $136 million programme to
tackle this issue. The catalyst for their 'Call to Action' had been
the so-called 'Montreal Massacre' — the slaying of fourteen women
engineering students at the University in 1989 by a man who objected
to their presence in what he considered to be a male domain, and who
loudly proclaimed his virulent anti-feminism as he gunned them down.
In response the Canadian Government devised a strategy for tackling
violence against women which incorporated public education, service
provision, and reforming the judicial service.

The three-pronged approach of the Zero Tolerance campaign reflects
this influence, and calls for the reduction and elimination of violence
towards women by:-

> PREVENTION — active prevention of crimes of violence against
> women and children
> PROVISION — adequate provision of support services for abused
> women and children
> PROTECTION — appropriate legal protection for women and
> children suffering abuse.

MALE ABUSE OF POWER IS A CRIME

The campaign is explicitly informed by a feminist analysis of male
violence, and articulates the irrefutable links with male domination
and power in society which create, sustain and perpetuate this abuse. In
drawing on the understanding of male violence as a result of structural
inequality and cultural acceptance, it insists that the root causes of
such violence have to be addressed if the problem is to be tackled
in any meaningful way. It is clear that seeking recourse to individual

and pathological explanations serves only to obscure, mislead and deny the reality of male violence, which ultimately merely assures its continuation.

Essential to the process of designing the campaign, was the consultation with women's organisations, particularly Women's Aid and Rape Crisis; not only because of their role in tackling male violence, but because it was reasonable to assume that a campaign of this nature would inevitably increase the demands on their services. Given the degree to which they are presently over stretched this was not a minor consideration, a fact that has been borne out by the responses to Zero Tolerance. Their support and advice were crucial in developing the campaign, the centrality of which remains one of the most important features in initiatives that have such an explicitly feminist base.

The political clarity of its creators determined the fundamental precepts upon which Zero Tolerance is based, and which are indivisible from its overall aims which are as follows.

To Illustrate the Continuum of Male Violence

Demonstrating the links between the different forms of male violence is pivotal to the attempts of Zero Tolerance to encourage people to view the issue in a wider context, and to see it as an abuse of power accorded men in society. In using the series of posters, and linking them together under the statement 'No Man Has the Right', the campaign challenges perceptions of these as discrete problems. In the inclusion of psychological, emotional and sexual violence in the definition of abuse, it covers some of the range of abusive behaviours experienced by women. This is a crucial element in explaining the analysis underpinning the campaign, and in ensuring that it does not get subverted into a narrowly restricted debate on the issue of physical brutality. In Strathclyde[3] this has been very important since the first stage of our campaign co-incided with the launch of a campaign by the Scottish Office which dealt only with the physical aspects of domestic violence. It is essential that this definition of abuse does not prevail. For whilst people may not be comfortable discussing domestic violence or its repercussions, they do seem able to mention it without visibly flinching. Replete with difficulties though this phrase is — for example, in its gender neutral terms, and narrow definition of abuse — it has at least been acknowledged as a growing problem. With sexual violence and child sexual abuse, however, this is less apparent.

Identifying the continuum of violence permits us to focus on why men abuse, why this violence exists on such a scale, and why the judicial sanctions which are in place to deal with it are so seldom invoked, and so seldom protect women and children.

Empower Women and Challenge Men

The use of victim imagery was rejected at the outset by the designers who had no wish to provide a voyeuristic spectacle of suffering, or a vision of powerless abused women. In contradistinction to the usual portrayal of 'victims', the posters show women in their everyday lives. No bruises, no dishevelled clothing, no piteous gaze for the camera. In using indoor locations, they challenge the belief that women are most at risk from abuse by strangers in the street.

Using predominantly white, middle-class images and settings, the posters depict comfort, security, warmth and 'normality'. An elegant woman perusing a magazine in her graciously appointed lounge. An elderly woman reading to a child. Nice, gentle images into which the text shockingly intrudes:

> From three to ninety-three, women are raped.
> She lives with a successful businessman, loving father and respected member of the community. Last week he hospitalised her.

Can they really have asked for it? Are they the archetypal victims? How are we to understand the abuse of these women? That is the point. There are no archetypal victims. They could be anyone. From any social class, ethnic background, age group. Logically, therefore, so too are their abusers.

The effectiveness of this iconography was noted in the evaluations of the Edinburgh and Strathclyde campaigns as the examples from Jenny Kitzinger and Kate Hunt from Glasgow University Media Group (1993, 1995) illustrate:

> It's not always a drunken bricklayer who comes home on a Friday night and beats up his wife. (1993)
> Middle-class men think that what they do in the house nobody knows about, and that poster displays that that's not the case. (1995)

Tellingly, they portrayed women as 'people with rights'.

Even where there is opposition to the campaign it has encouraged people to reconsider their assumptions of male violence, although not always convincingly so! One man within the Regional Council, for example, protested that while it may be commendable to highlight

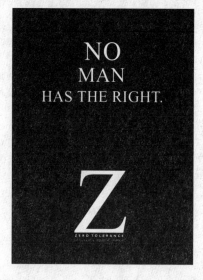

this problem, it was 'a bit over the top' sending it to his department because he worked alongside 'educated, intelligent men'. His female colleagues did not merit a mention. Clearly we should not be bothering this irreproachable group, but should focus on their proper target — the Great Unwashed. The rejoinder that men such as he worked with also abuse was received in silence. Middle-class men are clearly unaccustomed to being included in this debate, far less identified as possible perpetrators of these crimes. Some seem to take it as a personal affront. In shattering the illusion of this as a working-class problem, Zero Tolerance removes the comforting distance of higher social class and status.

There has been some criticism of the under-representation of black and ethnic minority women in the campaign. Whilst this was a conscious decision by the creators of Zero Tolerance to avoid re-inforcing racist stereotypes, and was discussed with black women's organisations, it is problematic. The fifth poster, designed in January 1994, does redress this a little, but there is concern that the relative absence of black women will serve only to silence their experience. It is noteworthy, however, to consider the responses of the focus groups during the Edinburgh evaluation: when looking at the child sexual abuse poster showing two little girls, they were predisposed to believe that it was the black child who had been abused. Defining the problem in terms of male power is of paramount importance in the campaign. As such it is clear that when attempting to challenge the prevailing ideology within society, the onus must fall on the dominant group to respond to the charge, and that responsibility must not be deflected by making this an issue of race or class.

There has also been some contrast of the campaign with the format adopted in London. The latter focused solely on domestic violence, particularly on physical abuse: 'He gave her flowers, chocolates and multiple bruising'. It used images of men, rather than women, although these too did not portray stereotypical notions of abusers. One perceived consequence, however, is that whilst challenging men, women have been rendered invisible.

NAMING THE PROBLEM

The boldness and innovation of the Zero Tolerance campaign lies partly in its unflinching insistence that this is not a gender free issue. Beginning with the premise that it is usually men who commit these crimes, and usually women and children who are the targets of their aggression, it identifies male violence as the primary issue. Some people have difficulty with this. They want the campaign to remove the word 'male' and simply conflate male and female violence. The women's movement recognised a long time ago the importance of naming. If we cannot name a problem, how can we solve it? 'One must speak truth to power' writes Andrea Dworkin (1988). Zero Tolerance recognises this. It has taken what is commonly defined as a women's issue — and therefore for many not particularly worthy of male gaze or attention — and insisted that it is a men's issue. It says that male violence is the responsibility of ALL men, as a social class to accept and act upon. Revolutionary. It dismisses the bad, mad or sad theories of male violence. It simply calls on all men — abusive and non-abusive— to end the violence.

STRATHCLYDE CAMPAIGN

The campaign has been tremendously successful in Strathclyde, and in other areas where it has run. This is a remarkable achievement for any movement advocating social change, but particularly for one which is avowedly feminist. It is all the more significant given the political context in which it has operated. There has been a Conservative, neo-liberal government in power in the UK for the last 16 years which has systematically been dismantling the welfare gains of the post-war period. Under the pretext of 'rolling back the state' it has peddled its ideology of rampant individualism and reaction. The backlash against the inroads made by women has accompanied this period of hostile government. Inimical to the interests of women, it has sought to debate the issue of equality within an arena dominated by discussions on the need to get 'back to family values' (the definition of 'family' being a two-parent, heterosexual, nuclear unit). The growth in lone parent families has been heralded as the most insidious social evil responsible for moral degeneracy, social breakdown, and economic decline. Women are getting out of control. Of men, that is. Clearly a situation that cannot be allowed to continue.

The ongoing struggle to protect the limited access women have to abortion in Britain is paradigmatic of the way in which our attempts to create a radical agenda are stymied. In having to deploy our energies and resources in preserving our few gains, it is difficult to shift the focus on to our rights to control over our own bodies.

Scottish politics have traditionally been more left wing than in the UK as a whole. Electorally we have consistently rejected the Tories, although the iniquity of our electoral system has meant this has been of little importance in a national context. We therefore operate within a system which is an anathema to most Scots, with a tradition of protest and a sense of our own distinctive identity and culture. Perhaps this explains to some degree the way in which the campaign has developed, unfettered by the constraints of the New Right.

The Strathclyde campaign has differed in structure and implementation from other areas, primarily because of its size and geographical diversity. The largest local authority in Europe, it has a population of approximately 2.5 million. It encompasses a major city, towns, villages, rural areas, and island communities. Planning and executing a public awareness campaign to cover such a vast area is thus a major task. The Regional Council opted to approach this as a partnership venture, but one in which it would provide the management and co-ordination. The support for the campaign across the region has consequently been of immense importance in ensuring its success. Of the nineteen district councils covering this area only two refused financial support. They cover the political spectrum in Strathclyde, thus underlining the fact that this is not a party political matter. The four Health Boards in Strathclyde are also key funders of the campaign. The significance of this collaborative approach lies not simply in the material provision, but in the acceptance of these organisations of their role in tackling the issue, and, crucially, in the tacit recognition of the scale of the problem and its causation. In supporting Zero Tolerance they acknowledge both the legitimacy of their role as service providers to abused women, and their remit in working to eradicate this violence.

The weight and authority ascribed to the campaign because it is a local government initiative is considerable. It has enhanced its delivery and scope, and has assured that the central message of Zero Tolerance — that this is a major social and political problem requiring social and political solutions — is disseminated. Within Strathclyde it has been incorporated into the Council's keynote policy for tackling poverty, disadvantage and discrimination — The Social Strategy. The Social Strategy is the jewel in the Region's crown. As an integral part of this, the legitimacy of the campaign is unassailable. A fact which has not been lost on those for whom it is an abomination: 'Fear and loathing on the rates' observed one incensed commentator (Warner 1994). In practical terms it has meant we have been able to distribute campaign material throughout all twenty-seven Regional Council departments, and insist that they are displayed as a part of the Council's policy. This has been of considerable importance particularly when those who oppose it seek to undermine it, or question its presence.

As in Edinburgh, the endorsement of the campaign by prominent men within the region has been obtained. For example, the Chief Constable and Chief Executive launched our bus campaign challenging the excuses used by men to minimise or deny their violence. Their public support has been useful in silencing the claims of some men that this is an anti-men campaign which only women could support. The inclusion of men in the campaign has been a shrewd , strategic part of this initiative. Men have not been asked to validate what we are saying, nor to co-opt this issue or take credit for the achievements of the women's movement — but to accept the centrality of their role in ending male violence.

STRUCTURE

The Strathclyde campaign was launched on International Women's Day, 8 March 1994 at the Royal Concert Hall in Glasgow. Over 400 women and children from all age ranges and backgrounds attended. In an atmosphere charged with hope and excitement there was a very early signal to us that the campaign had meaning for women. They felt ownership of it and identified with it. The advertising campaign throughout the next twelve months comprised of bus, train, subway and billboard advertising, supplemented by the distribution and display of over 150,000 posters, 400,000 leaflets, and thousands of information packs, car stickers, and badges. A distribution company was employed to display posters in pubs, clubs, shops cafes, laundrettes etc. across the Region. It's difficult to verbalise the emotional response to seeing a billboard saying simply 'No Man Has the Right'. One woman, on seeing the Edinburgh Campaign, said she stood there and simply said 'Yes'. How can you convey the sense of power — the power to name, the power to object, the power to reject male violence, the power to *be*? 'Yes' encapsulates the fist raised in defiance, the spirit raised in hope and the voice raised in accord with women. I have lost count of the number of times women have expressed their elation on seeing the campaign, and the value it places on their experience. For many it is a very visible and audible declaration of their rights to themselves. One woman, describing herself as middle-class and a typical 'victim', called us up to say that she had been abused by her husband for years. Driving behind a bus carrying a Zero Tolerance poster she decided that she would leave him. Zero Tolerance cannot assume credit for her decision. This was obviously an ongoing process. But what it seemed to do was provide the additional fillip to her decision to go — it re-affirmed her right to do so.

Whilst the campaign has succeeded in attracting funding which financed the outdoor advertising, the budget is still fairly inconsequential in comparison with other campaigns. It has been the degree of local community involvement in Zero Tolerance which ensured its success. To create and sustain a local profile for the campaign, twelve Implementation Groups were established across Strathclyde. The composition of these differed according to the needs of different areas, but generally included representatives from Strathclyde Regional Council, the local District Council, Health Board, Women's Aid and Rape Crisis Groups and other local Women's Organisations. The commitment and hard work of the women and men who made up the groups have been of immeasurable importance to the campaign. They have helped transform Zero Tolerance from being simply a public awareness initiative, to a process in which people, especially women, have investment and ownership.

In tandem with this has been the burgeoning involvement of all kinds of community groups who have responded to the focus it provides. Throughout the region, there have been theatre productions, safety days, writing workshops and discussion groups raising the issue of male violence. Stalls bearing Zero Tolerance leaflets, car stickers and badges have had a presence at every community venue imaginable. The material has been used with women who are experiencing abuse, with young people in schools and community centres and with offenders. One youth project, assisted by the local police and Procurator Fiscal, staged a mock trial of a young man accused of beating and raping his girlfriend. In Ayr, the four local Implementation Groups organised a major conference aimed at taking the initiative forward to tackle the issue of service provision, which included international speakers, and which attracted a tremendous degree of local interest. Since its launch there have been dozens of invitations for an input on the issue it raises at a huge variety of events held by different organisations, including Trade Unions, women's groups, church groups, and the Worker's Educational Association.

These represent just a few examples of the responses to Zero Tolerance. It has enthused, excited and and prompted people to take action. It has provided the space for the issue of male violence to be raised and debated. Accounts of arguments, conversations and discussions held about male abuse, simply because of the display of a poster, are often quoted to us. Whether or not these are supportive of the campaign, they signal the success of a central objective: to get people talking about the problem, and acknowledging its scale. People who hitherto would be embarrassed or uncomfortable with the subject, have engaged vigorously in discussing it; whilst others who may have considered it too esoteric have propounded their views on why and how it happens. In the evaluation of the Strathclyde Campaign this was reiterated:

The community health volunteers in Glasgow picked up on it. There was a lot of quite heated discussion — it was really very positive. It certainly helped some men who said they didn't realise the extent [of violence against women] and one of the men was quite disturbed by it because he had been violent to a partner in the past . . . (Kitzinger 1995)

A fellow that I used to work with approached me and said [. . .] 'My next door neighbour is beating his girlfriend, I hear it every night, I cannae listen to it any more . . .' He knew about Zero Tolerance and had seen the advert on the telly and that made him think about [doing something] rather than doing nothing. (Kitzinger 1995)

There have been young people who have raised the issue with me — not violence direct to them but within the family unit. Just through asking questions round what the badge means. (Kitzinger 1995)

Whilst the advertising campaign and corresponding work in communities has been successful, there have been a number of shortcomings in the campaign we are still seeking to address.

As mentioned earlier, the under-representation of black and minority ethnic women, whilst deliberate to avoid racist stereotyping of male violence, provoked concern that its corollary had been the silencing of their experience. To address this, the Black and Ethnic Minority Women's Zero Tolerance Forum was established in Strathclyde in February 1994. It is composed of representatives from a variety of statutory and voluntary organisations. Within the Forum, there has been much discussion on the most effective way of ensuring the visibility and accessibility of the campaign within different communities. The paucity of existing local data concerning violence relating to black and minority ethnic women has been raised consistently at the Forum as well as at a seminar held in October 1994 looking at the particular needs of black and minority ethnic women *vis-à-vis* the campaign. A preliminary research proposal was accordingly drawn up in response which identified ways of addressing this issue. The research focuses on ascertaining the nature and extent of service provision for black and minority ethnic women experiencing abuse; how, if at all, this is monitored to ensure it is responsive to their needs, and whether any gaps have been identified by agencies working in this field. It is also envisaged that it will provide an opportunity to recognise and highlight areas of good practice which currently exist. A consultant,

Rosina McCrae, was commissioned to undertake this work, scheduled for completion in October 1995, and which forms the basis for further consultation within agencies and minority ethnic communities. It is also hoped that it will contribute to the ongoing development of the Zero Tolerance campaign at a local and national level.

Another feature of the campaign as it is presently constructed, is the invisibility of disabled women. To generate discussion on the needs and experience of disabled women in relation to male violence, Jan McLeod of the Women's Support Project in Glasgow was commissioned to consult with disabled women in Strathclyde and outline the salient issues in a report. Entitled 'We're no Exception' this report has formed the basis for the establishment of a group within Glasgow to act upon its recommendations. We are presently at the stage of organising further consultations with disabled women to explore the most effective way of addressing these. Disability Awareness training is planned for women in voluntary organisations which work in the field of male violence and we are also hoping to work with disabled women to devise a proposal for more in depth research in this much neglected area. A similar approach has been adopted in relation to the issues facing rural women. Janette Foreman, also of the Women's Support Project, compiled a report — 'Making Us Visible' — following consultation with women from around Strathclyde. Again the recommendations of this are currently being explored. Training initiatives, and development of curricular materials for use in schools constitute further examples of development work within the Region.

IMPACT OF THE CAMPAIGN

The success of Zero Tolerance throughout Scotland and in parts of England where it has run, is undoubted. Whilst the evaluations which have been carried out attest to this, and to the support it has amongst the general public, it has also stimulated a great deal of debate and controversy. Some critics seem to have reserved their most bilious attempts at polemic in assessing the campaign : 'This Goebbels style exercise in hate propaganda is a disgrace to a mature and democratic society' was the tentative view opined by Gerald Warner. He bemoaned the impact of these 'grisly placards' which he considered will subliminally assault the senses of young women: 'Like water dripping on a stone, the insistent message is: men are evil . . .' (Warner 1994). Whatever could have triggered such an attack of apoplexy? Warner identified the instigation behind such malevolence: the Feminist Conspiracy: 'an attempt to create an abyss of distrust and fear between two halves of humanity' (Warner 1994). His splenetic tirade reflects some of the more extreme responses to the campaign, yet paradoxically highlights the very 'core' of the campaign's success: its feminism. Zero Tolerance challenges the existing order; it challenges the prevailing ethos in society on the causation, extent, and remedy for male violence. In eschewing notions of the typical abuser, the campaign's challenge goes right to the heart of the problem — if it is not the result of alcohol abuse, poverty, race, intergenerational transmissions of behaviour, then *why* does it happen?

The cleverness of the campaign lies in its radicalism presented in a straightforward, common-sense way. For example, 'No Man Has the Right' evokes an intense reaction for some. Yet it leaves the argument of its critics wanting. How can they object to the directness and simplicity of the message? Do men have the right to abuse? Most would retreat from affirming this right publicly even whilst assuming it privately. Even cloaked in the obfuscation of female provocation, enjoyment and collusion, they might balk at being so explicit. Similarly the strapline — 'Husband, father, stranger — male abuse of power is a crime!' How can this be refuted, unless by seeking recourse to the 'rantings' of the redoubtable Mr Warner who warns 'Fathers — the ultimate symbols of patriarchy . . . are not to be trusted' (Warner 1994). Yet, it is incontrovertible that it is predominantly men who abuse, and women and children who are the targets of their aggression. Nevertheless, we are presented with the clichéd, apocryphal epidemic of female abusers whose pervasive maltreatment of men is hidden by the latter's shame and humiliation. Messrs' Lyndon and Ashton find no difficulty in believing the extremely tenuous and discredited evidence for this hypothesis, and instead direct their visceral attacks on the overwhelming evidence of male violence. Claiming to 'expose' the true extent of this abuse they decry the 'ludicrous and baseless exaggerations . . . (which) . . . reflect a general pattern of grotesque misrepresentations of the domestic violence phenomena'. Instead they lambast the 'professional parasites on the domestic violence racket . . . (who) will be dismayed at the prospect of their easy money drying up' (Lyndon and Ashton 1995). No more world cruises for Women's Aid Workers then! Commenting on the exponents of the feminist conspiracy 'theory', Usha Brown wonderfully captures their loathing of the 'Hoods' (The Sisterhood that is)!

> In covens all over the country we crouch over our cauldrons —
> double double toil and trouble, fire burn and cauldron bubble
> — here we are, destroying the family as we know it, society as
> we know it, and for all *I* know, the world as we know it. . . .
> Perhaps someone should tell them we're only making the dinner
> — not boiling patriarch's parts or hatching the Gunpowder plot.
> (Brown 1993)

It makes you wonder if they see the atrophy of male power before their eyes, or perhaps have a more physical sense of this? But what they have identified, and so patently abhor, is our success in defining the parameters of the debate. Perhaps the singular most important aspect of Zero Tolerance is that it has changed the terms of reference in relation to male violence. It has created the agenda to which others must respond. Bold. Innovative. Trenchant and uncompromising in its analysis and integrity, Zero Tolerance has shaped the political discourse and deflected attention from those who would minimise and deny the experience and voice of women.

In some ways the plaudits accorded the campaign since its inception have overshadowed the radicalism of its approach, which is perhaps more obviously displayed in the outpourings of feminism's erstwhile opponents. The 'slogan' Zero Tolerance, (helped by the pervasive use of the Z logo) has now become almost idiomatic; it requires little in the way of preamble or explanation — for the campaign has been received less hysterically by people in general than the accounts quoted above would suggest. This has been accomplished in part by its ability to engage people in the debate who have different perspectives. It operates at a variety of different levels. Those who consider they take a 'logical' approach to issues like this recognise the economic imperative of dealing with the costs of male violence. Others see it as a moral issue, one of 'right and wrong'. For others it is political. But whatever the angle from which it is viewed, the clarity of the theoretical understanding which infuses the campaign is unmistakable.

The evaluations of the campaign in Edinburgh, Strathclyde and Central Region vouch for the correctness of this approach. In Edinburgh, 79 per cent of people had positive feelings about the campaign, whilst only 9 per cent agreed with the statement that 'Violence against women is not the sort of issue that should be publicly discussed'. Even amongst men there was broad support for the campaign; only 12 per cent were negative about it overall. The gender specific nature of the campaign has been received well, although some are discomfited by it. For example, one man commented:

> . . . taking the men out and saying you're at fault, predominantly, so we're going to have a campaign aimed at you. I don't think it's right. (Lyndon and Ashton 1995)

Other men, however, have recognised the legitimacy of this:

> There are undoubtedly other forms of violence within relationships, but the predominant one is male violence . . . so let's not cloud the issue. (Lyndon and Ashton 1995)

CONCLUSION

Zero Tolerance is probably the most successful local authority campaign ever undertaken in the UK. Radical and pioneering, it has framed the issue of male violence in terms of looking at men's behaviour — not women's. It insists that men take responsibility for their violence. Yet it also insists that the political, social and cultural context in which it occurs and is allowed to continue, must be changed. It has sought refuge in neither justification of its feminism nor in pandering to the injured feelings of men who feel personally indicted.

Whilst there is still a great deal of work to do, it is important that we recognise the importance of the women's movement, both in creating the conditions in which such a campaign could exist, and in providing the intellectual and political framework for its development. Zero Tolerance did not emerge from a vacuum. Its genesis is in the women's movement. Its integrity and future development depend symbiotically on its continuing identification with this. What Zero Tolerance has been able to do, is incorporate these principles, values and beliefs into a campaign which is endorsed by local authorities, health boards and trades unions. It presents an intrinsically feminist view of power relations in society, and the way in which these continue the subordination and oppression of women.

Andrea Dworkin, in writing about her work, said she writes because she believes 'that women must wage a war against silence: against socially coerced silence; against politically preordained silence; against economically choreographed silence; against the silence created by the pain and despair of sexual abuse and second class status' (Dworkin 1988). The Zero Tolerance campaign aims to be part of that process; to challenge and change the legitimacy of women's oppression, and to contribute to the struggles of women in Scotland and beyond for equality and justice.

Notes

1 The Women's Support Project/Evening Times Report was based on responses from 1,503 women to the survey on Violence Against Women, March 1990. The Women's Support Project is a voluntary organisation, based in Glasgow, which aims to raise awareness about rape, sexual abuse and domestic violence. It provides a development and education service on issues relating to male violence, and works to promote an improved and positive service for women and children who have suffered violence.

2 Franki Raffles, one of the creators of Zero Tolerance, died in childbirth in December 1994, aged 39. Her work as a feminist photographer and designer, for which she was renowned, reflected her commitment to women, and her belief in their ability to bring about change. Her warmth, humour, vision and creativity suffuses her work, and attests to the uniqueness of the contribution she made to women's lives, and stand as a poignant reminder of the extent of our loss.

3 Dates for release of posters in Strathclyde:

    March/April 1994 — 'She lives with a successful businessman . . .'

    May/June 1994 — 'From three to ninety-three . . .'

    July/August 1994 — 'By the time they reach eighteen . . .'

    September/October 1994 — 'When they say no, they mean no . . .'

    November/December 1994 — 'No Man Has the Right'.

Conclusion

Chris Corrin

In drawing together the interwoven threads throughout the chapters in this book, I wish to point up some areas in which feminist research and activism is continuing as we move towards the next millennium. Recognizing the many levels and arenas in which women are active against male sexual violence and the complexities and layers of struggle encompassed, I consider local, national, international and global connections and campaigns. Overlaps and interrelations are visible throughout and it is the focus of this work to point up the intermeshing of feminist analayses and resistance to male sexual violence at all levels. It is clear that through their politics feminist groups and campaigns challenge the power of patriarchy.

COALITION POLITICS

In the work in which many feminists have been involved, in local groups, in national campaigns and in international alliances and networks, we have been carrying out a form of coalition politics. Some time ago, in 1991, I presented a paper at a Women's Conference in Denmark about women's politics in Europe in the 1990s and concluded that politics in its broadest, feminist sense was increasingly visible on 'European' agendas:

> The politics of the powerful and powerless, rich and poor, knowledgeable and underinformed, citizens and non-citizens abound. So too do the politics of those who will not be silenced and accepting of the *status quo*. (Corrin 1994, p. 296)

This could not be more true than of feminist activism to end male sexual violence. In the work collected here there is ample evidence of the multi-dimensions that feminists bring together in recognizing the ways in which our knowledge and ourselves are linked. Nawal El Saadawi has pointed out that thinking in terms of separation and division dates back to the times of slavery (Saadawi, 1990, p. 23). Many examples of feminist activism in this book highlight women's willingness to enter the, often difficult and dangerous, world of coalition politics. This can mean working in ways we would not otherwise choose in order to achieve the goals we aim for. As Bernice Johnson Reagon (1983) long ago reminded us, there is no space that is 'yours only' or just for people who you want to be there. This is true of our work against male sexual violence — telling truths that many people (including some women) do not wish to hear. It is necessary for all of us to feel that 'our' world includes everybody we need to include for survival. This inclusion means listening to different voices and hearing other truths.

GLOBAL, INTERNATIONAL AND LOCAL INTERCONNECTIONS

In considering global concerns, the areas of trafficking in women and of women's human rights are highlighted. The former is an example of a global problem in which, despite the complexities and difficulties posed for feminist intervention and campaigning, much feminist work is evident. Changes within the 'European' dimension are highlighted as this is another area in which more feminist research is needed to document something of the consequences of these rapid changes for women's situations. The international perspective of Kathleen Barry's work (1995) and the European dimension of women's groups within the Council of Europe Committee on Violence Against Women are important in this context. In the field of human rights, feminists are actively intervening and changing the terms of debate. It is possible to witness the power of global feminist campaigning tactics and strategies (Morgan 1984, Davies 1994, Barry 1995, Peters and Wolper 1995).

At the international level my focus is on some of the work of the Women's Commission of the hCa on women's activities and strategies — women's campaigns for better reproductive health care for women; active resistance to the range of male sexual violence, ethnic violence and wars, and on work with refugees. Such international feminist networking is a testament to the belief in the strength of feminist solidarity, support and the creation of new ways of learning and developing across borders — imagined and real. It is apparent within the changing situations in many Central and Eastern European countries that there are few encouraging conditions for feminist research and activism, yet both are continuing, as has been illustrated.

Feminist resistance and solidarity work from all over the world has been apparent for many years. In the late 1970s women from over seventy countries worked together to produce *Sisterhood is Global* (Morgan 1984). This work is a testament to the resourcefulness and resilience of women worldwide. At that time Robin Morgan spoke of the risks in challenging the system with either/or thinking: 'On the contrary, we need to be in the legislatures **and** on the streets' (Morgan, 1984, p. 34). The work of women celebrated by Robin Morgan and in this current book highlights how women have been consistently striving at many levels, in long and short-term campaigns and in coalition-building and forging links between our struggles.

In considering links at the national level the examples of women's efforts in building coalitions include that of the women's non-governmental organizations in Poland in their preparatory work for the Beijing Conference, and the work of Southall Black Sisters both in highlighting changes in immigration laws in the UK and their active campaign against certain changes. In both countries the impetus from feminist activism highlights the emphasis on the need for collaboration amongst women's groups and campaigns and the recognition of unity across differences. That is, precisely because feminists think through the various lenses from which we experience the world, we are able to coalesce in our activism towards particular ends. It is definitely the issues that unite us — the goals we identify with — not our own identities.

On the local level my focus is on the city in which I live and am politically active with other feminists — Glasgow — and on the lesbian collective (Glasgow Lesbian Line) with which I have worked for the past five years. This work involves local one-to-one situations, collective work of eight to twelve women, networking with other women's groups and organizations within Glasgow, Scotland, 'Europe' and internationally.

CONTRADICTIONS AND CONNECTIONS

Whilst the focus of this volume is on 'European' countries, across which there are many, varied levels of difference, the international aspects of many of the issues under consideration are apparent. Some of the complexities of Swiss immigration law for minority women are highlighted in Stella Jegher's chapter and Hannana Siddiqui has shown the need for campaigning on various issues simultaneously when tackling the complex and interrelated problems facing South Asian women experiencing domestic violence in the UK. The male violence that women suffer as a result of trafficking in women and through ethnic nationalism and racism takes many forms and the meanings and consequences are different for individual women and groups of women.

It is apparent that enormous political changes have taken place across the world in the last ten years and these have been accompanied by restructuring in economic terms. Usha Brown recently posed a question from the *Guardian* magazine regarding inequality and poverty:

> What is the difference between Tanzania and Goldman Sachs? The answer was: one is an African country that makes $2.2 billion a year and shares it among 25 million people. The other is an investment bank that makes $2.6 billion and shares most of it between 161 people. (Brown 1995)

Within these global shifts there have been ever-increasing structural inequalities and changes in conceptions of nation states. With the dismantling of 'blocs' at the end of the Cold War era new nation states have been created. Over fifty-five countries are now listed in 'Europe'.[1] Certain political and media voices within Western Europe now appear to view the Cold War as having involved a 'set of rules', and because this has ended, certain peoples/countries are viewed as no longer following any rules. Media commentators throughout Western Europe and elsewhere have viewed the war in the former Yugoslavia as being concerned with 'ancient' or 'barbaric' beliefs or feuds. In this way the focus is centred on 'identity' as an explanation so that structural inequalities are marginalized and structural violence is ignored. The peace 'settlement' brokered externally for those at war in the former Yugoslavia is a case in point. Structural violence has been ignored and groups from various 'sides' in the conflict are arguing against the sense of injustice about being put through this 'settlement'. Such issues as access to land and extreme inequality and poverty remain much the same after such 'settlements'. Given that women and children are the majority of those displaced, the 'settlement' has signally failed to address their needs.

Several contributors to this book have noted an apparent vacuum of values (Kriszta Szalay, Natalia Khodyreva) and how sometimes simplistic solutions are sought (Hannana Siddiqui). Within this context, when we consider the trafficking of women and the violence done to women in the face of ethnic nationalism and racism, it is crucial to be conscious that the global nature of these problems can be addressed at various levels only when the interconnections are born in mind. As is apparent in trafficking in women, issues of racism, objectification of women, failures of legal and judicial systems to protect women's and children's interests and issues of poverty and inequality all play a part in making up the systems of exploitation. So too in terms of ethnic nationalism and racist violence it is apparent that women experience the consequences in different ways precisely because of male exploitation of concepts such as 'mother of the nation' and expectations around women as bearers and transmitters of cultures to future generations. These can be very dangerous situations for women in times when certain cultural values are becoming rigid, or are promoted more than others, or indeed when cultural 'traditions' are being (re)invented. It is also dangerous for women when babies from particular ethnic groups are more desirable than other babies. This can lead not only to enforced sterilizations but also to enforced pregnancies. Women's reproductive health in such harsh situations suffers as do the lives of children. The use of ethnicized rape as a war weapon has had horrendous consequences for many women and children in the former Yugoslavia.

TRAFFICKING IN WOMEN

Considering some of the issues raised by trafficking in women across 'European' countries, it is possible to draw together some of the connections between inequality and poverty and to show where more research on the changing 'European' dimension is being carried out. Much work has been undertaken with regard to international feminist intervention in this area emerging from grassroots feminist activism, as Kathleen Barry has pointed out with regard to the proposed Convention Against Sexual Exploitation:

> As a product of worldwide grassroots feminism, it is framed to reveal how sexual exploitation aggravates the harm of other existing inequalities, often taking the form of sexual slavery, torture, mutilation and death (Barry 1995, p. 305).

The follow-up work from Huairou/Beijing has become important in this connection with groups making alliances across the various 'regions' present in the UN documentation.

There is clear evidence that trafficking in women is increasing across 'Europe'. Recent political and economic changes, especially within Central and Eastern Europe, have made the circumstances of trafficking in women from East to West easier and cheaper, with movement becoming less restricted in terms of legal entry on tourist visas. Increasingly women from Central and Eastern European countries are now entering Western Europe where they are trapped into prostitution.

Whilst the term 'trafficking in women' has been current since the end of the last century, there is still apparent confusion about its meaning.[2] Many women are hired as dancers, waitresses or hostesses in their countries of origin and secure temporary permits from the countries of destination into which entry is therefore legal. The deception lies in the fact that many of the women are then forced into prostitution against their will. Whilst some women are actually sold outright, others are so manipulated and exploited by traffickers that only entry into prostitution enables them to survive.

Not all traffic in migrant women involves prostitution and not all foreign prostitutes in any country have been trafficked. There are many forms of exploitation of migrant women that do not involve prostitution. These include coercion, deception, material exploitation and abuse of migrant women for marriage or domestic work.

PRO-PROSTITUTION GROUPS

Distinctions are made within some groups active in prostitutes' rights work between 'forced' and 'chosen' prostitution. Certain laws and government policies have been enforced in some 'European' countries to support prostitution as a woman's right. In 1990 the government of the Netherlands reported its position on prostitution to the United Nations:

> It follows from the right of self-determination, which is enjoyed by an independent man or woman on whom no unlawful influence has been brought to bear, that he or she is at liberty to decide to act as a prostitute and allow another person to profit from his or her earnings. (Barry 1995, p. 233)

In the context of trafficking in women this would not arise, as coercion is used against these women, yet in the Netherlands distinctions are drawn between Dutch women (and Western women generally) whom they considered to be 'at liberty to decide to act as a prostitute' and 'Third World' women, who 'come to Europe apparently of their own free will to work as prostitutes, but are generally actuated by economic motives and are not genuinely acting voluntarily' (Barry 1995, p. 233). These statements are fraught with contradictions, not least in that they recognize that many women immigrants from 'Third World' countries are fleeing poverty yet they do not recognize poverty as a factor for Dutch or other Western European women. In all of this the situation of women from Central and Eastern Europe is not considered as the rapid changes since 1990 have not yet been documented and taken into account in the changing market of trafficking in women.

RECENT RESEARCH

In the study by the International Organisation for Migration (IOM) data was collected on 155 cases of women who were trafficked to the Netherlands in 1994.[3] Interviews were carried out with people and institutions concerned with trafficking, including the police, Non-Governmental Organisations (NGOs), government officials and researchers. Four countries — Belgium, Hungary, the Netherlands and Switzerland — were chosen to illustrate different trends and policy responses. The traffic does not just flow across to Western Europe as it also involves the recruitment of women from the poorer Eastern European countries to Central Europe. In this context some of the countries of Central Europe are both sending and destination countries for trafficked women. These countries can also become transit countries for traffickers bringing women from developing countries to Western Europe. It was found that the majority of migrant women assisted by NGOs in the Netherlands and Belgium were forced into prostitution or severely exploited as prostitutes. In Switzerland, trafficking in women for marriage also appears as a significant problem.

RISKS AND PROSECUTIONS

The risks for the traffickers remain low. There are few successful convictions against traffickers and sentences are light. Often this is the case because many countries choose to deport 'victims' immediately, so valuable witnesses are no longer available. Immigration laws and policies that consider trafficked women as clandestine migrants and therefore immediately deportable, discourage women in these situations from coming forward to the authorities. Both in Belgium and the Netherlands temporary residence permits for trafficked women have been introduced in recent years, to give the women some initial time to recover and to encourage them to testify against traffickers. As yet though, no government programmes have been introduced to help women ensnared in trafficking to remain in the country of destination, to prepare for their voluntary return home or to assist them when they return.

VIOLENCE AS CONTROL

There is evidence that many of the women recently caught up in trafficking from Central and Eastern Europe in the Netherlands are very young — mainly under twenty-five and many only fifteen to eighteen years of age. Informal recuitment through friends and acquaintances often led to women finding themselves indebted to a trafficker or club owner on arrival in the destination country. In many instances their passports were taken, their freedom was extremely limited and they were threatened with violence. Given the dreadful circumstances in which these women and girls have to live, working long hours, not being allowed to refuse clients, and living in fear of — or with the reality of — violence against them, many of these women experienced health problems. As Natalia Khodyreva points out regarding prostitution in Russia, such health issues generally include sexually transmitted diseases (especially amongst the teenagers) and high incidence of reported mental health problems. Given that many governments simply deport women trapped in trafficking, little is known about what happens to them once they return to their countries of origin.

Some trafficked women receive less than 25 per cent of their earnings and many no earnings at all. The table below shows that trafficked women are often forced into situations of extreme dependency comparable to being held hostage.

Trafficked Women's Conditions of Work

	Central Europe	Eastern Europe + CIS	Developing countries
Passport taken away	15	27	11
Restriction of movement controlled	20	22	8
Working hrs 9–12	5	10	3
Working hrs 13–18	3	3	1
No freedom to refuse clients	16	6	24
Forced to work without a condom	0	1	1
Physical violence used against victim	13	10	9
Victim threatened with violence	13	5	9
Victim's family threatened	0	1	2
Regular circumstances*	2	1	1
Unknown*	16	28	14
Total interviewed:	44	64	47

* These circumstances are not fully explained within the study (IOM Study 1995: 22).

The above data shows that, in many cases, violence or the threat of violence was used to control women's movement and take away their freedom. The high frequency of women being forced to live on the premises in which they work exacerbates the dangers for them. A much higher proportion of women from 'developing' countries were in situations in which they had no freedom to refuse clients.

Whilst the scale of the problem of trafficking in women remains largely hidden and under-reported, the measures suggested to combat such trafficking are often double-edged in terms of their consequences. As Stella Jegher points out, the revision of the Swiss nationality law in 1992 was in part aimed at preventing the practice of organizing false marriages to trafficked women who were then forced into prostitution. As the new law made the acquisition of nationality a longer and more complicated process this legislation remains controversial. The new law can be used to send home trafficked women who are detained. Before these legal changes, the women acquired Swiss nationality which prevented deportations. Stella Jegher explains that this law also affects women migrants who live with violent husbands. This means that Swiss men who 'purchase' women as wives are able to do this and exercise violence towards their wives without punishment. As we can see with other racist immigration laws, such rules as the 'one year rule' in the UK equally adversely affect migrant women who are suffering sexual violence. In such situations women have little recourse to protective legislation and risk deportation if they seek intervention because they are being beaten and/or abused in other ways. Deporting trafficked women serves only to perpetuate their problems and neither prevents nor curtails trafficking, making prosecutions almost impossible. It has even been suggested that deportation is advantageous for some club owners, being a cheap way to send women home (De Stoop 1994).

RESEARCH AND POLICY RECOMMENDATIONS

It is clear that the number of *known* women trapped in trafficking across 'Europe' is very much the tip of the iceberg. Statistics on trafficking remain patchy, yet media attention is high, focusing on the 'sex/scandal' aspects of the trade. Women constitute the largest group of those who are poor, throughout the world. Whilst poverty and the marginalisation of women are root causes of trafficking, so that measures to combat poverty and women's marginalisation are still very much needed, poverty alone does not explain the increases in trafficking.

Women from some poor countries are more likely to be trafficked to the West than women from other poor countries. The multinational aspect to trafficking, involving people from several European countries is such that operations can be moved at short notice. So national legislation may just 'displace' the problem, both in terms of changing immigration laws which moves activities further 'underground', or by implementing restrictions which result in a shift of activities to another country.

Some research is being carried out at local and national levels by womens groups and organizations. In Poland the work of the NGOs Committee has highlighted the plight of many Polish women forced into prostitution by trafficking groups:

> Some of them have fallen victim to organised, international gangs trafficking in women. Such women have signed contracts with non-existent firms such as, for example baby-sitters, cleaners, waitresses or dancers in night clubs. After their arrival they are usually stripped of their passports and forced, by beating, rape and deprivation of food, into prostitution. Even those women who agree to work as 'sex workers' only do so because they have run into debt and have been coerced into prostitution by the owners of the clubs. Yet they could not get out . . . because they were blackmailed by threats that their involvement in prostitution would be disclosed and by threats of violence against their families. (NGO Report 1995, p. 52)

Yet the Report notes that there is also a lack of information about women (often from the former Soviet Union) who work in Polish sex clubs. The registration of prostitutes by police in Poland was ended in 1989 so that there is no official data from which to base guidelines as to the scale of the situation. It is in this context that the state interest is juxtaposed to that of social or feminist interest:

> These spheres of social life seem to be beyond the state's scope of interest. Only women's and feminist organizations recognize prostitution and trafficking in women as a problem and have undertaken activities aimed at forcing the Polish government to comply with the United Nations' provisions counteracting violence against women. (NGO Report 1995, p. 53)

In their recommendations the Committee propose (amongst others) the implementation of mechanisms safeguarding the execution of existing Polish regulations and international laws.

A case can be made for stronger international legal instruments to combat trafficking in women, and certainly the Proposed Convention on Sexual Exploitation has become very important for feminists working in this area internationally. Yet in the 'European' context there are many United Nations and Council of Europe instruments in existence and feminist arguments centre clearly on enforcement. Much legislation is not enforced as intended. Programmes initiated to either ease the women's stay in the country of destination or their return to the country of origin highlight the care needed in acknowledging different women's needs. It has to be remembered that given the circumstances of her departure (to become a singer, to marry a Swiss gentleman . . .) the idea of returning 'home' may not be a healthy option for many women. Rejection by friends or family could be one aspect, as is the knowledge that another mouth to feed could push people back home into further poverty. Such factors are being highlighted by feminist activist research which is campaigning for inclusion of such considerations within the current national or international conventions and legislation.

FEMINIST RESPONSES TO TRAFFICKING IN WOMEN

Clarity in analysis and response is what feminist campaigns are demanding from politicians and policy-makers at national and international levels. Kathleen Barry explains that the Proposed Convention on Sexual Exploitation demands a feminist synthetic approach, as pro-prostitution regulations in certain European countries have actually promoted trafficking in women to the Netherlands:

> Successful campaigns to reduce and even eliminate prostitution and to help women get out of it are based on several factors: the understanding that prostitution harms women, the intention to interefere with market supply for male customer demand, and the determination to provide women with emotional, psychological, health-services *and* economic alternatives. Resocialization of both public attitudes and women in prostitution is possible, but it must supplant the pro-prostitution legitimation of the sex industry's reduction of women to whores. (Barry 1995, p. 249)

The complexities of the politics around prostitution are apparent in that European pro-prostitution groups promote prostitution but are against trafficking in women. This in turn can turn 'local' women against immigrant women and lead to a situation of apparent competition. Kathleen Barry notes that: 'German prostitute women are complaining that there are too many drug addicts, women from Asia, and "cheaper" women from Eastern Europe who "spoil the market"'(Barry 1995, p. 234).

In their work *Migrant Women: Quest for Justice* the Migrant Forum in Asia urge the ratification of the UN Convention Protecting Migrant Workers because the Convention has special relevance to the situations faced by women migrant workers, in that the states concerned should take steps to provide 'effective protection against violence, physical injury, threats and intimidation, whether by public officials or by private individuals, groups or institutions' (Article 16.2). Compelling arguments are made by the Migrant Forum concerning the need for women migrant workers to acquire political power through participation in public affairs in the sending countries. Yet the idea that: 'Since the Governments of sending countries will not be able to ignore the voting power of millions of migrant women, it will open a window of opportunity for them to lobby for their rights' (Migrant Forum 1995, p. 26) may seem rather idealistic in terms of the situation for women caught up in trafficking in women.

EUROPEAN INITIATIVES

In 1993 a major initiative on policies and strategies for the elimination of violence against women was agreed at the Third European Ministerial Conference on Equality between Women and Men. The twenty-eight point declaration (full text in *Rights of Women Bulletin* Autumn/Winter 1994) outlines policies and strategies for the elimination of violence against women in society at the Strasbourg Conference which was attended by all thirty-two member states of the Council of Europe. The declaration was accompanied by a Plan of Action at which the first stage, the formation of a Council of Europe Committee on Violence Against Women, had been achieved. The UK-based group *Rights of Women,* along with women's organizations in other member states, were invited to help promote the declaration and develop the Plan of Action. In the context of trafficking in women, Section 2 on legislative, judicial and police aspects paragraph (g) states the need for the:

> development of appropriate domestic legal sanctions and intensi-
> fication of international co-operation between police and judicial
> authorities with a view to prosecuting and dismantling transna-
> tional networks of traffic in women (ROW Bulletin 1994, p. 20)

This document could be important in gaining funding by feminist groups and organizations for further research work into the extent and realities of trafficking in women across 'Europe'. Yet as with many international documents the specificities of women's lives in terms of the needs of Black and minority ethnic women, lesbians and disabled women are not contextualised in terms of the prejudices apparent within the implementation of legislation, judicial and police procedures. Yet, it is clearly very important that feminist groups such as *Rights of Women* and others across 'Europe' are actively involved in the development and implementation of this work and thereby aim to transform such proposals from a feminist perspective.

HUMAN RIGHTS ARE WOMEN'S RIGHT

Despite the inclusion of women in the 1948 United Nations *Universal Declaration of Human Rights* as an 'at-risk' population, the reality is that almost fifty years later, the human rights of women with regard to male violence remain largely unrelated to the overall situations of women in society. Women's human rights are often viewed as civil rights, and thus superseded by cultural and religious family policies, which restrict and undermine women's autonomy. Yet it is clear that any narrow definition of human rights is exclusive. Women's lives are concerned with social and economic realities as well as civil and political rights, and women's interests in all of these areas need to be protected and promoted. In their campaigning work, feminist activists worldwide can, and are, tackling human rights organizations in terms of their definitions of women's oppression and analyses of its causes. In the Amnesty International report *Human Rights are Women's Right* the key issue of a government's 'right' to interpret human rights is highlighted as posing problems, for the Fourth UN World Conference on Women in Beijing, and subsequent follow-up work:

> Women's rights are human rights and human rights are not only universal, they are also indivisible. A woman who is arbitrarily detained, tortured, killed, made to 'disappear' or jailed after an unfair trial has no chance of exercising her social, economic and cultural rights. . . . Without respect for women's fundamental human rights, the themes of the UN Conference on Women — women's rights to peace, equality and development — are unattainable (AI Report 1995, p. 6)

There is much to be 'unpacked' here using feminist theories and practices in terms of 'universality'. As in all other areas, feminist arguments and analyses both broaden and challenge certain widely-held or unproblematized notions regarding universality. As Hannana Siddiqui noted in her interview after returning from the Beijing Conference —

feminists can influence debates regarding definitions of human rights abuses:

> There is a problem about the wording around 'universal' human rights — how do we define 'universal'. What we are saying is that universal includes notions of patriarchy, structured inequality and therefore women demand certain things which are specific to them, not to be watered down in the wider debate (Trouble & Strife 32, p. 61)

Charlotte Bunch puts this perspective forcefully in arguing that: 'The transformation of human rights from a feminist perspective is crucial to addressing global challenges to human rights in the twenty-first century' (Peters and Wolper 1995, p. 11). In the UK human rights perspectives have not been highlighted within feminist campaigns until recently, but just as feminists are working to change legal codes concerning issues of male sexual violence, so too feminist groups and campaigns are networking to restate issues of injustice, structural inequalities and women's rights to resist racist and fundamentalist political movements globally, from (amongst others) a human rights perspective.

INTERNATIONAL ARENA

The focus here is on our work within the Women's Commission of the Helsinki Citizen's Assembly (hCa) over the past six years. This has largely been coalition work, involving individual women and women's groups and networks from many countries in 'Europe', Canada, North American, Iraq and Kurdistan. The hCa was established in October 1990 following the 'Prague Appeal' to active citizens throughout Europe (hCa Publication 3 1992). This pan-European Citizen's Assembly is composed of individual citizens and representatives of social and political movements, civil institutions, non-governmental organisations, clubs, citizens' initiatives, groups and associations. From the outset the ambiguities posed for feminists working within this context were apparent. The Women's Commission did not occupy any designated space within the Assembly, meeting in lunch-times and evenings. For the feminist activists, the provision of 'women-only' space in which to discuss issues and campaigns of relevance to women was important. Several women present voiced concern at women's issues becoming 'ghettoized' or marginalized if women were not present in all other Commissions, including Human Rights, Economy and Ecology, European Integration, Nationalism and Citizenship, Peace and Demilitarization. For some women representatives of national committees with particular priorities it was important for them to attend other meetings. For others to be in a 'women-only' environment, to highlight issues of interest to women, was important. Some women attempted to be in two places at once and exchange news in this way! From this first Assembly the provision of space and time for Women's Commission workshops and campaigns was established.

It became apparent very early in 1991 that the Women's Commission was working most usefully as a networking umbrella group focusing on women's needs. We decided to raise funds to bring women and women's groups together across Europe. Our first weekend conference and workshop held in Liblice, Czechoslovakia in December 1991 concentrated on women's reproductive health in Central and Eastern Europe. Approximately sixty women participated from at least thirteen different countries — Albania, Bulgaria, Czechoslovakia, France, Germany, Hungary, Iraq, Ireland, Poland, Serbia, Slovenia, the UK and the USA. The workshops highlighted how decisions concerning women's reproductive rights were being made in changing political contexts and considered the options open to us, as active women, to challenge some of these developments. The aim here is not to detail the achievements of the workshop, as these are outlined in the hCa Publication 3. The key aspect for consideration was the coming together of women from various countries throughout 'Europe' some of whom had never met in a voluntary grouping of women, some of whom had not encountered feminist ideas, some of whom had not met women from 'Western' or 'Eastern'[4] countries yet all of whom were able to discuss shared experiences and discover new ways of working together. It was clear to us in this meeting and our follow-up in Bratislava, in March 1992, that one of the primary sites of oppression for women was the violence they experienced at many different levels within their societies.

Our workshop 'Issues of Violence Against Women' in July/August 1993 included women from Albania, Belgrade, Bosnia and Hercegovina, Bulgaria, Canada, Croatia, Czechoslovakia, Hungary, Poland, Russia (Moscow and St. Petersburg), the Transcaucasus (Armenia, Azerbaijan and Nagorno-Karabakh) and the UK. The extent of the commonalities that we discovered over the course of the weekend was striking, both in East–West and in East–East comparisons. Within a feminist analysis this is not surprising given the patriarchal systems in operation throughout these countries. Many differences were also apparent at this time for those women from Central and Eastern European countries where their rapidly changing situations with the dismantling of older systems of government, rapid marketisation, the spread of pornography and increasing prostitution were being experienced in very telescoped and chaotic situations. Much discussion centred on approaching the 'authorities' — the police, legal structures and officials. It was recognized that throughout 'Europe' women from many different communities do so with varying amounts of fear and suspicion. The most marked differences were in relation to the official recognition of male sexual violence as a crime. As Delino Fico noted in her report on Albania:

> How much protection do Albanian women ask of the State? Very little. Women are not educated to actively resist violence. No one has gone so far as to denounce violence officially. Unfortunately people do not even report cases of rape because they are afraid of revenge from gangsters, and feel better keeping it a secret, away from the eyes of others. . . . There is no office or special centre to deal with reporting cases of violence or to provide counselling or protection. (hCa 3 1993, p. 19)

Certainly the dire economic problems within Albania exacerbated this already grave situation for women.[5] In comparing Bulgarian laws on violence against women with those of the Declaration on the Elimination of Violence against Women adopted at the United National Human Rights Conference in Vienna in 1993, Velina Todorova (a member of the Bulgarian Women-Jurists' Association) noted that:

> Bulgarian legislation cautiously approaches the identification and punishment of acts of violence, such as rape in the family. No legal protection is provided for battering, psychological violence, etc. On the other hand, effective protection is made difficult by the court procedures envisaged in the Penal Code. A victim must lodge a complaint in cases where she has suffered moderate or light bodily injury. Yet complaints are often withdrawn at a later stage of the court proceedings because of pressure from the husband. Further violence ensues. (hCa 3 1993, p. 39)

There were parallels in the Albanian and Bulgarian situations in that no centres existed to shelter or care for women who have had to leave their homes because of violence. The increasing sexual harassment at work and trafficking in women are not touched upon in Bulgarian law and Velina Todorova also stresses that: 'our country bears the consequences of an economic crisis and political instability which will inevitably compete with women's problems in attracting the attention of the public and legislative organs' (ibid., p. 40). Our discussions focused on ways in which we could establish women's agendas as part of national policy-making. Communications between women's groups on the local level into a national arena was important as was consideration of how to network internationally.

In considering ways in which women can organize, several women spoke of the beginnings of voluntary work and self-help groups. Jirina Siklova and Jana Hradlikova noted the work of the 'White Circle of Safety (*Bili Kruh*) in the Czech Republic which provides counselling for all victims of crime. It is worthy of note that during 1992 this group advised 84 people, wrote to 135 victims of sexual violence and fielded 200 telephone calls related to these issues. In their view:

> The most important use for all the research and counselling work is to break through the silence about this form of violence against women, to discuss a subject that is publicly taboo, to speak out on international laws protecting women against rape in time of war, to stress to the courts and the police that it is necessary for them to learn about this topic and to educate specialists who will deal with these problems in ways that are more sensitive than those previously used. (Ibid., p. 54)

It is clear from the work of NaNE in Hungary and the Rape Crisis Centre in St. Petersburg that the need for research and education in the area of male sexual violence is extensive in many societies across 'Europe' in which public political discussion, within a pluralist and active political culture, has long been absent.

Two important workshops at this weekend were those on *Women in War* and *Setting Up Support Systems*. In the first, discussion took place in a question and answer form in comparing the situations of women in the Transcaucasus and in the former Yugoslavia. Some of the commonalities that emerged were the situation of hostage-taking which is mainly a civilian activity in the Transcaucasus whereas in the former Yugoslavia this was done through military means. The NGOs working with hostages in the former Yugoslavia are mainly government supported. It was clear that women make up the majority of those involved in anti-war movements and in groups working with refugees. As has been noted by Lepa Mladjenović and Rada Boric in this volume, many women become refugees in war, leaving them open to many forms of exploitation and violence. As suggestions were being proposed for a UN role in the Transcaucasus, women from this region and those present from the former Yugoslavia talked about the UN role in their experience. The response was that the positive effects of the UN were limited — whilst certain border maintenance was effected, their mandate was viewed as too neutral without the ability to evacuate people during fighting. There had also been an increase in prostitution in UN areas and other social problems. Another common problem discussed was the preponderance of war orphans which is becoming overwhelming in both regions. Different strategies for caring for these children were discussed. Within the overall considerations feminist analyses were apparent in the suggestions and campaigns taken up by the participants from the former Yugoslavia. Highlighting domestic violence in time of war was something that some of the participants from the Transcaucasus felt was somehow wrong or 'being disloyal' within their communities. In thinking through our 'belonging', some women echoed the words of Virginia Woolf — as a woman I have no country, as a woman I am a citizen of the world. Other women spoke of the need to be 'here' with women from other countries as 'women'. Such different ways of viewing women's situations became an ongoing feature of our further meetings.

In our workshop on setting up support systems the discussions were wide-ranging, and women from many different countries and projects contributed. As always, it was unfortunate that we did not have more time in which to discuss all of the aspects that we clearly wanted to. Discussion regarding setting up 'hot lines' centred on issues of: gaining premises, confidentiality, training for volunteers, listening skills, the need for non-judgemental non-directive support work, advertising the service, working with police (or not) and gaining funding. In some of the countries of Central and Eastern Europe many phone lines are government lines which presents problems in terms of offering a confidential service. Whilst women from Glasgow Women's Aid and Strathclyde Rape Crisis spoke of, for example, providing training to the police, this was inconceivable to many of the groups present because of the general distrust of them. Advertising the services was spoken of with regard to the possibility of getting space within newspapers or even national phone directories. Discussion about the advantages and possibilities, and disadvantages of state funding touched upon issues of control and 'strings' being attached to the development of the service. Non-governmental methods of fundraising were explored and international networking on locating sources of funding within and across our societies. As to ways of working, it was generally felt that feminist groups worked best collectively, and this was something to strive for even with its many drawbacks, as it was essential to constantly challenge patriarchal hierarchies. Working for overall direction and support of workers (both paid and unpaid) was discussed in terms of looking creatively at collective structures. Other groups felt that collective working wasted time and it was necessary to have someone in charge. This was an interesting point of discussion as several groups which worked on feminist principles felt that because they could not call themselves feminist organizations openly (due to general antagonism and prejudice which would preclude both funding and service take-up) they wanted to work collectively as this potentially gave all the women involved equal power in the group as well as joint responsibility.

This work was followed up within our Assembly in Ankara, Turkey in December 1993. At this time several overlapping themes were discussed within the Women's Commission including: Women, 'Race' and Religion, Women's Rights are Human Rights, Patriarchy and Militarism, Women in Conflict Situations, Women's Activities for Change and Gender Studies in Central and Eastern Europe. Issues of violence against women were apparent within and throughout these considerations. The interconnections were made between women's struggles against racism and their exclusion from political processes and how certain women's marginalization from society is increased as their cultures are viewed as inferior. Pragna Patel spoke of the 1986 'virginity testing' in Britain carried out on Asian women by immigration officials. The profound racism and sexism here was apparent in this violation of Asian women's bodies. Emphasis was on what women can do to continue to struggle on several fronts at the same time.

In our work on women in conflict situations Teuta Cuckova from Macedonia spoke of the work of women in the Committee for Peace in organizing settlement for refugees including many orphaned children and single mothers. Dialogues had been established between Macedonian and Albanian women working together. Macedonian women also participated in a joint meeting with Greek women's organizations in Ochrid and organized with women from Bulgaria and Women in Black in Serbia and Kosova. Leyla Zana, a Kurdish MP spoke about women working together across conflicts — that is was not enough to be upset, nor to struggle for Turkish women or Kurdish women but for the world's women. In speaking of the problems faced by Kurdish people in Turkey, Leyla Zana explained that because their party (The Democratic Party) prepared a communique about the situation for Kurdish people, their leader had been imprisoned. Leyla Zana, who was herself awaiting trial for treason for speaking publicly about the situation of Kurdish people, has since been sentenced to fifteen years in prison and has also received the Nobel Peace Prize. . . .

The ensuing discussion between Turkish and Kurdish women within the Women's Commission was a difficult and dangerous one for the women involved. Yet it was very much a tribute to the strength and courage of women who are prepared to take the first step in trying to find the commonalities across conflict, in trying to discuss what keeps communities apart — how the state monopoly in various areas such as the media, education and public relations with other states can prevent people either understanding each other's situations or believing that change could be accomplished.

Much of the work carried out within our meetings, conferences, workshops and Assemblies has had ongoing effects within many societies across Europe. In our last meeting in Tuzla, Bosnia and Hercegovina in October 1995 many of the women who have been involved for several years again gathered to discuss issues of violence against women in the context of war and ethnic cleansing. For the women who participated from Tuzla this was an important meeting as their multi-confessional and multi-ethnic town had been very much 'cut off' for several years by the conditions of war. It was not easy to get to Tuzla from Croatia by road and the Serbian and Russian participants travelled at risk. Evidence of war was all around us on the journey — at times the miles of totally devastated areas with bombed out homes and destroyed churches, shops and farms forcibly reminded us of the desolation caused by this war.

Quite a number of the women attending the workshops were refugees and all of those participating from Tuzla wished to stress that they wanted their town to remain multi-ethnic. Women present from Sarajevo discussed their similar situation. These women had put up with many horrors in order to stay together and were obviously anxious about the possibility of Tuzla being 'carved up' with certain groups being forcibly removed. The concern with mixed ethnicity of most of the women who spoke from Tuzla highlighted the extent to which Catholic women had married Muslim men, or Orthodox men and Muslim women had children together and that these children's identity was formerly Yugoslavian. One Muslim woman married to a Serb had to explain, when her daughter asked who was bombing them, that it was the 'bad' Serbs. They are proud to be living peacefully with many different cultures, faiths, ideas and identities. For the refugee women a key point was the violent injustice of their forced removal from their homes. Accounts of the violence these women and children (and their male relatives) suffered were hard to hear. Rights for refugees to return home was something that we discussed, as were the rights to find out what had happened to those who had disappeared. These issues are now being hotly debated since the cease-fire in working towards some sort of peace.

Visits were made to several women's projects in Tuzla and these included 'AMICA' (project for traumatized women), Bosfam (project for refugee women), Viva Zene (therapy centre for women and children) and The Association of Women of Bosnia and Hercegovina. Women present from Zenica spoke of their work within *Medica Zenica* which is a project which offers a place of refuge and new perspectives for life to traumatized women and their children in the war zone. Again discussions around ways of working with women and children who have suffered violence ranged across the whole spectrum from how women became refugees to what sort of expertise is required for working in trauma psychotherapy as well as how the media constructs stereotypes of women (as victims or in the case of Tuzla as 'all in headscarves' and therefore Muslim/fundamentalist), and ways in which to raise women's voices in ending the violence, at all levels and in brokering a peace.

In this connection the discussions fitted with other considerations made through our work regarding women's involvement in war situations and in creating some conditions for peace. From our early discussions we did conclude that there is nothing inherently 'peaceful' about women. When discussing this again in Tuzla several women refugees stated that they had been moved once too often and would fight to defend their rights to remain in Tuzla. Some theories which view women as having a peaceful 'role' take explanations from the political realm into the realm of psychology — about how it is 'madmen' that start wars, just as it is deviant men who beat or rape women. Decisions about violence are made by men in power within calculated risk situations. It is important for women to get their political voices heard and to keep the arguments centred on systems of power. Groups such as Women in Black in the former Yugoslavia are not just highlighting the desire for peace (on behalf of the vast majority of the populations) and solidarity with other women in conflict, but are actively challenging their government every week that they stand dressed in black. They are challenging the political and military decision-makers in Belgrade, Zagreb and elsewhere by showing dissent and forcing the power-holders to recognise that they could choose to make different decisions. It is clear too that in the current situation of ceasefire across the former Yugoslavia violence against women has, in certain ways escalated, with men returning from violence in battles, still carrying their weapons.

In the aftermath of conflict the 'settlements', especially when brokered from abroad, generally fail to recognize, or wilfully ignore, women's needs and rights as structural inequalities remain unresolved. Women in Tuzla and elsewhere will not allow these omissions to go uncontested.

FEMINIST ORGANIZING ON THE NATIONAL LEVEL

The focus here is on the work of women across communities and groups within their country, networking between different organizations and communities of women — emphasising the work of women at grassroots levels to challenge some of the decision-making and policy implementation within state structures. The focus is on Poland where the Committee of Women's Groups came together during 1995 to process much of the documentation for Beijing from a feminist perspective. This example of women's networking in Poland is chosen because of the ways in which struggles against violence against women are interwoven within their political demands and because they highlight how feminist grassroots groups can affect national agendas on these fronts.

The Situation of Women in Poland report was put together by the Polish Committee of NGOs who stated that the report was made because of the growing activity of Polish women which they wished not only to be valued within Poland but to be made public outside Poland in networking with other groups and campaigns. In 1995 there were approximately seventy groups — both representatives of the nongovernmental women's organizations and those working on behalf of women. The report was deemed necessary because the document on the situation of women in Poland which had been prepared for the 1994 UN Conference in Vienna, by the Office of the Government Plenipotentiary for Women and Family Affairs, discussed the situation of Polish women to only a very limited extent. Neither women's health issues, codified laws and their observance, nor the role of women in the family or the problems of violence against women were adequately addressed. Whilst the completion of the report was a primary objective the Committee also aimed to enable women members of Polish NGOs to take part in all events preceding the UN Conference and to play a significant part in the Conference itself. In addition they have been using the media to make available information about women's situations in Poland, about developments relating to the Women's World Conference and human rights and in networking with other women's organizations.

In considering violence against women, the report states quite openly that very little has been done within Polish society and state structures to recognize the problems associated with male sexual violence:

In Poland, violence against women has not yet been adequately recognised as being a grave social problem. So far only feminist circles have treated the issue with due interest. They have pointed out that the issue should be taken into account by the government in pursuance of its social policy. . . . There are no official statistics concerning violence and scientific inquiries into the subject of domestic violence and violence against women and children are scarce while their results do not allow us to estimate the full extent of this phenomenon. (NGO Report 1995, p. 50)

This situation is a critical one for women wishing to organise services and support and information for women suffering male violence. In order to get changes within social policy and to redirect resources towards women's needs basic statistical and experiential information is required. Some data referring to crimes of violence in Poland does show the high extent of violence against women. Article 184 of the Penal Code deals with ill-treatment of a family member and the greatest number of victims are women. In terms of rape or unwanted sexual relations within marriage these cases are seldom reported:

Cases of rape and forced sexual intercourse occur fairly often in marriages. Women do not report such incidents as crimes because they are ashamed of their situation and they are afraid of public opinion. Furthermore investigations in cases reported by women are not instituted on account of the low credibility of the evidence, according to the police or the prosecution (e.g. the police require women to procure numerous medical certificates and numerous visits to the police station). (ibid., p. 51)

The strength of the NGO Report lies not only in the large number of groups and individuals who have had input but in the ways that it ties different aspects of women's realities together.

In the Section on Violence Against Women, maternity clinics are considered as places where institutional violence is used against women. As most women in Poland give birth in maternity clinics it is well to consider that Polish women are often badly treated in these clinics:

With a plastic bag which, in accordance with the recommendations included in every book on pregnancy and birth, contains her identification card, pregnancy card, a towel, a bar of soap, and a tooth-brush as well as slippers, the pregnant woman enters the world of the totalitarian institution. (ibid., p. 51)

Not only does the admission procedure include strictly observed rules but the medical staff also impose strict rules during delivery. Violence against lesbians is also highlighted with reports of psychological treatment still promoted as a 'cure', extortion from family members, suicide attempts and lesbian mothers losing parental rights if their sexuality is revealed (ibid., p. 65).

As in certain other Central and Eastern European countries many Polish women have been forced to go abroad to seek some income and the phenomenon of the trade in women is rapidly growing: in 1989 there was one case reported; in 1992, there were three; in 1993, twelve; and with the first eight months of 1994, up to forty-nine, forty-eight of which have been brought before the courts (ibid., p. 53). The violence meted out to migrant women is alarming in Poland because of the weakness of state and local structures. Illegal immigrants (including women) are deprived of any forms of assistance such as legal and health care. In relation to illegally employed persons many violations take place, including breaking the labour code, extortion, robbery and rape. Many legal refugees leave the refugee centres in Poland without informing the authorities which suggests that despite having ratified the Geneva Convention, Poland is still not prepared to fulfill its obligations to refugees as it lacks a comprehensive programme protecting refugees and facilitating their integration into society. As is often apparent in this work, the overlaps between different feminist groups and campaigns across 'Europe' are apparent. It is within this area of concern — immigration law and rights to social benefits — that the work of a feminist group within the UK has initiated a national campaign against the one-year rule in British immigration law as it leaves some women with a stark choice — domestic violence or deportation (Southall Black Sisters, 1995).

LOCAL CAMPAIGNS AND SERVICES

In this section the work of Glasgow Lesbian Line (GLL) is viewed as a window through which to view another area of violence against women and to consider the networking at local and city levels that is carried out by this small group. GLL was established in April 1981 by women who had previously worked with Strathclyde Gay and Lesbian Switchboard. The misogyny of the male members of the Switchboard was such that the lesbians involved believed that they would run a much better service for lesbians in a lesbian-only group. GLL remains the only lesbian-run voluntary service for lesbians in Scotland. We provide confidential support and information to women who are, or think they may be, lesbian. We are willing to listen, and talk through, whatever women want to discuss around issues of being lesbian. Over the last fifteen years the collective (of between eight and twelve women) has offered a telephone service at least one night each week, monthly socials and discos and entered into regular correspondence with hundreds of women.

The very existence of lesbians in our societies provokes widely differing reactions, ranging from guarded 'acceptance' (so long as they are not too blatant) to hostility and violence. Our three main types of calls and letters fall into general categories of: requests for meetings/befriendings with members of the collective, often after a befriending women choose to come along to socials and are able to make lesbian friends; issues of health/legal/equal opportunities which can include custody of children, harassment at work, mental health problems; and finally calls about violence and abuse. The main calls and letters around violence are about the violence done to women because they are lesbian. Within family settings this violence ranges from school students being forcibly sent to psychiatrists by their parents, 'to make them normal again', to women being thrown out of their family homes for being 'queer', to brothers, fathers, uncles and other male relatives or friends assaulting women who come out (or are outed) as lesbian. This violence can be physical, sexual and/or emotional. Often the abuse suffered in the home or on the street includes such taunts as 'all you need is a good fuck' and many men are quite happy to attempt to 'turn' lesbians back to the heterosexual fold by way of violence. Lesbians also suffer the range of violence that many heterosexual women experience. We also work with women involved in violent lesbian relationships.

At work many women suffer harassment because they are lesbian. Again the range is broad from having to suffer sexual assaults to 'prove' they are not lesbian, to daily taunts about 'dirty queers' and how unhealthy 'that lifestyle' is for women being near children. Many of the women with whom we speak and correspond are in caring professions, often working with children and are well aware that if their employers found out that they were lesbian they would find ways to dismiss them (legally or otherwise). In a survey carried out through the lesbian and gay advisory forum of the Housing Equality Action Unit, with *questionnaires* collected at the monthly Lesbian Line discos in Glasgow and Edinburgh it was found that a high percentage of women in both cities suffered direct discrimination in terms of their housing situation because of their sexuality. Some homeless women taking emergency accommodation or short-let flats, retold harrowing stories of the violent abuse they suffered in certain settings. Other lesbians suffered violence and harassment from landlords and neighbours and were sometimes forced out of accommodation and made homeless. Cases of lesbian partners being able to hold joint tenancies in council and housing association flats are rare which makes passing on a tenancy difficult. For young homeless lesbians the attitudes of some housing agencies are very prejudicial.

Disabled lesbians in Glasgow often suffer a double risk of hostility. Many people seem frightened of disability and do not see disabled women as 'real' women and therefore as not having any sexuality. For lesbians with restricted mobility getting around can be a problem and getting away from violent situations can be very difficult. Disabled women face 'double the prejudice and double the struggle for both acceptance as disabled people and as lesbian with equal rights' (Gillespie-Sells 1992, p. 1). Children of lesbian mothers also experience hatred and prejudice from other schoolchildren and neighbours because their mother is a 'lezzie' or maybe a 'disabled queer'. Often some sections of societies view mothers as 'good' and lesbians as 'bad' so for them lesbian mothers become a contradiction reduced to 'bad mothers'. Children of lesbian mothers also suffer prejudice and discrimination from schoolfriends and sometimes teachers.

There are several areas of our work on violence towards lesbians in which we liaise directly with other women's groups in Glasgow. We get many calls from women who have suffered sexual abuse when they were younger and want to work through this. We work directly with several women's groups such as NEWSS (North East Women's Support Service), Centre for Women's Health (Lesbian Health Clinic and various support groups), SAY Women (provide accommodation for young women survivors of sexual abuse), CASA (Counselling Adults on Sexual Abuse), Strathclyde Rape Crisis Centre and we refer women to others — Women's Counselling and Resource Service and Women's Support Project. This is a very hard area for our volunteers to work on because it can remind us of things that have happened in our own lives. Our work around violence against lesbians also reminds us of how much prejudice, hatred and violence there is against women who choose to love women. We are thankful that our services such as the monthly discos that we run are good, social and relatively safe spaces for lesbians to gather and have fun.

The story comes full circle with the work of GLL as we are a local group based in Scotland yet our contact with our lesbian groups is global. This is true of many lesbian groups as lesbians are everywhere in every society that has ever existed and as time goes on we are able to become more visible, at least to each other. In various ways over the years we at GLL have been involved in writing to and welcoming lesbian visitors from many countries of the world. Members of GLL have also attended international lesbian, and lesbian and gay gatherings in Europe (Berlin 1991, Vienna 1992, London 1993) and the International Lesbian and Gay Human Rights Conference in New York in 1994. This gathering has since become infamous because of the misogyny and violence shown to lesbians who spoke out against paedophilia.

The range of anti-lesbian violence in Scottish society on some general levels can be seen to mirror that in certain other 'European' countries. Particular differences across 'Europe' include: discriminatory ages of consent, sexual offences laws, protection against discrimination, incitement to hatred, immigration and residence rights, political asylum, lesbian and gay partnerships, child access and custody, children in care, adoption of children, sex education, promotion of homosexuality, and importation of homosexual-themed literature (Tatchell 1990, pp. 30–2). Contexts and situations differ for each of us, as Lepa Mladjenović has pointed out in the context of Belgrade and 'cleansing' where a local gang beat her up because she is lesbian: 'You are dirtying my street' (Chapter 6). For minority ethnic women 'coming out' within their communities which are often vulnerable within wider dominant communities, can be difficult as it may be viewed as a form of 'betrayal' by their families and/or friends. Yet women from all sorts of backgrounds do come out, proudly as lesbians, and do have the strength to work together to overcome the prejudice and violence that is thrown at us.

FULL CIRCLE

The strength of feminist resistance to male sexual violence, in all of its many flowerings, from naming our abusers, to finding out statistics and writing down our truths, to fundraising to develop support groups and services, run campaigns and network with other feminist groups in challenging the myths and realities of male sexual violence, can be seen throughout the pages of this book. Yet, it is also apparent as we move towards the next millennium that the powers ranged against women in the exercise of violence against women are ever-strengthening. Just as the 'X' case in Ireland showed the intermeshing of various levels of violence against a young woman raped by a man known to the family, the national laws prevented her choosing an abortion in her own country or abroad and when international law ruled her right to terminate the pregnancy, the legal system still failed to adequately punish the perpetrator (*see* Chapter 3). The backlash against feminism and the pressures to reverse gains made by women in certain spheres

(Faludi 1991) coupled with the increasing impact of fundamentalist political movements and racist and ethnic violence does not make 'Europe' a safe place for women to be. It is for most women on a daily basis 'a violent world'.

Yet, the many examples of women's analyses of, and resistance to, male sexual violence show the strength of women's collective energies and initiatives. In seeking to explain violence against women in terms that are both accessible and useful to women in their everyday lives feminist approaches do not offer simplistic solutions. From the work that many feminists are carrying out in difficult circumstances it is clear that only by struggling on several fronts simultaneously, making links across various 'levels', can we work towards freedom for all women. Recognizing the great differences between us across the countries of 'Europe' the aims of the feminist voices collected here lie in continuing to work towards that freedom in whatever coalitions we can, in the knowledge that there are millions of women ready to join with us.

Notes

1 Countries listed in 'Europe':
> Albania, Andorra, Armenia, Austria, Azerbaijan, Belarus, Belgium, Bosnia and Hercegovina, Bulgaria, Croatia, Cyprus, Czech Republic, Denmark, Estonia, Finland, France, Georgia, Germany, Greece, Hungary, Iceland, Ireland, Italy, Kazakhstan, Kyrgystan, Latvia, Liechtenstein, Lithuania, Luxembourg, Malta, Monaco, the Netherlands, Norway, Poland, Portugal, Republic of Moldova, Romania, Russian Federation, San Marino, Slovak Republic, Slovenia, Spain, Sweden, Switzerland, Tajikistan, the former Yugoslav Republic of Macedonia, Turkey, Turkmenistan, Ukraine, United Kingdom, Uzbekistan, Yugoslavia (Serbia).

2 The provisional definition of the International Organisation for Migration of 'trafficking in women' for the purposes of their recent study is as follows:
> Trafficking in women occurs when a woman in a country other than her own is exploited by another person against her will and for financial gain. The trafficking element may — cumulatively or separately — consist of: arranging legal or illegal migration from the country of origin to the country of destination; deceiving victims into prostitution once in the country of destination; or enforcing victims' exploitation through violence, threat of violence, or other forms of coercion (IOM Study 1995: 7).

3 Data is based on completed questionnaires collected from 155 women who were assisted by the Dutch Foundation Against Trafficking in Women (STV). That data plus information provided by government officials and NGOs in Belgium, the Netherlands, Hungary and Switzerland forms the basis of the report. 44 cases were from Central Europe (mainly Czech Republic and Poland); 64 from Eastern Europe and the CIS (mainly Russia and Ukraine); and 47 from developing countries — 25 from Latin America, 13 from Asia and 9 from Africa (mainly from Thailand, Dominican Republic and Morocco).

4 Concepts such as western and eastern have never really been useful but are shorthand devices employed as descriptive not analytical forms.

5 From 1994 the Gender Unit within Oxfam has been working with Albanian women to establish a women's resource and information centre.

Authors' Notes

Rada Boric is a university lecturer in the Croatian language and literature of Southern Slavs. She has previously taught at the University of Zagreb, Croatia, for eight years at the University of Helsinki, Finland and for two years at Indiana University, Bloomington, USA. She is a co-founder of Women's Studies and is currently teaching Women's Studies (gender and language) in Zagreb and working at the Centre for Women War Victims. Rada is a feminist and peace activist and is a trainer in conflict resolution and nonviolent communication.

Chris Corrin is a feminist lesbian activist, teacher and researcher. She has long been active in women's politics within the UK and Ireland and since 1984 has been involved with women's groups and initiatives in Central and Eastern European Countries. She has researched and written about women's situation in Hungary, women's politics in Europe and on Women's Studies. Her current research is concerned with issues of violence against women and women's political participation. She is a Senior Lecturer in Politics and Women's Studies at Glasgow University.

Katie Cosgrove is currently the co-ordinator of the Zero Tolerance campaign in Strathclyde. She has a background in Social Work, which has focused primarily on counselling female survivors of rape and child sexual abuse, and training and consultancy work around these issues.

Mica Mladineo Desnica works for the Women's Information and Documentation Centre (Infoteka) in Zagreb.

Stella Jegher, born in 1960, is by profession a translator in French, Italian, and German. She has worked for many years as a staff member in peace and feminist organisations such as the Swiss Peace Council, the Peace Research Forum in Basle and the Women's Desk of the Christian Movement for Peace, Switzerland. She is co-founder of the Swiss Women's Forum on Foreign Politics — a pressure and lobbying group founded in 1987. Since 1991 she has been a member of the Counselling Group of Christine Goll, the only MP at a national level elected on an independent election list. Stella's main themes of activity and research are Feminism, militarism and war, Feminist dialogue in Europe, Switzerland and the European Integration, Democracy and Women's Rights.

Natalia Khodyreva was born in 1959 in Astrachan and gained her doctorate on psycholinguistics and speech perception in 1988. Since 1983 she has worked as a researcher in the psychology department of St. Petersburg University and is now an assistant professor in psychology. Since 1988 Natalia has taken part in one of the first Feminist groups in Leningrad; SAFO (Independent Association of Feminists) group in Moscow in 1990; the First Independent Women's Forum in Dubna 1991 and The Second Independent Women's Forum in Dubna 1992 (as coordinator of the section 'Women and Violence'). From 1992 she has been one of the organizers of the hotline for women experiencing sexual abuse and has conducted assertiveness and self-help groups for women. From 1994 Natalia has been Director of the St. Petersburg Crisis Psychological Centre for Women.

Divna Matijašević works with the SOS Telephone Hotline for Women and Children Victims of Violence in Belgrade.

Jadranka Milicevic works with the SOS Hotline in Belgrade.

Lepa Mladjenović is a feminist lesbian activist who was part of the international network to alternatives of psychiatry, then one of the founders of different women's groups in Belgrade: Women in Black, Arkadia, Women's Studies. Lepa works in the Autonomous Women's Centre against Sexual Violence and is an editor of three books on alternatives to psychiatry and violence against women.

Hannana Siddiqui currently works as a community/caseworker and counsellor at Southall Black Sisters. She has worked there for over eight years. Southall Black Sisters' campaigns have centred on tragic cases of women who have been killed, either through suicide or as a result of murder at the hands of their violent partners. More recently, the organisation successfully campaigned for the release of Kiranjit Ahluwalia, who killed her husband after suffering ten years of violence from him. The organisation's campaign for the reform of the homicide laws, particularly the Law of Provocation, is on-going. Southall Black Sisters is currently campaigning for the reform of Immigration laws which entrap women and children in violent relationships. Hannana is also a member of Women Against Fundamentalism and over the years has been engaged in campaigning on issues concerning equality, justice, freedom and human rights, particularly in relation to the question of race and gender.

Ailbhe Smyth is a feminist activist, writer and researcher. She is Director of the Women's Education, Research and Resource Centre at University College Dublin, where she teaches Women's Studies.

Kriszta Szalay is a lecturer of English literature at the School of English and American Studies of Eötvös University, Budapest. She has written on Wyatt, Virginia Woolf and eighteenth-century Hungarian literature. She has carried out voluntary work for various civic organizations, amongst them for NaNE, a group of women working against domestic violence.

Celia Valiente is Associate Professor of Sociology at the Autonomous University of Madrid. Her current research deals with public policies for women, state feminism and the women's movement in Spain. She received an undergraduate degree in history and a Ph.D. in Sociology from the Autonomous University of Madrid, Spain, and a M.A. in Social Sciences at the Instituto Juan March de Estudios e Investigaciones, Madrid. She has written a doctoral dissertation entitled *Public Policies for Women Workers in Italy and Spain 1990–1991* (in Spanish), under the supervision of Juan J. Linz. She is the author of a chapter in Comparative State Feminism (1995). She has presented many papers at international conferences on the role of women in Spanish society and politics.

Bibliography

Acker, H. (ed). (undated) *Sexual violence against women and girls* Brussels, Socialist Group of the European Parliament

Addis, E. 1989. 'What Women Should Ask of the Law: Italian Feminist Debate on the Legal System and Sexual *Violence.' Harvard University Center for European Studies Working Paper* Series Number 18.

Afanasiev V., and S. Skorobogatov (1994), *Prostitution in Saint-Petersburg: Saint-Petersburg in early 90s: crazy, cold, cruel* . . . Moscow Charitable Foundation 'Nochlezhka'

Allison, J. A. and L. S. Wrightsman 1993, *Rape: the Misunderstood Crime* Newbury Park (California): Sage.

Amnesty International (1995), *Human Rights are Women's Right* London, Amnesty International Publications

Antonyan Y., and A. Tkatchenko (1993), *Sexual Crimes* Moscow, Ameltea Publishing House

Asociación Española de Mujeres Separadas y Divorciadas 1985. 'Pago de emplazamientos a funcionarios de justicia.' In *Primeras jornadas: aplicación del Derecho y la mujer* Instituto de la Mujer, 21-3. Madrid, Instituto de la Mujer.

Baiges, M. (1985), 'Introducción.' In *Primeras jornadas: aplicación del Derecho y la mujer* Instituto de la Mujer, (ed). 9-12. Madrid, Instituto de la Mujer, pp 9–12.

Barry, K. (1995), *The Prostitution of Sexuality: The Global Exploitation of Women*, New York University Press

Bigley, B. (1995), 'Media Watch' *Women's Aid Newsletter*, No 5, (August) Dublin

Boland, E. (1980), *In Her Own Image* Dublin, Arlen House

Boric, R. (1995), 'The Oasis' London, *New Internationalist* August, pp. 12-13

Bradley, F. et al. (1994), 'Violence Against Women: An Issue for Irish General Practice' unpublished paper

Brown, U. (1993), 'Women and Power' Speech to the Scottish Labour Women's Caucus Conference

—— (1995), 'Women, 'Race' and Class' talk at the Women and Culture Plenary, *Desperately Seeking Sisterhood Conference* Stirling University

Bunch, C. (1995), 'Transforming Human Rights from a Feminist Perspective' in J. Peters and A. Wolper (eds), *Women's Rights Human Rights: International Feminist Perspectives* London and New York, Routledge

Bunch, C., and R. Carillo (1992), *Gender Violence: a development and human rights issue* Dublin, Attic Press

Bustos, J. (1991), *Manual de Derecho Penal (parte especial)* Barcelona, Ariel

Cabo, M. (ed) (1993), *Manual de Derecho Penal (parte especial) I* Madrid, Editoriales de Derecho Reunidas

Caputi, J. (1992) 'Advertising Femicide: Lethal Violence Against Women in Pornography and Gorenography' in J. Radford amd D. E. H. Russell (eds.), *Femicide: the Politics of Woman Killing* New York, Twayne, pp. 203–21.

Casey, M. (1987), *Domestic Violence Against Women: The Women's Perspective* Dublin, Federation of Women's Refuges

Cavanagh K. and V. Cree (with R. Lewis) (eds.), (1995), *Working with Men: Feminism and Social Work* London, Routledge

Clarke, C. (1983), 'Lesbianism: an Act of Resistance' in C. Moraga and G. Anzaldua (eds.), *This Bridge Called my Back* New York, Kitchen Table: Women of Color Press

Connell, R. W. (1987), *Gender and Power* London, Routledge

Connors, J. F. (1989), *Violence against Women in the Family* New York, United Nations Office at Vienna, Center for Social Development and Humanitarian Affairs

—— (1994), 'Government measures to Confront Violence Against Women' in M. Davies (ed), *Women and Violence: Realities and Responses Worldwide* London and New Jersey, Zed Books

Corcoran, C. (1989), *Pornography: The New Terrorism* Dublin, Attic Press

Corrin, C. (ed), (1992) *Superwomen and the Double Burden: Women's Experience of Change in Central and Eastern Europe and the former Soviet Union* London, Scarlet Press

—— (1992), 'Women's Experience of Change in Hungary in S. Rai, H. Pilkington and A. Phizacklea (eds.), *Women in the Face of Change* London, Routlege, pp. 167–185

—— (1993), 'Is Liberalisation damaging Albanian women's health?' *Focus on Gender: Perspectives on Women and Development* Oxford, Oxfam Publication 1:3, pp. 35–7

—— (1994), *Magyar Women: Hungarian Women's Lives 1960s-1990s* London, Macmillan

—— (1994), 'Women's Politics in Europe in the 1990s' *Women's International Studies Forum* vol 17 Numbers 2–3 (March–June), pp. 289–98

Council of Europe (1991), *Seminar on Action Against Traffic in Women and Forced Prostitution as Violations of Human Rights and Human Dignity* European Committee for Equality Between Man and Women, Strasbourg

Cova, L. M., and A. Soledad (1985), 'Aplicación del Derecho.' In *Primeras jornadas: aplicación del Derecho y la mujer* Instituto de la Mujer (ed), Madrid, Instituto de la Mujer, pp. 35–7

Cronin, J. and M. O'CONNOR (1993), *The Identification and Treatment of Women Admitted to an Accident and Emergency Department as a Result of Assault by Spouses/Partners* Dublin, Joint Project: Women's Aid and St James' Hospital

Dallos, R. and E. McLaughlin (1993), *Social Problems and the Family* London, Sage Publications

Davies, M. (ed), (1994), *Women and Violence: Realities and Responses Worldwide* New Jersey and London, Zed Books

Delphy, C. (1984), *Close to Home: A Materialist Analysis of Women's Oppression* London, Hutchinson

De Stoop, C. (1994), 'They Are So Sweet, Sir' in International Organization for Migration (1995) *Trafficking and Prostitution: The Growing Exploitation of Migrant Women from Central and Eastern Europe* Budapest, Migration Information Programme

Dobash, R. E., and R. P. Dobash (1993), *Women, Violence and Social Change* London, Routledge

Dublin Rape Crisis Centre (1993), *Annual Report* Dublin, Rape Crisis Centre

Dworkin, A. (1988), *Letters From A War Zone, Selected Writings 1976–1987* New York, Secker & Warburg

El País 1978–March 1995

Elman, R. A. and M. L. Eduards (1991), 'Unprotected by the Swedish Welfare State: A Survey of Battered Women and the Assistance They Received' *Women's Studies International Forum* Vol.14, Number 5: pp. 413–21

Enloe, C. (1993), *The Morning After: Sexual Politics at the end of the Cold War* University of California Press

Faludi S. (1992), *Backlash: The undeclared war against women* London, Chatto and Windus

Fennell, C. (1993), 'Criminal Law and The Criminal Justice System: Woman as Victim' in A. Connelly (ed) *Gender and the Law in Ireland* Dublin, Oak Tree Press

Funk, N., and M. Muella (eds.), (1993), *Gender Politics and Post-Communism: Reflections from Eastern Europe and the former Soviet Union* New York and London, Routledge

Getman, V. and N. Khodyreva (1993), 'The Rape Myths' and 'The Myth of the Protector' unpublished research papers

Gillespie-Sells K. and D. Reubain (1992), *Disability* London and Cardiff Broadcasting Support Services Channel 4 Television

Gittins, D. (1980), *The Family in Question: Changing Households and Familiar Ideologies* London, Gerald Duckworth

Glinka E. (1989), *Kolyma's 'tramway' of middle heaviness* Moscow, Neva

Government Reply to the Third Report from the Home affairs Select Committee (1993), Session 1992–93, London, HMSO

Government Publications (1995), *Task Force on the Travelling Community* Dublin, Stationary Office

Gutiérrez, P. (1989), 'La administración de la justicia ante el problema de los 'malos tratos' en el ámbito doméstico' (unpublished paper)

—— (1990) 'Violencia doméstica: respuesta legal e institucional.' In *Violencia y sociedad patriarcal.* V. Maquieira and C. Sánchez, (ed) Madrid, Pablo Iglesias, pp. 123–36

Hall, R. E. (1985), *Ask Any Woman: A London inquiry into rape and sexual assault* Report of the Women's Safety Survey conducted by Women Against Rape Bristol, Falling Wall Press

Hanmer, J. and M. Maynard (eds.), (1987), *Women, Violence and Social Control* London, Macmillan

Hanmer, J. and S. Saunders (1984), *Well-Founded Fear: A Community Study of Violence to Women* London, Hutchinson

Hanmer, J., J. Radford and E. Stanko (eds.), (1989), *Women, Policing and Male*

Violence London, Routledge

Heise, L. L., 'Freedom Close to Home: The Impact of Violence Against Women on Reproductive Rights' in J. Peters and A. Wolper (eds.), (1995), *Women's Rights, Human Rights: International Feminist Perspectives* New York and London, Routledge

Heise, L. L., A. Raikes, C. H. Watts, and A. B. Zwi (1994), 'Violence Against Women: A Neglected Public Health Issue in Less Developed Countries' *Social Science Medicine* Vol.39, Number 9: pp. 1165–79

Helsinki Citizens' Assembly (1992), *Reproductive Rights in East and Central Europe* Prague, hCa publications 3

—— (1993), *Violence against women in Central and Eastern Europe* Prague, hCa publications 8

—— (1994), *Ankara Report: Where does Europe end?* Prague, hCa publications

Henderson, S. and A. Mackay (1990), *Grit and Diamonds: Women in Scotland Making History 1980–1990* Edinburgh, Stramullion Ltd and The Cauldron Collective 1990

Hill Collins, P. (1990), *Black Feminist Thought:Knowledge, Consciousness and the Politics of Empowerment* London, Harper Collins Academic

hooks, b. (1984), *Feminist Theory from margin to center* Boston, South End Press

Hoff, J. (1994), 'Comparative analysis of abortion in Ireland, Poland and the United States' *Women's Studies International Forum* vol 17 No 6, pp. 621–46

Hyden, M. and C. McCarthy (1994), 'Woman Battering and Father-Daughter Incest Disclosure: Discourses of Denial and Acknowledgement' in *Discourse and Society* vol 5(4)

Instituto de la Mujer, (1985), 'Conclusiones de las primeras jornadas de aplicación del Derecho en relación a la mujer.' In *Primeras jornadas: aplicación del Derecho y la mujer* Madrid, Instituto de la Mujer pp. 69–75

—— (1986), *El Instituto de la Mujer 1983-1986.* Madrid, Instituto de la Mujer

—— (1994), *La mujer en cifras: una década, 1982–1992.* Madrid, Instituto de la Mujer.

International Organization for Migration (1995), *Trafficking and Prostitution: The Growing Exploitation of Migrant Women from Central and Eastern Europe* Budapest, Migration Information Programme

Irish Council for Civil Liberties (1987), *Report of the Working Party on Child Sexual Abuse* Dublin, ICCL

Jeffreys S. (1994), *The Lesbian Heresy: A feminist perspective on the lesbian sexual revolution* London, The Women's Press

Juviler, P. (1977), 'Women and sex in Soviet law' in D. Atkinson, A. Dallin and G. W. Lapidus, (eds.), *Women in Russia* Stanford University Press, pp. 243–65

Kelleher, P. et al. (1992), *Patterns of Hostel Use in Dublin and the Implications for Accommodation Provision* Dublin, Focus Point

Kelly, L. (1988), *Surviving Sexual Violence* Cambridge, England, Polity Press

Kelly, L. and J. Radford (1991), 'Nothing Really Happened' in *Critical Social Policy* No. 30

Kelly, M. (1989) 'Orange Horses' in A. Smyth (ed), *Wildish Things: An Anthology of Contemporary Irish Women's Writings* Dublin, Attic Press

Kelly, R. (1989), 'The Patriarch' in A. Smyth (ed), *Wildish Things: An Anthology of Contemporary Irish Women's Writings* Dublin, Attic Press

Khodyreva, N. (1983), 'Russia: Regional Report' in Helskinki Citizen's Assembly *Violence Against Women in Eastern and Central Europe* Prague, hCa publication 8

Khodyreva, N., Korneva I., and I. Lunin (1993), 'Soviet statistics on rape' unpublished research paper

Khodyreva, N., and S. Kuznetsova (1994), 'Study of lawyers' and doctors' attitudes to sexual and domestic victims of violence in Petersburg' unpublished research paper

Kiswar, M., and R. Vanita (eds.), (1984), *In Search of Answers* London, Zed Books

Kitzinger C., and S. Wilkinson (1993), 'The Precariousness of Heterosexual Feminist Indentities' in M. Kennedy, C. Lubelska and V. Walsh *Making Connections: Women's Studies, Women's Movements and Women's Lives* London, Taylor and Francis, pp. 24–36

Kitzinger J. (1995), *Interim Evaluation of Strathclyde Regional Council's Zero Tolerance Campaign*, Glasgow University Media Group

Kitzinger J. & K. Hunt (1993), *Evaluation of Edinburgh District Council's Zero Tolerance Campaign*, Glasgow University Media Group

Knezevic, D. (1993), *'We' versus 'I' in Feminism: Problems of Political Identity in Croatia* unpublished paper, p.1

Kornblit, A. L. (1994), 'Domestic Violence: An Emerging Health Issue' *Social Science Medicine* vol.39 No 9, pp. 1181–88

Kozlova E., and E. Slucski (August 1994) St. Petersburg, Vedomosti. Unpublished research paper

Law Reform Commission (1988), *Report on Child Sexual Abuse* Dublin, LRC

Law Reform Commission (1990), *Report on Rape* Dublin, LRC

Lees, S. (1992), 'Naggers, Whores, and Libbers: Provoking Men to Kill.' *Femicide: the Politics of Woman Killing* J. Radford and D. E. H. Russell (eds.), New York, Twayne, pp. 267–88

Leonard, M. (1993), 'Rape: Myths and Reality' in A. Smyth, (ed), *Irish Women's Studies Reader* Dublin, Attic Press

Levin, E. (1989), *Sex and society in the world of the Orthodox Slavs 900–1700* Cornell University Press

Levitskaya A, E. Orlik and E. Potapova (1993), *A Study of violence happening at a rendezvous:a crime or a moment of sexual game?* Moscow, Sociologicheskie Issledovania, (Social Researches) No. 6

Lipsky, M. (1980), *Street-Level Bureaucrats* New York, Russell Sage Foundation

Lyndon N. & P. Ashton (1995), 'Knocked for six: the myth of a nation of wife-batterers' London *Sunday Times*, (29 January)

López, J. (1992), *Manual de Derecho Penal (parte especial) III* Madrid, Akal

Lorde A. 'There is no hierarchy of oppressions' (1993), in R. Cleaver and P. Myers (eds.), *A Certain Terror: Heterosexism, Militarism, Violence and Change* Chicago, Great Lakes Region American Friends Service Committee

McKay, S. (1993), 'Report on the Kilkenny Incest Case' *Sunday Tribune* (9 May)
—— (1993) *Bringing it Out in the Open: Domestic Violence in Northern Ireland* Belfast, HMSO

McKiernan, J. and M. McWilliams (1994), 'Domestic Violence in a Violent Society: The Implications for Abused Women and Children' *Rights of Women: Bulletin* (Spring)

McWilliams, M. (1995), 'Struggling for Peace and Justice: Reflections on Women's Activism in Northern Ireland' *Journal of Women's History* Vol 6, No 4 / Vol 7, No 1.

Macleod Jan, Patricia Bell and Janette Foreman (1995), in M. Davies (ed), 'Bridging the Gap: Feminist Development Work in Glasgow' in *Women and Violence* London, Zed Books 246–53

Mamonova, T. (ed), (1984) *Women and Russia: Feminist Writings from the Soviet Union* Boston, Beacon Press

Martin, D. (1976), *Battered Wives* San Francisco, Glide Publications

Maynard, M. (1993), 'Violence Towards Women' in D. Richardson and V. Robinson (eds.), *Introducing Women's Studies* Basingstoke and London, The Macmillan Press Ltd, pp. 99–122

Mertus, J. (1995), 'State Discriminatory Family Law and Customary Abuses' in J. Peters and A. Wolper (eds.), (1995), *Women's Rights, Human Rights: International Feminist Perspectives* New York and London, Routledge

Migrant Forum in Asia (1995), *Migrant Women: Quest for Justice* Hong Kong, Migrant Forum in Asia

Ministerio del Interior and Instituto de la Mujer (1991), *Violencia contra la mujer* Madrid, Ministerio del Interior

Minnesota Advocates for Human Rights (1995), *Lifting the Last Curtain: A Report on Domestic Violence in Romania* Minneapolis, Minnesota Advocates for Human Rights

—— (1996), *Domestic Violence in Bulgaria* Minneapolis Minnesota Advocates for Human Rights

Moraga C. and G. Anzaldua (eds.), (1983), *This Bridge Called my Back: Writings by Radical Women of Color* New York, Kitchen Table: Women of Color Press

Morgan, M., and M. Fitzgerald (1992), 'Gardai and Domestic Violence Incidents: a Profile Based on a National Sample of Investigations' Paper presented to the Conference on Women and Safety, Dublin

Morgan R. (ed) (1984), *Sisterhood is Global:The International Women's Movement Anthology* Middlesex, Penguin Books

National Report of Ireland: United Nations Fourth World Conference on Women (1994), Dublin, The Stationery Office

National Federation of Women's Refuges (1994), *Policy Document for Women's Refuges* Dublin, NFWR

'National Inter-Agency Working Party Report on Domestic Violence' *Victim Support*, July 1992

O'Connor, A. M. (1994), *The Health Needs of Women Working in Prostitution in the Republic of Ireland* Dublin, EUROPAP/Eastern Health Board (Women's Health Project)

O'Connor, M. (1992), 'Foreword' in C. Bunch and R. Carillo (eds.), *Gender Violence: A Development and Human Rights Issue*

O'Connor, M. (1995), 'Violence Against Women: An Issue for Medical/Health Personnel' *Women's Aid Newsletter* No 5, (August)

O'Malley, T. (1993), 'Perceptions of Sexual Violence' in *UCG Women's Studies Centre Review* vol 2

Patel, P. (1990), 'Southall Boys' in *Against The Grain: A Celebration of Survival and Struggle, Southall Black Sisters 1979–1989* Southall, Middlesex, Southall Black Sisters, pp. 43–54

Peters, J., and A. Wolper (eds.), (1995), *Women's Rights, Human Rights: International Feminist Perspectives* New York and London, Routledge

Polish Committee of NGOs (1995), *The Situation of women in Poland: The Report of the NGOs Committee* Polish Committee of NGOs: Beijing 1995, Warsaw

Popular Education Research Group 'Talking Feminist Popular Education' in M. Davies (ed) *Women and Violence* London, Zed Books, pp. 223–5

Radford, J. (1992), 'Womanslaughter: A License to Kill? The Killing of Jane Asher' in *Femicide: the Politics of Woman Killing* J. Radford and D. E. H. Russell (eds.), New York, Twayne, pp. 253–66

Radford, J. and D. E. H. Russell (eds.), (1992), *Femicide: The Politics of Woman Killing* Buckingham, Open University Press

Reagon, B. J. (1983), 'Coalition Politics–Turning the Century' in B. Smith (ed),

Home girls — a black feminist anthology New York, Kitchen Table Press
pp.356–68

Regan, L. (1994), 'The Effects of Violence in the Home on Children' in *Policy
Document for Women's Refuges* Dublin, NFWR

Report of the Second Commission on the Status of Women (1993), Dublin
Stationary Office

Rich, A. (1977), *Of Woman Born: Motherhood as Experience and Institution*
London, Virago Press

—— (1980), 'Compulsory Heterosexuality and Lesbian Existence' *Signs* 5(4), pp.
631–60 (Also published 1981, London, Onlywomen Press)

Richardson, D. (1992), 'Constructing Lesbian Sexualities' in K. Plummer (ed),
Modern Homosexualities London, Routledge

Richardson, D. and V. Robinson (1993), *Introducing Women's Studies* Basingstoke
and London, The Macmillan Press

Rights of Women *Bulletin: Rights of Women* Autumn/Winter 1994

Rodríguez, L., Alvarez, F. J., and P. Gómez (1988), *La justicia ante la libertad
sexual de las mujeres* Madrid, Instituto de la Mujer

Ruddle, H. and J. O'Connor (1992), *Breaking the Silence: Violence in the Home:
The Women's Perspective* Limerick, Mid-Western Health Board

Russell, D. E. H. (1984), *Sexual Exploitation: Rape, Child Sexual Abuse and
Workplace Harassment* Beverley Hills, London, New Delhi, Sage Publications

Saadawi, N. el (1980), *The Hidden Face of Eve* London, Zed Books Ltd

—— (1990) Interview in *Spare Rib*, London, Spare Rib Collective p.23

Scanlon, G. M. (1990), 'El movimiento feminista en España, 1900–1985: logros y
dificultades.' In J. Astelarra (ed.), *Participación política de las mujeres.* Madrid,
Centro de Investigaciones Sociológicas and Siglo XXI, pp. 83–100

Shanahan, K. (1992), *Crimes Worse than Death* Dublin, Attic Press

Shelly, L.I. (1987) 'Inter-personal violence in the USSR' *Violence, Aggression and
Terrorism 1(2)*, pp. 41–67

Sillard, K. (1995), 'Helping Women to Help Themselves: Counselling Against
Domestic Violence in Australia' in M. Davies (ed), *Women and Violence*
London, Zed Press, pp. 239–245

Smart, C. (1989) *Feminism and the Power of Law* London, Routledge

Smyth, A. (1994), 'Paying Our Disrespects to the (Bloody) States Women are in:
Women, Violence and the State' in Griffin, G. et al (eds.), *Stirring It* London,
Taylor and Francis

—— (1995a), 'States of Change: Reflections on Ireland in Several Uncertain
Parts' in *Feminist Review*, No.50

—— (1993), 'The Women's Movement in the Republic of Ireland 1970–1990' in
A. Smyth (ed) *Irish Women's Studies Reader* Dublin, Attic Press

—— (1992b), 'A Sadistic Farce: Women and Abortion in the Republic of
Ireland' in A. Smyth (ed) *The Abortion Papers: Ireland* Dublin, Attic Press

—— (1992a), 'The Politics of Abortion in a Police State' in A. Smyth (ed) *The
Abortion Papers: Ireland*, Dublin, Attic Press

—— (1995b) 'Haystacks in my Mind: Beating the Backlash or how to stay
SAFE (Sane, Angry and Feminist) in the 1990s in G. Griffin (ed), *Feminist
Activism in the 1990s* London, Taylor and Francis

Southall Black Sisters (1990), *Against the Grain: A Celebration of Survival and
Struggle, Southall Black Sisters 1979–1989* Southall, Middlesex, Southall Black
Sisters, pp. 43–54

Southall Black Sisters (1995), *A Stark Choice: Domestic Violence or Deportation?
Abolish the One Year Rule!* London, Southall Black Sisters

Spanish Senate (1989), 'Informe de la Comisión de Relaciones con el Defensor del Pueblo y de los Derechos Humanos encargada del estudio de la mujer maltratada.' *Boletín de las Cortes Generales Senado* May 12, Number 313, pp. 12182-211

Stacey, J. (1993), 'Untangling Feminist Theory' in D. Richardson and V. Robinson (eds.), (1993), *Introducing Women's Studies* Basingstoke and London, The Macmillan Press Ltd, pp. 49–73

Steiner Scott, L. (ed), (1985), *Personally Speaking: Women's Thoughts on Women's Issues* Dublin, Attic Press

Stetson, D. McBride (1987), *Women's Rights in France* Westport (Connecticut), Greenwood Press

Stiglmayer A. (ed), (1994), *Mass Rape:The War against Women in Bosnia-Herzegovina* University of Nebraska Press

Stout, K. (1992) " 'Intimate Femicide': Effect on Legislation and Social Services" in J. Radford and D. E. H. Russell (eds.), *Femicide: the Politics of Woman Killing* New York, Twayne, pp. 133–40

Tatchell P. (1990), *Out in Europe: A guide to Lesbian and Gay Rights in 30 European Countries* London and Glasgow, Broadcasting Support Services, Channel 4 Television

Threlfall, M. (1985), 'The Women's Movement in Spain' *New Left Review* 151, pp. 44–73

United Nations Security Council (1994), *Final Report of the Commission of Experts Established Pursuant to Security Council Resolution 780 (1992)*

Valiente, C. (1995), 'The Power of Persuasion: The *Instituto de la Mujer* in Spain', D. McBride Stetson and A. G. Mazur (eds.), *Comparative State Feminism*, Newbury Park, California, Sage

Varian-Barry, S. (1995), 'Raped' in *The Cork Literary Review* vol 1

Vasilyeva L. (1993), *Kremlin Wives* Moscow, Vagrius

Walby, S. (1990), *Theorizing Patriarchy* Oxford, Blackwell

Walsh, C. (1993), *Media Coverage of Rape* MA Dissertation, WERRC, University College Dublin

Ward A., Gregory, J., and Yuval-Davis, N. (1992), *Women and Citizenship in Europe: borders, rights and duties* London, Trentham Books and EFSF

Ward, P. (1993), *Divorce in Ireland: Who Should Bear the Cost?* Cork University Press

Warner, G. (1994), 'Time to Give Zero Tolerance to the Sex Warriors' *Sunday Times Scotland* 9 October

Wingfield, R. (1996), 'Fundamental Questions: From Southall to Beijing' *Trouble and Strife* No. 32, p. 61

Women's Aid (1994), *Submission to the Joint Oireachteas Committee on Women's Rights* Dublin, Women's Aid

—— (1995), 'Domestic Violence: the Northern Ireland Response' in M. Davies (ed), *Women and Violence* London, Zed Books, pp. 27–31

—— (1995) *Pre-Budget Submission* Dublin, Women's Aid

—— (1955), *Zero Tolerance: A National Strategy on Eliminating Violence Against Women* Dublin, Women's Aid

Women's Support Project/Evening Times (1990) *Report on Responses from 1503 Women to the survey on Violence Against Women* (March)

Yllo, K. (1988), 'Political and Methodological Debates in Wife Abuse Research' in K. Yllo and M. Bograd (eds) *Feminist Perspectives on Wife Abuse* London, Sage

Yuval-Davis, N. et al. (1995) 'The Potential Uses of Religion, Culture and Ethnicity: Cairo 1994' *Women Against Fundamentalism Journal* No. 7, P. 13

Yuval-Davis N. and F. Anthias (1989), *Women–Nation–State* London, Macmillan Press

Zajovic, S. (1992), 'Patriarchy, language and national myth: The war and women in Serbia' *Peace News* (March) p. 7

Zhenschchiny v SSSR (Women in the USSR) (1992) Goskomstat, Moscow

Index